I AM DANGER

I AM PRISONER

BURNING BRIDGE

PUBLISHING

I AM DANGER
I AM PRISONER

Sergeant Danger Geist

www.BurningBridge.com

Book art and cover designed by Chris Beatrice
Burning Bridge Publishing logo designed by Ryan Rizzio
Cartography by Mapping Specialists, Ltd.
All photographs property of Danger Geist

Printed in the United States of America.

2nd edition, April 2012

Publisher's Cataloging-in-Publication Data

Geist, Danger.
I am danger, I am prisoner : a memoir / Sergeant Danger Geist.
p. cm.
ISBN: 978-1-937691-00-4 (hardcover)
ISBN: 978-1-937691-01-1 (pbk.)
ISBN: 978-1-937691-02-8 (e-book: ePub)
ISBN: 978-1-937691-03-5 (e-book: Kindle)
1. Afghan war, 2001—Personal narratives, American. 2. United States. Army—Biography. 3. Illinois—Biography. I. Title.
DS371.413 .G45 2012
958.104`7—dc22

2012900167

This book is dedicated to the lives sacrificed from the 2-130th Infantry Battalion in Illinois.

Blackhawks. Always Ready.

1LT Jared Southworth

SSG Jason Burkholder

SGT Scott Stream

SSG Josh Melton

SPC Christopher Talbert

SPC Gerrick Smith

AUTHOR'S NOTE

The following story is a true one that started off with the sole intention of being bi-weekly email updates to my loved ones while I was deployed. As my time in Afghanistan progressed, however, the emails quickly became something more than just updates about my responsibilities as a Chaplain Assistant; they became moments of reflection and a means of explaining the conflict to American minds that haven't had the opportunity to experience its ramifications firsthand. Every account you read in this book is true and unembellished. Only minor details were altered on rare occasion to help the story flow in a coherent manner.

Matters of faith are a steamy subject, and the following pages are loaded with this reality. Please note that none of the religious interpretations in this story have been evaluated by scholars. The presentations of Christianity and Islam are based off a small group of people's understandings of each respective faith and are not necessarily agreed upon by all who claim to ascribe to these religions.

All Biblical references come from the New International Version (NIV), unless otherwise noted.

The names of specific soldiers have been changed to protect their identities. However, none of the names of the fallen soldiers have been changed because I want you to overtly recognize the real names of real heroes who have died for you, even though they never met you and never will.

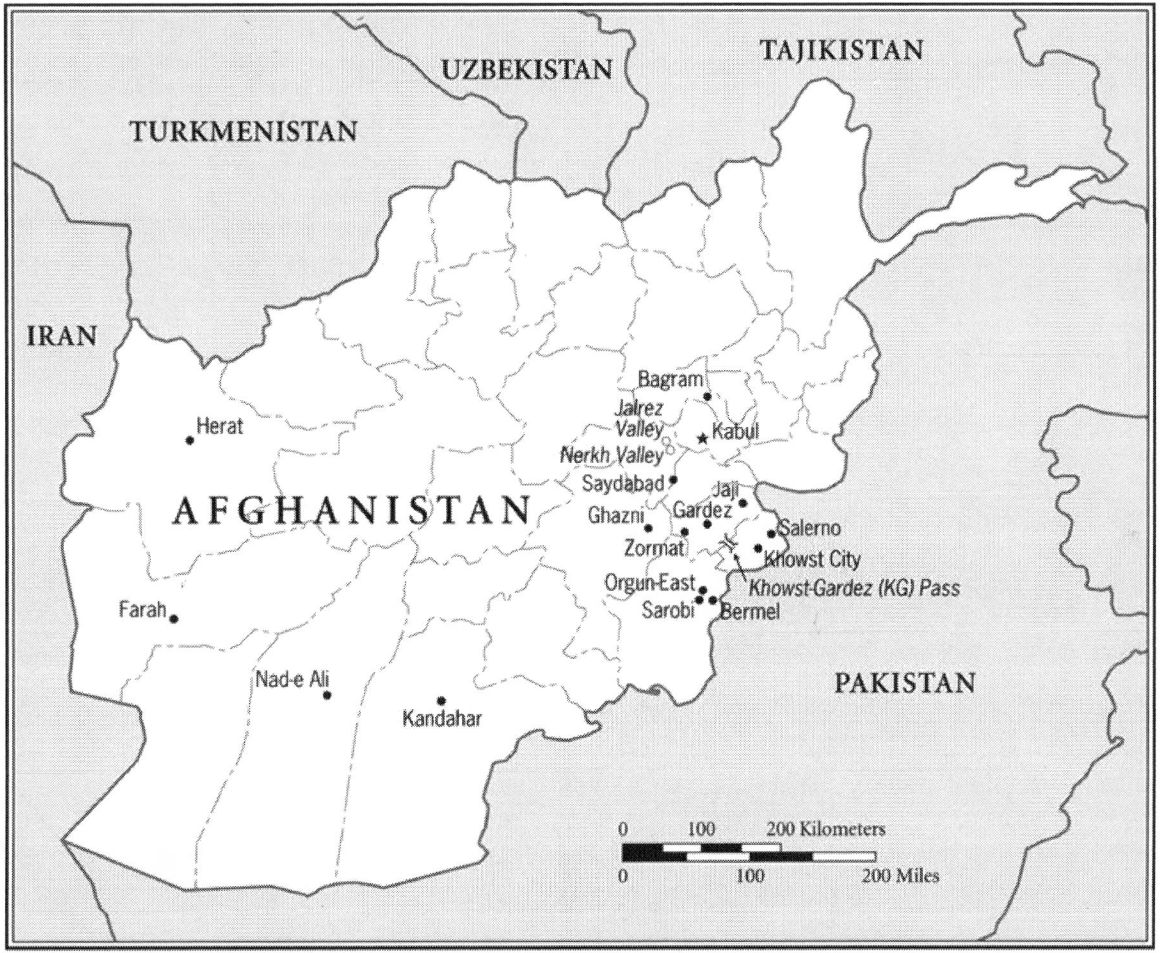
TURKMENISTAN
UZBEKISTAN
TAJIKISTAN
IRAN
AFGHANISTAN
PAKISTAN
Herat
Farah
Nad-e Ali
Kandahar
Bagram
Jalrez Valley
Kabul
Nerkh Valley
Saydabad
Jaji
Ghazni
Gardez
Salerno
Zormat
Khowst City
Orgun-East
Khowst-Gardez (KG) Pass
Sarobi
Bermel
0
100
200 Kilometers
0
100
200 Miles

TABLE OF CONTENTS

**A glossary of acronyms can be found on the last page of the book, though each one is spelled out the first time it's used.*

.: *prologue* :.

Doubt, Despair, Pain
September 2008

Put on your uniform, Danger. Welcome to death row.

I was filled with regret. I wanted to escape from reality and go back in time to when I made the choices that led me here. If I got a chance to do it over, I promise I wouldn't be here right now.

I looked over at my girlfriend, Joanna, and her eyes told me she was going through the same pain.

I began considering the fact that I couldn't sit in the passenger seat forever. Mustering all the modest willpower I had, I got out of Joanna's car and staggered over to her driver's side window. Pulling the door open, Joanna leered up at me, knowing it was time to render her last goodbyes to her condemned boyfriend. I crouched down until we were at eye level, and we just stared at each other as tears flowed down our cheeks.

I leaned over and held her close to me, squeezing her as tightly as I did the night we first met. I could smell the faint scent of her vanilla perfume, which was now all-but-worn-off by the tears that trickled down her neck. I whispered to her words of hope, "It's all temporary."

But what if I'm wrong? I wondered. *What if I was wrong all along?*

"It's all temporary," I reasserted. "This pain, this suffering, it's but a small blip on eternity, Joanna."

What if I die? What if I misread the prophecy?

Joanna nodded with hopeful optimism.

No, God won't allow me to die. He wouldn't let that happen, not after everything He put me through already, not after what He told me. This isn't how it ends.

I kissed Joanna one last kiss, clamped her hand with mine for a moment, and then backed away so she could drive out of my life.

As I watched her car disappear into the distance, the night sky clotted into one dense mass and, pressing down like a giant fist, crushed my soul to the ground. Obversely, my body stood tall and waved goodbye, refusing to show any sign of frailty.

After Joanna's headlights vanished completely, I sauntered off to my parents' car to be taken to my final destination.

◊

I thought that when we arrived at the armory, the worst would have been over; I was confident that I wouldn't cry again. And so, despite the knots in my stomach demanding more of an emotional response when I hugged and kissed my mom goodbye, I let a few tears roll down my cheek and nothing more.

An inaudible voice whispered hopelessness, "She could be holding her son for the last time. The next time she sees you, you'll be dead, blown to tiny pieces. If she's lucky, she'll get to hold the hand of your pale corpse."

Shut up! Shut up! You're wrong. I'm making it back.

I gave my dad a flaccid embrace, too shaken to offer a substantial final hug. He picked up on this weakness and atoned for it by gripping me tighter than he ever had before, burying my head into his chest and cradling my back like I was still his baby. I tried turning my head to the side, but every tear I had been holding back seemed to find its way onto his shoulder. I broke down on him, having stayed strong for the two women in my life, but now powerless against this stinging grief I couldn't suppress any longer.

My dad felt the immensity as well, spastically kissing my head as he enveloped me in his arms. He later told me that, during that final hug, he accepted that I would soon be dead. Every day from then on, he looked for that government car to pull up to our driveway to hand him a letter of lament. To him, this would be his last chance to tell me how much he loved me; the last hug he could give to a son that was as-good-as-dead.

"You are strong," he whispered to me. "So strong."

A minute later, I was staring at an empty spot where my parents' car had been. By now, they were probably a couple of miles away, yet it was as if I could hear my mom wailing right next to me.

I peered past my shoulder to the structure towering over me. Tonight, it could pass as a dank dungeon instead of a military armory.

I nodded towards the sky, finally accepting my destiny: I was a soldier who was ordered to go to one of the most volatile areas in Afghanistan, and my journey began in the morning.

"Okay, God. This is it."

I meandered towards the armory front door, weighed down by invisible shackles clamped all over my body. It was as if I was walking down the final hallway before my execution, and by sunrise, I'd be gone.

The armory was empty. It seemed the other soldiers had opted not to stay overnight, so it'd just be me tonight. I found a room that was full of boxes of pocket-sized Bibles and an arbitrary loveseat, and I rolled out my sleeping bag and tried getting some shuteye. It felt less like I was getting rest in a supply room and more like I was letting my condemned body bleed out in the basement of a morgue.

I was alone. And not just alone in the armory, but also in awareness. I was living with a knowledge that none of my family were afforded; a secret that only made this deployment all-the-more unbearable. If they knew what I knew, they would've never driven away.

I began to snivel again, overwhelmed with my fate and chained to my distress by indestructible handcuffs.

But this wasn't the first time I cried myself to sleep in a foreign place. Oh, *yes.* I've been here once before, indeed.

.: 1 :.

The Beginning of the End

June 2004

I collapsed to the confined bathroom floor, certain I had just made the biggest mistake in my 17 years of life, a mistake so immense that it would ultimately cost my life. I cradled my head in my hands, weeping bitterly onto the tile floor.

For the first extended period of my life, I was leaving my hometown of Zion, Illinois. Moments ago in a hotel lobby just outside of Chicago, I had said goodbye to my family for what felt like forever. Just a month-and-a-half earlier, I had enlisted in the U.S. Army National Guard[1] for six years, and now I was in this doleful hotel room awaiting a flight to go to South Carolina for basic training. I wasn't even a high school graduate, and I had already signed my life away to the U.S. government. I had just finished my junior year of high school, and by the time my senior year rolled around, I would be a bona fide United States soldier. I was a cicada; I had waited the last 17 years to finally surface and maximize my potential for one fleeting summer.

The last month of my junior year was a tough one, because even though I would only be gone for a little over two months, it felt like it was the beginning of the end of my life. I had been admonished by teachers for enlisting to serve under the "evil Bush regime," and several friends told me that I made a fatal decision. My parents, who had to co-sign my enlistment papers as I wasn't even a legal adult yet, were criticized and told that I was going to die and that my blood would be on their hands.

---

[1] **Army National Guard**: a component of the regular U.S. Army; unlike active duty soldiers, National Guardsmen are considered reservists (i.e., part-time soldiers), except during certain periods of stateside or overseas deployments, in which said Guardsmen temporarily become full-time active duty servicepersons.

When I lifted my head out of my palms, I couldn't see a thing through my teary vision, save for the toilet that was smack in front of my face. Just like so many of my friends and family and teachers, I was sure that even the toilet was judging me for my decision.

At 17 years old, you've already thrown away your life. How does it feel to know that?

"Stop. I don't regret what I did."

You're going to regret it when you have to kill somebody. Will you be able to live knowing you ended someone's life? What will you do when you realize you're innately a wild boar; a brute; a predator? How might you answer God when He asks you why you willingly became a killer?

"That's a low blow. Don't make this about God's judgment."

But your whole life is about God! If you really believe in what you say you do, then how can any decision not be a matter of faith to you?

"It *is* a matter of faith, but what I'm saying is I can still be a Christian and be okay with killing during war."

You're lying to yourself. Let's be realistic: why'd you really do it? Don't you have any common sense?

"Yes, of course I have common sense! I know what I'm doing."

You think so? Then you must be aware that this will be the death of you. Your death will spiral your family into a deep depression. All because you wanted to be something better. Is that worth it?

"It's not about me. I'm a patriot. I'm doing this for my country. And if I die for my country, so be it. I have a duty to give back to the people what they have so graciously given me."

What people? You think anybody ever went to war because they genuinely cared about you? People go to war because they had nowhere else to run to, not because they want to protect anyone.

"You're wrong. You just don't get it. It's about justice. The September 11th attacks were an atrocity; I'll never forget the fury I felt when I watched those towers fall. I want to bring those who propagated that evil to justice."

You think you're really going to help bring terrorists to justice?

"I *will* bring them to justice. My family has a history of military service, and it's up to me to continue that tradition. I just have a servant's heart; I love serving others."

So go and serve others! Why did you need to serve in this capacity? You could've served in a million different ways, ways that you would actually be good at.

"Stop it! Will you just stop it? You're missing the point. I enlisted because..."

Because why?

"Because... because I, I... want, I mean that I wanted ... I wanted to... you know..."

Wanted to what?

"I wanted... I had to make..."

Why are you here?

"I did... I just..."

Quit sputtering!

"I enlisted..."

Why?

"I enlisted because I wanted to make the world a better place!"

Private Geist, June 2004

.: ⊾ :.

Live from Fort Bragg, it's Sergeant Geist!

29 November 2008

Joanna,

After two months of training, we finally leave to Afghanistan in a few days. I loathe Fort Bragg so much that I'm actually looking forward to going to a dangerous third-world country. The comfort level here is so low that I can't imagine the war zone will be any worse.

When we first arrived to Bragg, we were herded into tents like cattle. These tents were constructed to comfortably house eight soldiers, but 16 soldiers inhabit each one; this situation would become our living conditions for the next couple months. The issue isn't as much that we barely have room for our gear, but rather we're more infectious than the undead. Besides catching illnesses from one another, we've also been shot up with anthrax, tetanus, and the highly-contagious smallpox vaccines, tanking our immune systems so low that we feel the rancor of every germ out here.

The good news is we haven't spent much time in our disease-infested tents. The bad news is our days have usually started around 5:30am and we work until 8:00pm. This is true of all seven days of the week, and we don't get "days off." One day, we started work at 3:45am and didn't get time for ourselves until 9:00pm.

It's also been frigid. On the first night we arrived to Bragg, none of our gear had arrived from Illinois yet, and so I swiped rolls of port-a-pottie toilet paper to use as pillows, while my dirty laundry functioned as my blanket. You would think that North Carolina is warm year-round, but I can tell you that's not the case. Soldiers who go to the water supply to top off their canteens right after they wake up find the entire water supply's been frozen. No water means no showering, no rinsing your mouth while brushing your teeth, and no option but to dry shave. It didn't take long for me to wise up and start filling my canteens between mid-afternoon and midnight, so I'd have a full (albeit musty) water supply for the next day. One soldier cracked a joke, "I can't wait 'till we get shipped to a third-world country, where our living conditions will improve."

That being said, you and I both know that I didn't sign up to be comfortable, and I certainly don't mean to complain. Rather, I hope this puts it into perspective as to why I'm so zealous to get onto that plane that'll zip me over to a country where I'll have to be at the top of my game just to survive.

As non-ideal as the conditions are, I can't help but appreciate the knowledge I've gained. Though I've never had trouble grasping the fundamentals of being a chaplain assistant, I've learned more in my two months on active duty than I had in my five years as a part-time soldier. I always knew the chaplain assistant's main job is to provide religious support to soldiers, but now I fully grasp the execution of its three main responsibilities.

The chaplain assistant's first responsibility is to be a counselor for troubled soldiers. On paper, this is solely the chaplain's job, but often the chaplain isn't available, and so the chaplain assistant gets handed the duties. These can range from girlfriend issues, financial problems, work stress, and deaths or illnesses back home, to name a few common ones. In a war zone, the chaplain and chaplain assistant must travel from base to base to perform this duty, which I imagine will constitute the riskiest part of this job.

The second responsibility is to essentially be an altar boy. We help set up services for the religions of the soldiers that are under our care, and we get the holy books that are associated with each of those religions. The most requested books are the Bible, the Qur'an, and the Tanak. Generally, most soldiers going on this deployment identify as Protestants, though there are a handful of Catholics, a few Jewish soldiers, and one Wiccan. I haven't worked extensively with a Muslim or Buddhist in this job yet, but I know there are some Muslim soldiers within our unit.

In my opinion, these two responsibilities are less important than our third role: the bodyguard. Now, I've been scolded before for using the term "bodyguard," but the fact of the matter is that we are charged with the safety of our chaplain. In a battle, our primary mission is to make sure the chaplains aren't injured or killed, and we have to be ready to put our lives on the line to ensure that happens. If that's not the description of a bodyguard, then I don't know what is.

The reason it's so important to protect the chaplain is because if they became incapacitated, religious support gets flushed down the toilet. By the Geneva Conventions code,[2] chaplains are not allowed to carry firearms, nor can they even pick up firearms from a dead soldier in self-defense during a battle. Because of this code, the combatant role of the chaplain assistant emerged. We carry the weaponry that chaplains are forbidden to have. Even before it was an official job in the military, soldiers were selected to be chaplain assistants as a side-job. In essence, I have a somewhat different mission than everyone else: I am to ensure the chaplain's survival.

The Illinois National Guard's 33rd Brigade Combat Team is sending 3,000 of its soldiers to Afghanistan, the largest deployment in the state's history. As such, we're sending more chaplain and chaplain assistant teams from one single unit to war than there have ever been before. We have six teams going (constituting a total of 12 people), and we've all been training together since January to prepare for this deployment. But, even though we're sending so many ministry teams, we'll still be stretched thin when we get into theater. Afghanistan is roughly the size of Texas, and so imagine six undermanned churches having to minister to 3,000 people stretched across the entire state.

Though there are some commanders who undervalue the ministry role of the chaplain team, most appreciate our role and take us seriously. We want to be respected as knowledgeable and useful assets to the teams we're put on, which is why we've been practicing bodyguard techniques during our minimal down time. This training consists of throwing our chaplains to the ground to provide them cover and learning how to reload our weapons without looking away from the enemy, allowing us to maintain awareness of

---

[2] **Geneva Conventions code**: a 1949 agreement that established international wartime rules, as ratified by 194 cooperating countries. One of these precepts offers the definition of a *combatant* versus a *non-combatant*; a chaplain is explicitly specified as a non-combatant.

our chaplain's location in the heat of battle. It gets intense, especially because we wear our heavy gear whenever we train.

We've also spent much of our time practicing our rifle and pistol marksmanship. Because this revolves around using live bullets (as opposed to blanks), I always hope to be paired with the most adept soldiers whenever training teams are put together. One day, we practiced kicking down doors, rushing into rooms, and shooting cardboard cut-outs of terrorists with real bullets. The training facility's walls are composed of rubber to prevent ammunition from bouncing off, but those rubber walls still wouldn't stop a less-than-proficient soldier from accidentally shooting another troop. As if that exercise didn't make us nervous enough, we returned that night after sundown to repeat the task, this time executing it in pitch black while wearing night vision goggles.

Conducting training in which one person's split-second mistake could be the difference between life and death for a bystander forced me to realize what my greatest fear is in regards to this deployment: killing a terrorist, only to find out later that I had made a mistake and shot an innocent local. If this happened, I'd have great difficulty learning to forgive myself. I pray that my fellow soldiers and I aren't put in a position where we accidentally kill an innocent citizen or, even more devastating, each other.

Not all of our exercises are centered around killing, though. Some of our best training involves identifying what improvised explosive devices (IEDs) look like, and how to prepare yourself in situations where you believe you might run into one. The term "IED" is interchangeable with "roadside bomb," which the media most likes to use. They're the most efficient way of killing soldiers because they're bombs that don't look like bombs until you get up close to them, at which point it's usually too late to react. There are so many forms of IEDs, it's ridiculous. Terrorists can turn practically anything into a bomb, from bicycles to car trunks to paper bags to patches of dirt to roadkill to dead bodies. We've been told that if we didn't put something on the ground, don't pick it up. In an attempt to familiarize ourselves with the different variations, we've practiced searching houses for IEDs and we've been exposed to deactivated bombs.

Because there are a lot of soldiers who are dying overseas when their vehicles roll over, we've spent some time preparing for such situations. You see, many soldiers who have died in rollovers didn't die necessarily because of the physical impact, but rather because they were trapped inside their humvee as it filled with water or was engulfed in flames. We have a simulator that's similar to a roller coaster that lacks securing mechanisms. In the simulation, we enter the humvee, and then it physically flips upside-down and we're tasked with escaping the vehicle. After the vehicle flips, we hang upside-down and try to unbuckle ourselves. The first time I did this, I fell on my head and then a nearby soldier fell on me while I was twisting my body to get positioned for my escape. As it would turn out, this was also the first time I've ever been grateful for my helmet.

I reflect on the rollover training and am surprised that more soldiers don't get hurt from the simulation. Several soldiers have had injuries here and there throughout training; I've only had one recurring injury. One day while I was out in the field visiting soldiers with my chaplain, my body unexpectedly gave out under the weight of my gear and I collapsed to the ground.

Earlier that day, I'd been given additional side-rib plates that added several pounds. The body armor alone weighs between 30 and 40 pounds, not to mention the extra weight of all the additional ammo, firearms, and water on my body. I've been told that, altogether, that equipment can weigh anywhere from 60 pounds upwards to 100 pounds. My skeletal frame has always been weaker than the average person's, and though I've generally had success in overcoming my inferiority, that wasn't the case this time: the drastic change of weight on my shoulders was more than I could handle.

Because we're simulating a combat zone, we're not allowed to take the body armor off in the field, so after I floundered to the ground, I rallied myself back to my feet and lingered over to a vehicle that was deemed to be a makeshift garrison, and then took my body armor off as I lied in a lump on the vehicle floor. Each time I put my armor back on, my shoulder was in unbearable pain.

Not but a few days later, we were all issued new body armor that was invented to help offset the weight on the shoulders to be distributed throughout the rest of the body (specifically onto the hips). While this did help a little bit, my back has been in poor condition ever since my collapse. Military doctors have examined my back several times since this incident and have been unable to help me, though they instantly recognize the problem: body armor frequently destroys soldiers' backs, they say. Yet, all they can do is prescribe medication to ease the pain.

Understanding that I need to just work with my equipment, I've tried my best to ignore the pain as I continued training in the field. One night, I forgot all about my back pain when I endured a different kind of discomfort that I've only heard about in stories from other soldiers who've had to cuddle with one another to survive the night. There's an old military anecdote that "there are two kinds of soldiers in the field: the warm and the proud."

As I was packing my gear to sleep in the field one night, I underestimated how ruthless the cold would be. I had been told I would at least be in a tent, so I figured it couldn't be much chillier than what I was used to. What I didn't know was that the tent would be paper-thin and retained less heat than a mortuary. I had naïvely grabbed the thin layer of my sleeping bag, misjudging the extent of the conditions I would be facing. By midnight, I was sleeping in 30° weather with the temperature dropping as low as the 20s by morning. My shivering was so intense that it woke me up every hour that night; I was so desperate for heat, I would've gladly cuddled a live bear had one been available.

Aside from growing icicles on my nipples, we've spent some time mentally preparing ourselves for cultural obstacles we're sure to come across. For instance, every soldier is going to have to interact with local Afghans on some level, and so the government has invested money into training us to speak Dari, the most-used language in the areas of Afghanistan we'll be making our locales. I've taken this classroom training seriously because I can't help but feel I'll need to use this knowledge at some point over the next year. We've been given a translation book to study, and I've picked up on a few key phrases, like "drop your weapons," "thank you," and "good day." I've also learned a few interesting words, including "Khatar," which is Dari for "Danger." Soldiers have been calling me "Sergeant Khatar."

When we get to Afghanistan, every soldier will be placed in a Camp, a Forward Operating Base (FOB), or a Command Outpost (COP). The difference between each of these bases is size and luxury; in oversimplified terms, think of Camps as hotels (usually having things like fast-food restaurants, laundry services, and massage parlors), FOBs as motels (usually having things like contracted chefs, makeshift theaters, and small libraries), and COPs as homeless shelters (usually having things like port-a-potties, makeshift kitchens, and electrical outlets).

Despite the varying degrees of luxury, every base is prone to indirect fire on the base itself and direct fire just outside of it.[3]

◊

In the weeks leading up to Thanksgiving, we've been enduring the Mission Readiness Exercise, a 4-day simulation that tests our readiness to go to war. During this exercise, our base comes under attack by hired actors playing terrorists, to which we have to throw on our gear and protect our base from. These battles can last a couple of hours, and we practice everything from flanking our enemies to providing first-aid to wounded buddies. Most nights between the hours of 1:00am and 4:00am, we'd be woken up to the whistle (and explosion) of dummy mortars, then have to sprint to our chaplains' bunkers to account for the chaplain we're assigned to.

I've been assigned to Chaplain (CH) Fardpot, a man in his upper-40s who's as stout as a sack of plums and as handsome as one of its shriveled fruits. While a compassionate minister to soldiers and well-trusted by leaders, his homely appearance parallels his much-to-be-desired attitude towards me.

---

[3] **indirect fire**: artillery projectiles, like rockets and mortars, that fly into the air and land in the general vicinity of where the shooter wants them to land. Used most frequently to attack bases because of its ability to induce sizable damage while safely keeping a shooter as far away from his target as possible.
direct fire: straight-shooting projectiles, like rifles and machine guns, that are shot at a specific target. While its ballistics are not as powerful as artillery, it allows for much greater accuracy.

While it's improper to directly address a chaplain by his rank, CH Fardpot is proud to hold the rank of Captain and has made it clear that he doesn't appreciate how seriously I, a lowly enlisted soldier, deem my job to check in on him, a superior officer, after a battle.[4]

You see, CH Fardpot wasn't always a chaplain. He often boasts about once being a soldier in the Special Forces; nevermind the fact that he wasn't actually an SF soldier, but *support to* a Special Forces battalion. So, because he once had the esteemed job of cleaning the toilet bowls in a Special Forces barracks while the team was away conducting covert operations, CH Fardpot seems to believe that he can do any enlisted soldier's job better than them, especially mine. To him, I'm just a scratched cassette tape: an obsolete piece of equipment that's defective in the first place.

Another chaplain from the 33rd Brigade picked up on the fact that I wasn't being taken seriously.

"Geist," he candidly explained, "you're just a kid, and your youth is gonna work against you. There's nothing you can do about that. But here's what you *can* do: take your appeals to God. Check this out..." He flipped open his Bible and pointed to a passage. "This is Proverbs 21:1. Read it aloud."

He handed me the Bible and I squinted to read the words, "The king's heart is in the hand of the Lord; He directs it like a watercourse wherever He pleases."

"Exactly, Geist," he pushed my chest. "This is your verse for this deployment, understand? I want you to focus on this. You can't change the

---

[4] **enlisted**: soldier who takes orders from officers; must have a high school education; the subordinates who are the "brawn" of a military operation; in civilian terms, they can be compared to blue-collar labor workers.
officer: soldier who gives orders; must have a college education; the leaders who are the "brains" of a military operation; in civilian terms, they can be compared to white-collar management.

hearts of the leaders above you, but you can pray that God will change their hearts."

I certainly appreciated his encouragement, but it seems God doesn't care to change CH Fardpot's heart just yet; I'm still being treated like a deck of cards missing its ace of spades, expected to keep collecting dust on the shelf until the chaplain has no other option but to invoke my services. What CH Fardpot doesn't acknowledge is that the government has spent tens of thousands of dollars to specifically train me for his sake, so I have a duty to protect him at all costs.

At least I know it's nothing personal, as CH Fardpot doesn't seem to value any of the training being provided, either. Recently, after reporting to my bunker during one of our early-morning pseudo-attacks, I looked around at the soldiers and realized I didn't see my chaplain's face anywhere. I checked a couple of other bunkers and didn't see him there, either. So, I jogged over to his tent, which I knew was inhabited by officers ranking from Lieutenant to Major. Not only did I find CH Fardpot still snoring away in his bunk, but so was every officer in the tent.

"Gentlemen," I flicked on the lights, "you would now be dead. Report to your bunkers."

After putting on their protective gear, the officers flooded out of the tent, stumbling to the bunkers like a group of drunken men who had gum sticking to their boot soles.

Whenever I'm done accounting for CH Fardpot during these notional attacks, I have lots of time to evaluate the simulation before we receive the "all clear" that permits us to go back to bed. I consider how quickly my body becomes alert and fully operational in the dead of the night; if I'm this frightened when I hear dummy mortars now, how terrifying real mortars must feel! The dummy mortars provide an intense sensation in which the blast hits you with a strong wall of wind, flapping your clothes against your skin, even when they're a respectable distance away. I can't imagine what a real mortar attack would feel like, and more importantly, how would I react? I feel like my first inclination wouldn't be to account for my chaplain, but instead to find the closest bunker, suck my thumb, and close my eyes until the attack stops.

Thoughts like these pressure me to evaluate how important I deem our mission. That is, do I believe in it enough that I'm willing to risk my life? Well, let's examine why I've been slated to go to Afghanistan in the first place.

The 33rd Brigade was activated for a specific purpose: we are to train the Afghan National Police (ANP) and Afghan National Army (ANA) so they can stand up to the Taliban bullies on their own, thus allowing the United States to safely pull out. The mission we face is unique compared to other missions in wars past and the war on al-Qaeda in Iraq right now.[5] What I mean by that is the government of Afghanistan has pleaded for our help; we aren't simply invading their country and forcing our ideals on them. Instead, our desire is to equip them so they can be considered a viable military presence, compelling the Taliban to reconsider their efforts to overthrow the Afghan government.

A key piece to achieving this mission is that we need to learn about their culture and ensure that we don't force our methods down their throats. We've been beat over the head again and again that our goal is to "win the hearts and minds of the Afghan people." To do this, we've been learning about the country's rich history and have been getting educated on their contemporary culture.

---

[5] **What is the difference between al-Qaeda and the Taliban?** Though both rooted in Islamic extremism, there are many differences between the two terrorist organizations. Perhaps the biggest contrast is that, while al-Qaeda operates globally, the Taliban is believed to operate mainly in Afghanistan and Pakistan. Osama bin Laden was the leader of al-Qaeda, but following the September 11th attacks, it's understood that the Taliban harbored and protected him and other al-Qaeda leaders in Afghanistan, uniting in their hatred of western culture and democracy.

One thing we've been warned about is that we'll see things that might particularly bother us, but we shouldn't overstep our boundaries and criticize their practices. For instance, we've been told that many women wear burkas, often against their will. Women who don't wear the burkas are looked down upon in society, and in a Taliban-influenced society, "looked down upon" can sometimes spell death.

For a freedom-inclined America, this is bothersome, but we've been taught to just grin and bear it. In the late 1980s, Russia invaded Afghanistan to set them up with a civil government. However, Russia forced Marxist ideals upon Afghanistan, enticing the Afghans to rebel against the Russians. The Russians lost the fight largely because they didn't have the support of the locals. According to the U.S. Army, the Russians killed 30,000 insurgents *per year* during their war in Afghanistan, but the Afghans' operations weren't slowed down because for every one insurgent they killed, several more were created. Imagine if a soldier killed your father: would you, your brother, your sister, and your mother not want vengeance against the government that murdered your loved one?

This Afghan retaliation was highlighted in the 1988 action flick, Rambo III. In one scene, an American Prisoner-of-War (POW) explains to his Russian captor the futility of trying to take over Afghanistan:

> There won't be a victory. Every day, your war machines lose ground to a bunch of poorly-armed, poorly-equipped freedom fighters. The fact is that you underestimated your competition. If you'd studied your history, you'd know that these people have never given up to anyone. They'd rather die than be slaves to an invading army. You can't defeat a people like that. We tried; we already had our Vietnam. Now you're gonna have yours.

The U.S. has tried learning from the Russians' mistakes, and now our aim is to work hand-in-hand with the Afghan government. We didn't invade Afghanistan; we allied with them. We have no desire to give the Afghans reason to dislike us, therefore we aren't interested in enforcing our own morals and standards on them. The only kind of thing we won't allow Afghan locals to do is train to be terrorists or strap IEDs to kids. Because we're so serious about being partners instead of rulers over the Afghan people, Americans have steadily been gaining support from local Afghans every year.

I've been soaking up any and all potentially useful tidbits about Afghanistan. For instance, I've learned that 80% of Afghans are Sunni Muslims, while 19% are Shi'ite Muslims. There is one registered Jew in all of Afghanistan, and no registered Christians (though there are underground churches).

Most Afghans are illiterate; there's an 80-85% illiteracy rate in men, and a 90-95% illiteracy rate in women. Though, my understanding is that this is leaps-and-bounds better than the rates they had just a few decades ago.

Many Afghans don't know their birthday. In their culture, this piece of information simply isn't important. When Afghans travel to the United States, they often make up a date to use as their birthday for their passport. Most of them choose January 1st because it's easy to remember. Furthermore, many Afghans are unaware of how old they are, so sometimes they also have to guess what year they were born in.

Afghanistan runs by the Islam calendar, in which they're in the year 1387. Just like Western calendars revolve around the estimated birth of Christ, the Islam calendar revolves around the year that Muhammad traveled to Medina from Mecca. Nearly every year since their Year One, Muslims have been at war in some capacity.

Muslims have a diet that has a similarity to that of the original Jews; the consumption of pig products is forbidden. *(Mental note: don't share my pork rinds.)* We need to keep this in mind so we don't insult the country's citizens. What a paradox: we're allowed to shoot at its natives when necessary, but first soaking our bullets in bacon grease constitutes a *faux pas*.

Interestingly, Muslims believe that Jesus will accompany Muhammad at the end of times, though they don't revere Jesus as the Christ or any status above "prophet." Muslims accept Abraham as their great ancestor, just as Jews and Christians do. The breakdown of agreement between people of Judeo-Christian beliefs and Muslims begins in Chapter 16 of the Book of Genesis; Muslims believe that Ishmael was the chosen son of Abraham, not

Isaac. Jesus came from the seed of Isaac, while Muslims believe that Mohammad came from the seed of Ishmael.

Seeing as how Jesus Christ is such a huge part of my life as a Christian, I'm particularly interested in learning about the religious aspects of Afghanistan when I arrive. So many people are quick to point out all the dissimilarities between the two faiths, while others are just as quick to solely acknowledge the parallels. I feel both those approaches are somewhat reckless, and I hope to reflect on both the unifying similarities and the divisive differences. I personally only know the basics of Islam, and so if I have a chance to talk with any locals about their religion, I'm going to jump on that opportunity.

As I've hopefully conveyed, I've learned so much about the Army and about Afghanistan and about myself over the past couple months. Joanna, now we'll learn about our relationship and the strength that binds it. I thank God that I got to spend time with you over the week of Thanksgiving. Saying goodbye to you on the night of my deployment, I thought that would be the last time I would see you until I came back. After all, that's what the Army told us, that we wouldn't have any breaks. To say that I feel blessed to have seen you one last time is an understatement.

The next time you hear from me, I'll be corresponding from Afghanistan. Until then, stay safe, and I know I don't have to tell you that I love you because you know it well. But, I'll tell you anyway.

I love you.

Bon voyage,

Sergeant Khatar

Sergeant Geist, October 2008

.: 2 :.

The Wreck
January 2006

I sat in my car, waiting for my Guest to arrive, but I didn't see anybody.

Go figure. Stood me up.

I was just starting the second semester of my freshman year at a college in the St. Louis area, and I was dealing with major depression. Anxiety disorders and depression ran in my family's history, as well as in my own. In fact, I was almost hospitalized just four years earlier in high school because of an overwhelming onset of obsessive-compulsive disorder (OCD), something that I never completely outgrew.

But this was a little different than the depressive episodes I had before. My sorrow ran so deep that my left bicep was bloody and scarred from cutting myself to cope, and I had been fantasizing about suicide. I daydreamed about the different ways I could kill myself like a teenage girl daydreams about marrying the perfect man.

I was a mess, which is why I was in my car this night. I had driven to my church and sat in its empty parking lot, hoping God would literally meet me where I was at. I listened for His voice and swiveled my head to watch for Him, but He wasn't there. He had stood me up. I came to His house, knocked on the door, and He left me out in the cold.

Something else caught my attention: the parking lot had a large lightpost to illuminate the entire area, but much like my spirits, the light was off.

What if I hit that lightpost? I began to wonder. *I bet I could get up to 55 in this parking lot.*

I wasn't necessarily intent on killing myself. Rather, I was interested in hitting that lightpost full-force, just to see what would happen. And, if I happened to die, then so be it.

I resolved that I would smash my car into the post. I grabbed the steering wheel tightly enough to turn my knuckles white, then began to drive.

If I died, who would care?

5 mph.

God didn't even care to show up to intervene.

15 mph.

I bet people would be talking about me for a little while.

20 mph.

Then they'd forget me.

25 mph.

And what if this doesn't even kill me? I'll be so embarrassed.

30 mph.

This is really happening. I'm about to crash my car.

35 mph.

I need to be stronger than this. It can't end like this.

35 mph.

You're stronger than this.

35 mph.

Stop this.

30 mph.

This isn't how it ends.

25 mph.

This isn't how it ends!

15 mph.

I told you. This isn't how it ends. Pull over.

I slowed down to 5 mph and swerved to the left of the lightpost, then put the car into park. I turned my head to the right and, as if I could see into a parallel universe, saw a car that had its hood smashed in and its windshield caved into the front seat, smoke rising to the sky. I saw my mangled torso on the hood, my lower body and legs wrapped around the lightpost. My dying carcass was panting, gasping for air as blood dripped down my mouth; my glossed eyes were wide open, staring back at me. We exchanged glances with one another, and the distorted version of myself moved its lips to tell me something.

This isn't how it ends, he said. *This isn't how it ends.*

◊

Despite a few particular nuances, this hopeless situation was not unlike my confinement in the hotel bathroom; I felt as trapped now as I had the night I left for boot camp. I wanted to remind myself how I weathered through that period in my life, just putting one foot in front of the other and marching on. I had huffed and puffed my way through basic training, wanting to quit every day, but holding onto the hope that there would be something better for me if I just finished this trial. Eventually graduation day came, and I stood as a proud soldier, ready to face whatever the world threw at me.

Aye, but back then I actually believed in what I was doing, that I was doing my patriotic duty. But now, I realized that while I appreciated America as a nation, I'd never be willing to die for her. The mere thought of dying for my country seems unappealing and terrifying.

Back then, I rationalized that the September 11th attacks were my motivation for enlisting. But when I really think about it, I was barely 15 years old when those attacks happened, much too young and naïve to truly comprehend what happened that day. I had tricked myself into believing I was angry when I watched those towers fall; being honest with myself now, the only emotion I can remember feeling that day is confusion.

I used to justify my enlistment by saying I was carrying on the family tradition of military service. Who was I kidding? True, both of my grandfathers served in World War II, but since then, not a single family member on either side of my extended family had been in any branch of the military. Collectively, my grandfathers had 25 descendants after them, none of which had any involvement in the military. I was the 26th descendant, the one who broke that mold. So to say that there's some kind of "family pride" that I was living up to was a crock.

I would deceive myself, saying that if nothing else, I was enlisting because I liked serving others. But when did my actions ever speak such a concept? Against my idealistic assessments, I have now come to accept that I'm a selfish person who feels no duty to give back to anybody who hasn't first served me. To utter anything otherwise is a lie.

I didn't realize it when I signed the papers, but I had always been living a life that constantly yet subtly drove me towards enlisting.

Throughout my childhood, I was poked fun at for being weak. My older brother would taunt me for being puny, and my baby brother would take those cues and tease me, too. I felt so inferior, and I resented them for it. So, I sought to be better than my brothers, to find ways to become stronger than them.

One day during junior high recess, I was hanging around my friends who were talking about the upcoming pee-wee football season. They all seemed to have a camaraderie that I was excluded from.

"Hey, you guys," I piped in. "I want to be on your team. I'm going to join the football team."

Several of the kids started snickering. My best friend at the time put his hand on my shoulder.

"Nathan," he tried finding the words, "You're... the problem is... I don't think you can play."

"Well why not?"

"Football is hard. Football is for guys who are... well, football players are strong. You're not built for it."

"Can't I at least try? Can't the coach decide if I'm not good enough?"

"Well, Nathan, I just don't think you'll... you won't survive the practices. They're too hard for you. You... you're too weak."

Two weeks later, I was out on the practice field in pads, ready to play some football. Nobody believed I could persevere through the rigorous calisthenics, so I became determined to survive the football season. Not only did I survive my first year, but I signed up and played the following two seasons as well. I dreaded the coming of autumn every year because I was so much weaker than the other kids, but I needed to prove I could be strong. When I was done with my junior high football career, I hadn't achieved anything remarkable, and for its entire duration, I had been a talentless player. *But I was still a player.*

In high school, I shifted my focus from sports to theatre, having always dreamt of being a film actor.

"Alright, everyone ready to rehearse this?" the director asked.

In one scene, six Thespians were needed to grab the arms and legs of the lead actress, lifting her over their heads and carrying her across the stage. Along with another guy and several girls, I had been chosen for this task. I was honored to do it.

"Hoist!" the director screeched.

We picked the actress up and started carrying her to the other end of the room. It was easy at first, but something started going wrong in the middle of our practice: the actress was slipping, and our ensemble was about to drop her.

Mustering all our strength, we gently set her on her feet while we gathered ourselves. What had gone wrong?

"Nathan!" the director snapped. "You dropped her. That was your fault! Now, try it again. Hoist!"

We picked the actress back up, finding the same results: we had no trouble at first, but she started slipping and we had to set her down again.

"Nathan, that's it. You're being replaced by someone else."

I didn't know what to say. I didn't think it was my fault alone, but I didn't know for sure. The director picked up on my embarrassment.

"Nathan, you're just too weak," her eyes exuded disappointment. "You're letting your team down."

I dared not look around. I had just gotten fired in front of everyone, being told that I was weaker than even the girls in the play. I was pathetic and humiliated; the exact opposite of what someone would expect from a future soldier.

Throughout my entire life, I never felt like I was good enough. While there are many actual reasons that I enlisted, all of them have one thing in common: pure, unadulterated hubris. I wanted to prove to the world that I was stronger, braver, and crazier than they gave me credit for. And Uncle Sam whispered in my ear that he would give me that chance, so I took his hand.

At no point in my life would anyone have guessed that I'd be one to enlist. But I did enlist. And I did because no one thought I ever would. I enlisted telling very few people beforehand, so when I announced my decision to everyone else, nobody could scoff at me, insisting I wouldn't actually go through with the paperwork.

I went to boot camp in hopes that I could prove I had value. But only being 17 years old, I didn't grasp tactical concepts as well as the other soldiers did. From the beginning, I received a lot of extra attention from the drill sergeants; my lack of inherent soldier qualities made me their special project. Halfway through boot camp, I broke down in tears, realizing that the drill sergeants and my fellow recruits thought I was a poor excuse of a soldier. But I refused to quit; I refused to return to my senior year of high school without wearing a soldier's beret. The drill sergeants recognized my determination, this inability to give up, and helped me achieve the standard that the U.S. Army expected of its soldiers. I barely graduated boot camp, *but at least I graduated.*

Ultimately, I liked to rationalize that I enlisted because I wanted to make a difference in the world. Now that I was less naïve, I understood the grim truth: I didn't enlist to make a difference in the world. I enlisted to make a difference in my world.

I wanted to be strong. I wanted to be worthy. I wanted to be unafraid. I wanted to prove that I wasn't the same pathetic kid that I'd been all my life. Haughty and superfluous reasons, to be sure. But I've already admitted that I'm selfish and only interested in serving myself, so perhaps this shouldn't be as much a shock. But despite these faults - and they are faults, don't be fooled - maybe someone would respect me. Maybe someone would let me be a hero, even for just a moment. That's all I've ever wanted, really. Maybe someone would let me be their hero.

◊

I almost forgot that I was parked in my car, now hypnotized by the snowbank in front of me. I wasn't sure what I was doing here, but I was here nonetheless, and so I just accepted it. I took my hand off the shift, curled up into a ball in the driver's seat, and fell asleep in the desolate church parking lot.

When I woke up in the morning, I had no confusion about where I was. I knew physically I was in a church parking lot, but mentally, emotionally, and spiritually, I was at rock bottom. My life was a wreck.

I pulled out my cell phone and called home.

"Mom, Dad? Hey, it's me. Um... I need some help. No, not money. I need you to call Dr. Callaghan. Uh huh. Yea...yeah, it's... yeah. It's pretty urgent."

.: 2 :.

Ernest Goes to War
11 December 2008

Hello my America-dwelling girlfriend,

I'm currently writing to you from the future. That is, my day is 10½ hours ahead of yours. As you're getting up in the morning to do your thing, I'm getting ready for bed. And when I'm getting ready to do my thing, your day is closing.

I, along with several other soldiers being shipped off to different parts of the country, arrived into the combat zone on December 6th. After a flight that burned up about a day, we touched down in Manas, Kyrgyzstan (a country just south of Borat's Kazakhstan). From there, we boarded a C-17 military plane and flew to the outskirts of Kabul, the capital of Afghanistan. The C-17 flight was nerve-racking; you kind of feel like you're on a ride at a Six Flags amusement park, except you can't see what's coming next and you're wearing body armor and holding a weapon the whole time.

We landed outside Kabul and were told that we had to jump on a convoy into the city. If you're unfamiliar with the term, a military convoy is where you get a bunch of vehicles in a row to travel together to wherever you're going. It's like caravanning with your family to a vacation spot, the only difference being that someone might blow you up.

Before we began the convoy, we were briefed about the route we would be traveling. Every route is rated on a color scale. A green road means that there's virtually no threat at all, an amber road may have potential for an enemy encounter (though there is no specific concern at the time), a red road is expected to have some likely enemy activity, and a black road means that you will most certainly be attacked if you try to travel it. On that particular day, the route was classified as red. Even though it was just a 15-minute ride, there was a lot to beware. They told us that there were three known VBIEDs in the area (VBIED = vehicle-borne improvised explosive device = car bomb), and they gave us the license plates of the cars to look out for. Beyond that, regular IEDs were possible, and there's always the potential of small arms fire (automatic weapons being shot at you) and BBIEDs (bicycle-borne improvised explosive devices). Realizing that the threat of attack was finally real and not just some nebulous training exercise on Fort Bragg, we began packing ourselves into an armored bus (known as a Rhino) that would take us on our first convoy.

I was one of the last soldiers on the Rhino; all the seats were occupied by the time I got in, so I had to just grip an overhead handrail with my left hand as I clutched my rifle in my right. As we jaunted through the streets of Kabul with our helmets bouncing off one another, I hunched down to survey the streets outside the windows.

My initial reaction was that I'd landed in a dump. Buildings were in poor condition and there was excessive trash in the streets. But at the same time, it was exhilarating to see the locals browsing the market kiosks and to watch the little Afghan children playing on the sidewalks. If any of us forgot why we were there, we remembered then.

We continued into the fields just outside of the city. My eyes widened and my forehead began glistening as several Afghans wearing backpacks bicycled towards us.

Think quick, Danger. What are you going to do? If those are explosives in their backpacks, you'll be hurled against the side of this bus.

I swiveled my head around in hopes of devising a quick plan that I could implement if we would get blown up, but I found no viable solutions to prevent myself from harm; we were packed sardines with no control over anything that was about to happen.

I bent my knees, clenched the handrail, and controlled my breathing as we whipped past the bicyclists. Hearing a *whoosh* instead of a *boom*, I looked out the back window to see the peaceful Afghans pedal away from us.

We were safe this time, but my mind was being transformed, starting to comprehend the potential threats that existed all around me.

We arrived into the heart of Kabul safely, only to experience the worst air quality you can ever imagine. The air tasted like carbon and smelled like car fumes, and hovering over the city dangled a cloud that was the color and enormity of a herd of elephants. Afghans have to burn tires in Kabul just to stay warm, but with the way the air circulates in Kabul, the smoke from the burnt rubber collects together and forms a menacing haze that remains suspended over the crestfallen capital. And, as if the city needed an extra pinch of dreary, dust is omnipresent; tents that haven't been occupied in days look like they haven't been occupied in years.

If at any point we forgot where we were, we were reminded when loudspeakers blared melodic Muslim prayers throughout the city. One of the "pillars of faith" for Islam is the Salaat, which is a practice in which Muslims pray five times a day, no matter where they are or what they're doing; with these loudspeakers, no Muslim (or non-Muslim) would forget when the Salaat was.

As enlightening as it was to be in Kabul, it was not the final destination for CH Fardpot and me. We had to find a way to get to FOB Lightning, which would become our home base. However, getting there is tricky: in Afghanistan, there are only a few paved roads, one of which we took into Kabul. The only paved road from Kabul to Gardez (the city that FOB Lightning resides) usually flickers between being a red and black road, and is surrounded by other black unpaved roads. My chaplain and I have been in communication with those already stationed at our future FOB, and we've always been told that we would fly into Gardez on a helicopter because the roads are nearly impassable because of terrorist activities.

Over the next couple days, we weren't having any luck finding flights going to Gardez. After we were told that there probably wouldn't be flights to Lightning for a couple weeks (which was problematic, as we needed to shadow-train and ultimately replace the current ministry team by the time they left in ten days), we found out that the road between Kabul and Gardez had briefly changed from black to red. We decided that the red road was our best option, so we signed ourselves up for a convoy to Gardez. (If you've never heard anyone pray a desperate prayer before, go ahead and tell a soldier that, for his first convoy, he'd be going down the road that we were slated to go down.)

The next day, we got all our gear and headed out of Kabul and down the only road that could take us to Gardez. The route at first was great. Again, we got to see the "city life" of Afghanistan, and as we drove by, kids would stop and give us thumbs-up or wave to us.[6] They were so excited to see soldiers going by in their town, and it was great to know that even if it came to the point where nobody in our own country supported us, at least these little kids felt we had value.

As we treaded on, there were fewer and fewer Afghans, and more and more dirt fields. After several hours, our convoy stopped to a jerking halt. I shared glances with the other first-time-deployment soldiers' faces, and we all seeped with fear that we were already going to have to use our weapons.

"Everyone, get out," called the troop commander from the front. "There's a wire in the middle of the road, and it's screaming 'I-E-D.' "

I dismounted the vehicle and chambered a bullet, ready to shoot when needed while patrolling the immediate area. We knew from our Fort Bragg training that we were supposed to pull security during circumstances like these.

We were in-between two large mountains, so I began carefully scoping out the area to see if I could spot any snipers, hoping we didn't fall into a trap.

An Iraq-war veteran sidestepped towards me, keeping his eyes on the mountains. He leaned in towards me.

"Right now, if any Talib wanted to fuck us up," he slowly raised his chin, "they could fuck us up."

---

[6] **Isn't the "thumbs-up" gesture meant to be offensive in the Middle East and Southwest Asia?** Not anymore. Several years ago, this was the case in these countries, but the gesture has since taken on a much more friendly meaning, especially in areas with an American presence. Today, most of these areas have adopted westernized hand signals, with "thumbs-up" being a positive gesture and the middle finger becoming the negative version.

He was right: had a group of terrorists prepared for an attack, we would've been stuck in a bad choke point.

My heart beat faster with each passing minute we were out in the middle of the danger zone. I looked at the veteran for some assurance that what he said wasn't actually going to happen, but his eyes didn't stray from the mountains, even as he spit his chewing tobacco to the ground.

I noticed an opaque bag lying beside our vehicle, spurring my suspicion. And if I learned anything from Bragg, it was to trust your suspicions.

"So," I tried maintaining my cool with the veteran, "you see that bag?"

The veteran glanced at the bulky bag, then back towards the mountains.

"Yeah, I seen it."

I cleared my throat.

"How, uh... how do you think it got there?"

The veteran picked up on my unease.

"You talking about *this* thing?"

He zeroed in on the bag and darted its way, as if he was going to stomp on it. Filled with apprehension, I stumbled backwards to distance myself from the potential bomb, almost tripping and falling on my rifle in the process.

The veteran had no such qualms. With one swift kick, he sent the bag flying into the air, its contents flying all over the road. It wasn't a bomb; just a bag filled with candy wrappers, a leftover slab of beef, and a can of pop.

Without saying a word, the veteran returned his eyes to the mountains.

After 20 minutes of security operations, we were told to mount up back in the vehicles. I felt relieved because my back was killing me under the weight of the armor. I couldn't wait to sit down again under the protection of our vehicle.

It was an interesting sensation as we continued our drive: as we climbed higher and higher into the mountains, I became more and more tired. It got to the point where I couldn't keep my eyes open for more than a few seconds because of how thin the air was. Us "newbies" weren't acclimated for the altitude, which was one reason we were riding down with those who had already been in those mountains for quite some time as we struggled to stay awake. And, of course, the jet lag wasn't doing us any favors, either.

When I woke up, it was over an hour later, and we had reached a daunting altitude, just under 9,000 feet above sea level. At this point, it was starting to get dark, but the view was gorgeous as I looked down into the valley below. We entered FOB Lightning well after sundown, with no significant activity[7] to report.

I imagine you can't be happy with the story I just told you, Joanna. I don't doubt that you're gasping to yourself, "Oh my gosh... my poor little baby is in such a dangerous place, he could've been killed!" Yes, your little baby had an intense experience, but now baby is safe at his FOB, and doesn't have to make that trip again. When the Army found out that I was college-educated and proficient on the computer, they deemed me an asset that they didn't want to lose. They've told me that I'm not to go out on combat missions for any reason; that my mission is to stay on the FOB and take care of the mental tasks that I'm particularly gifted at.

Besides the fact that I won't be leaving the base, the chaplain assistant that I'm replacing told me that FOB Lightning itself is particularly safe, and other Lightning natives have corroborated on that. With the way the FOB was built, I have to agree: we're on a hill and thus have the advantage to any attacks that may come our way. Also, our FOB has both the ANA and our own American soldiers pulling security, and there is a presence of soldiers from other allied countries that could step in and help us in the case of an emergency.

---

[7] **significant activities,** or **SIGACTs**: incidents worth reporting to the command, particularly regarding attacks that occurred during a mission.

So far, the FOB seems nice. We have porcelain toilets and warm bathrooms, and instead of having to eat Meals Ready-to-Eat (MREs) all the time, we have a DFAC[8] in which contractors serve food for us. And despite Afghanistan's low health standards, the local nationals who serve meals put on chin covers, so our food doesn't get beard in it. I appreciate the gesture (not because I'm afraid of accidentally eating beard, but because the attempt at sophistication brightens my day for reasons I don't understand, kind of like seeing a dog wearing a sweater). The DFAC is also always stocked with a modest array of *free* cold cola products (which makes me wish I brought my grenadine so I could make myself some kiddie cocktails).

Overall, I anticipate a tolerable year here. It does get difficult to walk around at night because most FOBs (including ours) are "blackout FOBs," meaning the sun and moon are our only sources of outdoor light. We're allowed to carry flashlights, but besides that, there are no unnatural lights to guide us around the FOB after dark. We keep it this way because American forces are the most elite nighttime-ready forces in the world; it's often said that we "own the night" because we're so efficient at nighttime operations. And then, of course, there's the obvious: terrorists can't shoot a rocket into a base they can't see.

It's a little bit difficult remembering where everything is in the dark, but in a couple days, I should know the layout by heart, sun or moon. Because we have had full moons the past couple nights, the visibility hasn't been bad. Come next new moon, I shouldn't need my flashlight anymore to guide me.

There are only two things that I've found may be ongoing problems: one of them is the water supply. None of our water is potable, meaning if we drink it, we'll get sick. This is a fact of life for all soldiers living in Afghanistan. You know how annoying a boil order is; imagine having to deal with one that lasts a year. It's not ideal to have to brush my teeth using a water bottle, but I imagine I'll get used to it.

---

[8] **DFAC,** or **dining facility**: more commonly known as a mess hall.

Instead of tap water, they supply water bottles around the FOB. Apparently, the tap water here has quite a bit of fecal matter in it, so we don't drink that crap. It's always in the back of my mind when I take a shower that I'm washing my body with Afghan poop, but when I think about what soldiers had to do during the initial OIF[9] and OEF[10] campaigns, I really can't complain.

The other thing that is less-than-appealing is the altitude. The air is exceptionally thin up here, and so it screws with our bodies in ways I didn't expect. Of course you get your standard shortness of breath, but it goes beyond that. For one, my sinuses are going nuts. My nose constantly shifts from running like a waterslide to being clogged up like a mud pit, which then turns into a sore throat at night.

Also, we've all been experiencing bladder problems. Because the pressure is so low here, it's like someone is pushing on our bladders, and so we have to pee all the time. The altitude even causes bags of chips to puff up to the point where they feel like a blown-up balloon. I've found that when your body alerts you that you gotta go, *you better get going.* Some soldiers don't even attempt to make it to the bathroom; they just keep empty water bottles next to their bed for when nature calls, then dump their homemade apple juice in the morning.

As someone with OCD, I don't take to this practice. Though, I can't say I necessarily blame those who do. Last night, I had to pee three times during the night, and I have a *young* bladder. I can't imagine what some of these older guys are experiencing.

Because of the thin air, I also get tired a lot earlier, but when I finally go to bed at night, I can't sleep for long because I'm either trying to breathe too hard or my mouth is too dry (there's approximately 0% humidity in the mountains here). Also, we have to take pills everyday to prevent malaria,

---

[9] **OIF,** or **Operation Iraqi Freedom**: anti-terrorism campaign launched in Iraq in 2003.

[10] **OEF,** or **Operation Enduring Freedom**: anti-terrorism campaign launched in Afghanistan in 2001.

which makes our skin drier, and with us being so high up in the air and close to the sun, it's a double-whammy of dermatology issues. So, whoever came up with the phrase "your attitude determines your altitude" obviously never took a trip to Gardez, Afghanistan.

CH Fardpot and I are still getting into the groove of things here, trying to soak up information from both the soldiers who have been here for awhile, as well as the interpreters who permanently live here. Today we met the oldest interpreter on the FOB, an Afghan in his early 60s; his ash-colored hair makes him particularly respected among the Afghan people. Those with "mature" hair are regarded as wise folk, which makes me wish I could grow out my sexy cowlicks and show the Afghans my locks that've been sprouting silver since I was 17.

Anyway, this older interpreter expounded that he, as well as the other Afghans, want us here. He guesstimated that, of the Afghan people, at least 98% of them appreciate the American presence. We were *invited* to the country and have liberated them from a lot of the tyranny and fear they were living under when the Taliban ruled their country. He respects us, as do more than most of the Afghans. The Taliban is becoming less successful here because of American efforts, and the Afghans are becoming less fearful as a result. In fact, most of the suicide bombers these days aren't even Afghans – he said that they're Pakistani terrorists who found a way across the border. It's gotten to the point where the terrorists are running out of volunteers for suicide missions, and those that did it once before don't answer their phones for a second round – go figure. But, hearing this man's appreciation for America gave me a newfound distaste for the media, rarely showing that side of the story because it doesn't sell. It's a huge encouragement to know that the Afghans support us.

So, the prognosis is good. From the moment a soldier signs the dotted line, he gets tossed onto Uncle Sam's conveyor belt. You can try running backwards to where you started, but there's no escape from the inevitable: you're going to get dumped out onto a foreign land.

I've finally reached that dumping point, and now I'm safe in Afghanistan. Surprisingly, it's a laid-back atmosphere, and much more pleasant than Fort Bragg. Not to mention, it's a beautiful country; the FOB is surrounded by monstrous mountains, many of them snow-capped. If only this were a secure country, it'd be a tourist attraction that would rival Ireland and Italy.

Joanna, I know this is a big lifestyle change for you, having me over here, not being able to talk to me every day. Not to mention, while I have the luxury of being occupied all the time, you don't. I'll be praying for you, not that you learn to live without me, per se, but that God comforts you in your loneliness and anxieties. But don't worry about me. I believe God is on high-alert for my sake, and though I always appreciate prayers, I'm at a point where I believe I am exactly where God wants me. There's much comfort in that.

I'll be home for Christmas... just not this one.

Love,

Sleepless in Battle

Kabul and the smog that hangs over it

.: 3 :.

The Girl from the Playground

February 2006

TICK. TOCK. TICKETY-TICKETY-TICK. TICK. TOCK. TOCK.

The family room was all but quiet, save for the clock in the corner that barely functioned. It had been a few days since I almost crashed in the church parking lot, and I should've been 300 miles away at college, but instead was back home to see my psychiatrist.

As the fickle clock crept from late night into early morning, the tone of a text message chimed in my pocket.

Who's contacting me at such a peculiar hour?

My intrigue only deepened when I didn't recognize the number.

The text simply read, "Nathan?"

I responded, affirming that the sender had reached a "Nathan." Seconds later, I found out who had been texting me.

"It's Joanna from Kilmer."

Joanna from Kilmer? Wow! What a surprise…

◊

Joanna from Kilmer.

Before my family moved to Zion as I was entering third grade, we lived in a Chicago suburb named Buffalo Grove. Back then, I was a student at Joyce Kilmer Elementary; back then, *I was a Cougar*.

The Cougar was the school mascot. Every morning, each student would recite the Cougar Pledge, a litany of admirable traits that every Kilmer kid was to strive to achieve: we would pledge to treat others with kindness and respect, to be cooperative and responsible, to use proper manners, to follow school rules, and to be the best Kilmer student that we could be. Our daily oath would conclude with all of us kids shouting, "Once a Cougar, always a Cougar!" Reflecting on the pledge, I found that last bit a little peculiar: my college mascot also happened to be a Cougar, so the proclamation of "once a Cougar, always a Cougar" held particularly true for me.

Joanna had also been a Kilmer Cougar. Though, we weren't friends or even acquaintances as children. For all I know, it's possible we never had any interaction: we weren't in any of the same classes, and there really should be no way that we would remember each other.

But, back in the spring of 2005, I had found my old 2nd grade Kilmer yearbook, brushed the dust off, and started searching for recognizable names so I could track down other Cougars on the newest fad: social networking sites. I was discouraged at first, as most of the faces and names in the book weren't ringing any bells for me. Except there was this one picture of a cute little girl, and even though I couldn't put my finger on how, I knew I knew her. There were no specific memories of her, but I felt like I must've known her from somewhere. Something drew me to her. So, I searched for her online, found her, and messaged her.

Similarly, Joanna didn't know how, but she recognized me, somehow, someway. We began corresponding, but our virtual relationship wouldn't last long. I was getting ready to ship off for the summer to train to become a chaplain assistant in what was essentially a second iteration of boot camp, and Joanna was in a committed relationship with a guy. The contact ended there.

That is, until I got that text in the first few minutes of a frigid February morning.

◊

"It's Joanna from Kilmer. I was just lying in bed and I realized how important it is to keep in contact with people, because you never know."

Over the next several days, we corresponded more and more through texts and continued playing "catch up." At the time, the thought of a significant relationship was all-but-absent, considering we didn't know each other and that we both were dealing with the aftermaths of break-ups.

But in that time, we learned to appreciate each other. We had recalled ancient memories of Kilmer that had been locked-up way in the back of our brain's filing cabinets, from our fond memories of Mr. Ryan the gym teacher, to the solemn atmosphere of the school the morning after the Kilmer secretary died, to the "Jump Rope for Heart" fundraiser that took place on the school's tennis courts. We also discovered that we grew up a few blocks from one another, and Joanna had even been neighbors with my aunt who lived just a few houses south of her.

The more we talked, we realized how many times there was a possibility that we had met as kids, and just didn't remember it. In a matter of a couple weeks, late-night phone conversations between us two Cougars became a regular thing.

On one particular night, we talked not only all night but well into the morning of February 18th. After finishing our phone conversation at 4:00am (and stopping mainly because my phone battery was dying), a strange feeling came over me. But not just a feeling, though. It felt much more than that, much more… divine.

As if a flash of lightning hit the room, I felt a warm breath speaking to my soul.

"Nathan… Nathan, this is the one… this is who you will marry…"

Okay, Nathan, you're getting a little too tired, I rationalized.

"This is who you will marry…" it repeated.

You're just woozy. You're experiencing an emotional high, and you probably should get some sleep.

"Let it be, Nathan… you *will* marry her…"

Okay, you're going crazy. You are going crazy.

"You *will* marry her…"

I logically came to the illogical decision that God must be speaking to me. But as I considered this, I experienced something more than a voice: it was like I was inexplicably afforded a knowledge of the future, but a future that already happened. It felt as if I had already married this girl and now was thinking about the years we'd been together; though there were no specific memories, it was like I'd been with this girl for years.

Then came the phenomenal. Like a train heist gone bad, my broken heart derailed into a love-filled lagoon. Drowning in ecstasy, this ruptured heart flooded with unconditional adoration.

I love her. I love a girl I've never met. I love Joanna.

But then I realized my biggest obstacle: marriage takes two.

What about Joanna? No way she's gonna be receptive to this. She's not even religious! How would she react if I suddenly proclaimed my love for her, telling her that God said she would get married to some guy she hasn't even met?

There was only one way to find out, so I did just that. I suddenly proclaimed my love for her, telling her that God said she would get married to some guy she hasn't even met.

Joanna's response?

"I know. I feel it too."

She believed what I had been telling her, a miracle in its purest form.

But this exciting news didn't come without responsibility, as the voice indicated next.

"Tell everyone… no matter what they might think of you…"

What?

"Tell everyone..."

What do you mean?

Silence.

Hello?

More silence.

What do you mean?

No response.

The still voice said to tell everyone. But what does "everyone" mean?

Regardless of who "everyone" entailed, I figured my parents had to be first on that list. Besides, after going through something like I just did, I knew I had to talk to them right away anyway. So, at 6:00am, I called home, assuming my parents would be up for work.

"Heh... hello?" answered my groggy father.

That's when I realized it was Saturday; my parents would be sleeping in this morning.

"Oh, gosh. Sorry Dad, I forgot it was the weekend."

"That's okay," he responded, fighting his desire to sleep, instead listening to what I had to say. "What's up?"

"This is gonna be worth the early wake-up, Dad. Believe me. An emergency came up..."

"An emergency?" he seemed alarmed, as I undoubtedly elicited his memories from the last time I called him with an "emergency."

"Yeah, but not a bad one. No, it's great, Dad. Really! You won't believe it."

"Okay…" Now he was wide-awake.

"But I can't tell you like this. I need to come home next weekend. You guys have to hear it in person."

"Have you been taking medicine?"

"Dad, stop and listen to me. Everything's fine, something so great just happened to me, the best thing that's ever happened to me in my whole life."

"Oh, so… uh, does it involve quitting school?"

"No, no," I laughed. "But Dad?"

"Yes?"

"Can you make sure everyone in the house knows I'm coming home? Can you round everyone up and make sure they'll be there when I get home? I need everyone to hear this."

"Yeah, sure. I'll prepare everyone and let them know that… uh… I guess you have news. Some… *big* news."

◊

That next weekend, I did end up going home, but not without first making a detour to Joyce Kilmer Elementary.

I sat on top of the playground slide, my hands more jittery than if I had downed a cup of joe but as numb as if the cup was made of ice. While I hugged myself to smother my shivering, I saw a head poke around the corner of the school.

All of a sudden, the biting cold was bearable.

My heart started beating almost as fast as I was sprinting down the slide. After nearly falling off the edge and onto the woodchips, I scrambled towards the girl, my legs wobbling with raw anxiety.

In the dark, the two of us were finally able to see each others' faces, of which we shared matching bright grins.

She was more beautiful than she looked in pictures: her giddy smile was as striking as her shapely figure; her hair was straighter than a meticulous winemaker's vineyard, a brilliant tint of sepia; her cheeks were an alluring shade of pomegranate, ridged with an adorable little dimple, to boot.

Our bright blue eyes met; looking at her was like watching a steamy waterfall cascading amidst a frozen tundra. Though there technically was a time and date, it felt as if time ceased to exist, the rest of the world stopping altogether to allow us one brief moment all to ourselves.

The night's veil harbored us as we embraced, the brutal wind unable to tear down our spirits.

"It's been too long…" I muttered to her.

"I know…" she replied.

.: Ɛ :.

A Very Islam Christmas

25 December 2008

Hey Santa Baby,

Things are going okay here in Afghanistan. I've spent much time learning about the culture and Islam; one of my responsibilities here as a chaplain assistant is to work with the locals who live on the FOB, so I often meet with the interpreters during my down time.

The interpreters have welcomed me with open arms, excited that I'm taking the time to befriend them in a way that most soldiers don't care to. I've grown closest to the interpreter who is assigned to the ministry team; he goes by the nickname "Rambo Three," in reference to the third Rambo installment that focuses on the 1980s conflict in Afghanistan.

But that's not to say I haven't gotten to know the other interpreters, most of whom are roughly the same age as me. They've learned to call me Danger because they wanted to call me what my friends call me; they're always trying to make me feel comfortable around them. Whenever I walk into their little hut, I announce upon entering, "Natersade! Khatar injast!" In Dari, that means, "Don't be afraid! Danger is here!"

In the Afghan culture, when you enter someone's house, you're offered chai tea, and you shouldn't decline it. Unfortunately for me, I detest tea, and the mugs they use aren't washed well as I can see lip marks from the previous person who drank from the cup (a real nightmare for someone with OCD). The first time I visited Rambo Three's hut, he asked me if I wanted some tea, and I politely refused. He looked more disappointed than a Chicago Cubs fan in October, and so I asked, "Am I being rude because I did not accept your tea?" He looked me straight in the eyes and said, "Yes." Since then, I've not declined their tea or their dirty mugs, learning there's no such thing as a "polite refusal" in Afghanistan.

Also noteworthy is the Afghans' take on affection. The people here aren't afraid to hug and kiss and hold hands and even lay their head down on one another's thighs. An American would quickly classify such behavior as inherently gay, but upon reflecting on their attitudes toward one another, it seems Afghans are just more affectionate to one another than Americans are, regardless of gender. Yet, as much as I recognize this as a cultural thing, don't expect to hear any stories of your boyfriend kissing any Afghans.

Sitting down with the interpreters (who we call "Terps" for short), I've found they have a particular fascination with writing acrostic poems in English (in the Dari language, it's impossible to create an acrostic poem because all their letters flow into one another, somewhat similar to our cursive writing style). Though some of the Terps' adages don't make a lick of sense, I can't help but smile as I read their poetry:

WHAT IS A FRIEND?
Faithfulness
Respect
Intelligence
Earnestness
Nobility
Division

WHAT DOES LOVE MEAN?
Land of sorrow
Ocean of tears
Valley of death
End of life

WHAT IS THE PURPOSE OF PEPSI?
Pay
Every
Penny to
Save
Israel

WHAT DOES FAMILY MEAN?
Father
And
Mother,
I
Love
You.

WHAT IS A WOMAN?
Window of paradise
Origin of life
Model of patience
Academy of manners
Nearest of heart

Besides spending time with the local Terps, I've also had brief moments of limited interaction with the Afghan soldiers. FOB Lightning is home to an ANA boot camp, the Afghan military's first step in training how to fight against terrorists. At the same time, it's speculated that a few Taliban have infiltrated the ANA, and so when you walk by a formation and look into the eyes of an ANA soldier, and he shoots back a glare of contempt, you can't help but wonder if you're but a few feet away from a terrorist who wants your head on a platter.

One of the other responsibilities I have is to meet with the local mullah.[11] That, too, has been eye-opening. We often talk about politics, culture, terrorism, and religion in order to better the already-successful relationship between the American forces and Afghan leaders. I asked the mullah if he

[11] **mullah,** the Muslim religious leader of a village. Sometimes referred to as an imam.

believed that there were terrorists within his own ANA troops, and he said he can't be sure, but if he found one in his ranks, that Taliban member would be executed within hours of his discovery. On the flip side, if the Taliban were to somehow take control of Afghanistan again, then every Afghan who ever helped Americans would be killed: every interpreter I've met, every ANA soldier, every peace-preaching mullah, and every remaining freedom fighter within the country would be hunted down to be hanged.

Doesn't it seem contradictory that the 2% of the population that hates Americans could eventually control the other 98% that appreciate us? Well, you've heard the phrase, "if you can't beat 'em, join 'em." For many, the fear of a Taliban resurgence outweighs logic, so if there was an atmosphere that suggested that the "good guys" were losing, many locals would pledge allegiance again to the Taliban in fear for their lives.

Speaking of the atmosphere, I've found that there exists a violent ambiance to this place. I don't know if it's just my mindset, or if it's a seething unholiness that's indelible to Afghan soil. But just the other night, I dreamt a dream that felt so real, I was sure it actually happened:

I lied in my bed feeling less-than-lucid, the state of mind you get when you have trouble discerning if you're really sleeping or not. I calmed my heartbeat to a steady pace, controlling my breathing.

Thud, thud. Thud, thud. Thud, thud. Thud, thud. Thud, thud.

KPUUUH!

Without warning, a mortar crashed on the opposite side of my hut, blowing our quarters to bits. I could barely open my eyes, but it was just enough to see a limp arm from the corpse of CH Fardpot. I was pretty sure that everyone else in the hut had been killed in the explosion, and the fact that I wasn't also dead was a miracle in itself. Unable to move, I closed my eyes and waited in what used to be my bed, hoping help was on its way.

Just as suddenly as the mortar had crashed on the hut, my eyes opened and I gasped for air as I realized I'd just been dreaming. I put my hand on my heart.

TH-THUD. TH-THUD. TH-THUD. TH-THUD. TH-THUD.

I pray that, if I ever have to endure such a tense experience, that I'm ready for it. If I find myself in a situation where enemies are dropping shells on my head, may God grant me the strength to overcome my fears to make the right decisions.

◊

A small group of us banded together today to form the Lightning Tabernacle Choir – a tandem of soldiers, airmen, and sailors – to sing carols in an attempt to help quell the constant tension on the FOB. But as I send this, the sun is setting on my Christmas while it burns brightly over yours; it's time to trade back my Santa hat for my field cap. And even though I miss America incredibly so, and I miss you all-the-much-more, I know God has me exactly where He wants me. There's so much peace in that. It's difficult to have a bitter Christmas in that sense. I have no pity on my situation, and I would request that you don't either.

Thank you, God bless, and have a merry, merry Christmas. Remember, Jesus was born in humblest of circumstances to be a servant to this world; let's strive to mimic His meekness.

Love,

Kilmer Kid

Danger exercises security precautions on an intruder who infiltrated FOB Lightning, December 2008

.: 4 :.

Foul on the Court

February 2006

After the night I met Joanna, life felt so different; to say I was happy would be an understatement. Rather, if the days leading up to my incident in the church parking lot were my rock bottom, then these days after hearing that God wanted me to marry Joanna were my cloud nine.

Even though I was excited to tell my family about Joanna, I was also nervous. I had driven 300 miles away from school to make myself more vulnerable than ever. My family and I have clashed with our religious differences before, and I wasn't sure how my good news would be received.

My dad had fulfilled my request to round up the family. My siblings looked at me with eyes that displayed hope that the news wouldn't take long to tell, my dad reserved in demeanor, and my mom excited yet nervous to hear what I wanted to say.

With everyone's attention, I broke the news.

"God told me who I'm going to marry."

"I knew it," called out my younger brother. "Didn't I tell you, Mom? I knew you were gonna say you got engaged."

"No, I'm not engaged. In fact, I think that's going to be a far ways away. God is going to direct me when I should take that next step with her, but it's not now."

"Is this the girl you just broke up with?" asked my mom, remembering how badly that relationship ended.

"No, it's not. Actually, the girl is someone I went to Kilmer with."

"Kilmer?" my mom asked, her eyes bulging from her skull. "What's her name?"

"Joanna. I stopped in Buffalo Grove on the way here so we could finally see each other in person."

"So you had never... *met* before?" my mom asked. "You're going to marry a girl that you just met?"

"Right, but like I said, that'll happen when God wants it to happen. I'm not jumping the gun on this one."

"So, is that it? Can we go now?" my little brother asked, hoping to get away from his nutty brother.

"Yeah, is that it?" my big brother resonated.

"Yeah, I guess that's it. I wanted to tell you all first. God told me that I need to tell everyone I know, no matter if they'd believe me or not."

"Why does He want you to tell everyone?" my dad inquired.

"I don't know, Dad. I don't understand that part either. But I feel a heavy conviction that it's what I'm supposed to be doing."

My dad solemnly examined me, one arm resting on his well-nourished belly and his other hand stroking his soot-shaded beard as if he was a court juror contemplating the verdict.

◊

Over the next several days, I tried telling anyone who might be a part of "everyone," friends and extended family and even some strangers included. But they weren't any less skeptical of my story. While there were a select few individuals who believed in what I had to say, the majority had less-than-enthusiastic reactions. There were some that were tolerant with what I was saying, verbally telling me that they believed me, but otherwise indicating that they wouldn't be willing to put stock into it. Other particularly religious people labeled me as "misguided," while some friends missed the point altogether and simply said, "If that's what makes you happy, then go for it," as if I was making a career choice. Others didn't care one way or the other, feeling my story wasn't worth their time to hear. Yet there were others who became angry, telling me that I needed to stop shoving my beliefs down their throat.

By the time I had told everyone around me, many of my relationships were broken at worst and strained at best. For those that didn't just tell me to shut up and not contact them anymore, I was still just one of those close-minded religious guys that people generally like to avoid.

If I had had any reputation before, it was dragged through the mud now. I was frustrated and hurt that any respect I had earned from my loved ones was all-but-gone now.

◊

Before I headed back towards St. Louis to return to college, my dad could tell I was feeling dejected, and so he sat down and patted me on the back.

"It's not going well, is it?" he asked.

I bit my lip, and not even looking at him, shook my head. My dad knew the answer before he even asked; in fact, the Zion High School principal reached out to him after I emailed all of my former teachers with my story. I had created a buzz at my alma mater, and not in a good way: I received several emails back from teachers who I once had the respect of, emails all flowing with concern and a few dripping with anger.

"I did everything I thought I was supposed to be doing, but it feels so embarrassing," I vented. "I don't want people to think I'm some religious nut."

"Nate," my dad laughed, "you're *way* past that point. You *are* a religious nut. But… maybe that's not such a bad thing."

"I guess what I mean is… I'm… I just don't know. Did I make a wrong move?"

"Well," he reasoned, "is it wrong to commit a foul in basketball?"

I looked up at him, flabbergasted by his comment. I didn't understand what he was saying, nor was it helpful. He might as well have said, "When's the next Leap Year supposed to happen?"

"You don't remember?" he seemed surprised. I shook my head again, looking no less confused.

"It was your first year playing basketball in junior high, and you had never been called for a foul all season. The entire year, you were such a timid player. You were so afraid of being the reason that your team lost that you would avoid playing aggressively, so as not to get called with a foul and give your opponent a chance at some free throws. Nevermind the fact that your passive defense was allowing your opponents easy shots at the basket anyway," he laughed to himself. "The night I drove you to your final game of the season, I explained to you that if you commit a foul, it doesn't mean you're a bad player; even your favorite Chicago Bulls athletes regularly commit fouls. Would you classify NBA stars as passive or aggressive?"

"Aggressive." Of course they were aggressive. What a stupid question.

"Right. They're aggressive. But you know what? When you play aggressively, you're going to get called for a foul every now and then. It's just a part of what happens."

I was starting to recall this conversation we had when I was in 5th grade.

"After we talked in the car that night, it was like it clicked for you. You realized you needed to be a bolder player. You realized you needed to play more aggressively. So, you said to me, 'Dad, during this last game tonight, I'm gonna get fouled.'

"Well, during that last game, you were a different player. You were all over the ball; nobody could get near the basket without you getting a hand on the ball first. And then, the inevitable happened: the referee blew the whistle to stop play and he called a foul on you for a reaching violation.

"As the teams got set to start play again, you glanced over in my direction and shot me a mischievous smirk. You had committed the first foul of your basketball career. I smiled back at you, so proud of you for challenging your opponent. I knew you finally figured it out: if you were gonna be effective, you'd inadvertently commit fouls here and there. It's the nature of the beast."

I remembered that story now. Hearing it again renewed the pride that I had felt that day. But what did it have to do with me now?

"This prophecy that you're telling people about now," my dad continued, "it's not going to go over well. When you play someone in basketball, they have one mission: to get that ball in the basket via the easiest route possible. But when you come at them, you frustrate their plans. Likewise, the people you're telling this story to have one mission: to live their life via the easiest route possible. But when you come at them, you frustrate their plans.

"If God did indeed tell you to do this, then you need to do this. You need to be bold. But you also need to understand you're going to upset people. You're going to commit fouls. But if you're not aggressive enough to commit fouls, then you're not trying hard enough, are you? Follow your heart and trust God's plan. If you're gonna be effective, you're gonna inadvertently commit fouls here and there. It's the nature of the beast.

"But," he set up the punch line, "when you do commit fouls, know that I'll still be proudly smiling back at you."

I nodded my head. He had made his point.

"Nathan," he then tried to put his skepticism in perspective for me, "as I consider your story, I can't say whether or not God spoke to you. He didn't speak to me about this, so I can't know. I won't tell you that you're right, and I won't tell you that you're wrong. But in time, your story will either prove to be one or the other. All I can do is wait and see."

I appreciated his candidness. And he was right, too. God never commanded me to convince anyone that what I was saying would come to pass, but rather that I just needed to tell it to everyone. I did what I was told to do, and that was enough.

"Besides," my dad added, "it's not like what you're saying is harmful. Nobody's going to die if you're wrong."

"Well," I swallowed hard, "there's more to this story than just the idea that I'm going to marry a stranger, Dad. What benefit would it be for God if there was no risk?"

"What's that supposed to mean?" he asked as his eyes drooped.

"If God promised me that I'm going to marry Joanna, then that means I'm going to marry Joanna. And nothing can stop that."

My dad's tolerant demeanor changed, not liking where this conversation was going.

"Not even death," I added. "I believe God wants me to be fearless until I marry Joanna. God wants me to know that I can't die until His promise comes true."

My dad hated hearing this. He knew that I was often a wild child in high school, known for being quite the reckless teenager. And if I was dangerous before, how much more dangerous I'd be with this newfound belief.

"Nathan... you're planning something, aren't you? You're going to act on this 'invincibility' belief, aren't you?"

He knew me too well.

"Are you familiar with East St. Louis?" I asked.

"East St. Louis, the city just across the river from St. Louis? East St.

Louis, debatably the most dangerous city in the country? That one?"

"Yes, that one."

"Nathan… what about East St. Louis? What are you going to do?"

I smiled at my dad, who wasn't returning the gesture.

"I think God wants me to reach out to them."

.: 4 :.

Take Me Down to the Gardez City, Where the Grass is Brown and the Girls are Gritty

11 January 2009

Hey baby Cougar!

I hope you're well. My outlook is good right now: I survived a difficult Christmas season away from home, I now have my combat patch for serving in a combat zone for over 30 days, and I've completed 100 straight days of this deployment.

Over the Christmas season, we received a lot of cards from teachers and children in schools and churches, wishing us well and praying for safety. But there were a few humorous ones that jumped out at me. For instance, one kid sent us a card exclaiming "I hope you win!", like we're playing a game of capture-the-flag with the terrorists. Another child seemed to think that our success or failure would have a direct and immediate effect on his life, as he pleaded, "Save me! Save me!" Another person understood how difficult it would be for us to enjoy Christmas, writing "Hoping your holidays are filled with (some) fun." Yet, my favorite card came from a young boy who was frank and right-to-the-point, packing all the important aspects of a Christmas card into six words: "Good luck. My name is Jared."

I've got some good news: our ministry team has been given an additional chaplain assistant. His name is Sergeant (SGT) Nicholas Bandee, and he'll be conducting the "operational" side of this duty; he'll be the one going out on convoys and taking flights all over Afghanistan, and in fact has already treaded over the dangerous Khowst-Gardez (KG) Pass of Afghanistan just one day after a group of soldiers were ambushed on that route.

The KG is a mountain pass where you're driving in a vehicle, literally just a few feet away from an edge that drops off at least 6,000 feet. I've heard the KG often referred to as the most dangerous mountain pass in all of Afghanistan, and it's with good reason. Besides the possibility of veering over the edge (the room for error is a mere few feet), you also have to worry about getting choked out by the enemy there. One explosion could send a vehicle plummeting off the edge into oblivion, and your most basic firearms attack often puts soldiers into sticky TICs.[12] Oh, and the entire pass is unpaved – plenty of places to hide IEDs or for an edge to crumble at an untimely moment.

Construction has been ongoing throughout the KG; it's taking an exceptionally long time to pave the entire mountain pass because contractors are constantly being shot at as they work on it; the terrorists want to do everything in their power to prevent it from being completed. Our base commander believes that once the KG is finished being paved, "the war will be won." While I'm not sure that I agree with such a bold proclamation, I understand his rationale: many of our supplies come westward through Pakistan, up-and-down the KG Pass, and then are distributed throughout all the bases in Afghanistan. Unfortunately, the trucks transporting these supplies are often attacked and then torched because of the driver's defenselessness while on the KG. Once the KG is paved, though, the ease of attacking will be substantially reduced: it'll be much more difficult to hide IEDs, and trucks can speed through a lot quicker, especially when under attack. Terrorists will find much greater difficulty in garnering dominance over the KG Pass once its construction is finished.

But as it stands today, crossing over the KG Pass in a coalition vehicle is as risky as strutting through the inner-city projects while pimping rival gang colors. Of all the ways SGT Bandee could've kicked off a tour in Afghanistan, it seems he was tasked with a combat mission that required him to dive headlong.

Bandee encountered a different breed of gut-twisting on his second mission: less than an hour before his flight left for the city of Ghazni, Bandee began uncontrollably puking. During our training on Fort Bragg, we were told that Afghanistan has low health standards, and that their food is probably undercooked and full of bacteria; Bandee decided not to heed this

---

[12] **TIC**, or **troops-in-contact**: term used to refer to situations in which servicepersons are being actively engaged by an enemy.

warning. He puked four times in a five-minute period a day after eating an authentic Afghan meal. He knew he wasn't going to abort his mission, so he packed his stuff and headed to the helicopter pad, spitting and wiping his mouth after each upchuck. Because I run the administrative side of our team, he reported back to me later about the rest of his trip:

> To get to Ghazni, I had to stay overnight to wait for a flight at an air base that was somewhere between the Jalrez and Nerkh valleys in Wardak Province. Well, that next morning, I was sitting in one of the huts, just killing time before the chopper arrived. That's when I heard the flapping sound of air being beat into submission: my Chinook had arrived 45 minutes early, and I was at least a 10-minute run away from the flightline.
>
> I dashed to reach the chopper before it lifted off, but the air is even thinner there than it is in Gardez. I was exponentially losing energy with every step I took, finding that I didn't have the strength or the lung capacity to make it to the flightline. To make matters worse, there had been heavy snowfall; each step I took was met with several inches of snow. It wasn't long before I collapsed, gasping out, "Help me," but only the frost heard my cry; nobody was around. It had felt more like I was wading through a thick swamp with an ape on my back than trudging through snow with my gear.
>
> I knew that if I was going to make this flight, I needed to get moving. I mustered all the strength I had and picked myself up, sloshing through the snow. I didn't make it very far, collapsing again under the elements. But this time, I had shuffled far enough that some soldiers were within view of me. They ran over, and finding my face downed in the snow, helped me to my feet and picked up my bags for me. That's when a golf-kart-like vehicle called a "Gator" came by and picked me up. I crawled onto the front of the Gator and laid on its hood as it carted me down to the helicopter, like I was

a dead body on a gurney. I barely made it to the bird in time, which had been getting ready to lift off. I arrived to Ghazni shortly after.

After his mission in Ghazni was complete, Bandee got on another helicopter the next day to return to Gardez. But during that flight, he got re-routed to Bagram Airfield in northern Afghanistan because of foggy weather conditions over the mountains between Ghazni and Gardez. Over the following days, no flights were able to get him back because of the ongoing harsh weather conditions between Bagram and Ghazni. He's now gone well over a week without a shower and has been wearing the same clothes for three days and counting because his 3-day trip to Ghazni turned into a week-long excursion all over central Afghanistan. At this point, the weather is only expected to get worse as Bandee only gets grungier.

I've found that Bandee is a valuable asset to our ministry team, enabling me to focus on the logistical side of the mission; that is, maintaining the chapel, planning Bandee's movements, overcoming administrative hurdles, meeting with the mullahs and locals, and taking part in humanitarian missions.

A humanitarian mission is a mission in which we gather a bunch of goods (specifically food, clothes, shoes, writing utensils, and toys) to hand out to the local Afghans. I've been privileged to have already gone out on one in the short time I've been here. A group of us traveled outside the FOB to a little village within Gardez to hand out the supplies we've collected over the past several months.

When we arrived to our destination, I hopped out of the humvee and saw children lining the village. The houses looked like they were made of adobe brick, and even though there were only about 50 houses, there were about 1,000 children sitting in the dirt, anxiously fidgeting for us to start handing out candy and other goods.

I approached some of the children to try to communicate with them, but my Dari is so limited, and for that matter, such is the case for the kids, who hadn't spent a day in school yet. I tried using hand signals to communicate with them, which they seemed to respond to; they understood "thumbs-up," and shot back the two-fingered peace sign as I waved to them. It broke my heart to see the children; many of them had tattered clothes and some didn't even have shoes. The girls of the village are too young to be wearing burkas, which they customarily don when they become teenagers, but their faces were veiled with dirt in its stead. The girls seemed afraid of me, but the boys were more lax.

One of the officers told me to go grab a bag of candy from the truck. I whipped the bag over my shoulder like a natural Santa Claus and began strolling towards the gaggle of kids. Before I got there, I felt a tugging on my bag and turned around: a little boy was trying to poke a hole in the plastic bag to get its contents to pour out like it was a piñata. As I told the boy "Nay," I felt more tugging and turned around to find two more boys trying to pull the bag off my shoulder. With command, I shouted "Nay! Nay, stop it! Nay!" The undisciplined children kept trying to get my bag to break open, and I started shuffling away like I was a wounded minnow in a tank of sharks. As I doddered towards the officer that requested the goods, I turned my head and found what had been just three or four kids chasing me before were now a couple dozen bloodthirsty ruffians. I began sprinting towards the officer, but the bag ripped and my hands were left with a few pieces of sweaty plastic. I turned around to find a kid had pulled the bag out of my hands as I'd started running. I tried my best to gather the bag and scamper away, but not before the dozens of children caught up to me and started digging into it. It was no use; I had failed my mission. I stumbled backwards and watched helplessly as candy flew everywhere. I felt like I was watching a pack of jackals tearing apart a poor innocent zebra. Within a matter of seconds, the pack dispersed and all that was left were pieces of the shredded zebra skin.

After the ambush, I headed over to another group of kids in hopes that I could slip some suckers to a few of them without getting mugged again. As I walked among the children, one boy jumped up on a pile of bricks, and establishing himself as king of the village children, yelled to me.

"Chocolate!" the boy cried.

"Chocolate?" I asked. "Nay, no chocolate. I have no chocolate."

"Chocolate!" the child king yelled louder.

"Nay!"

"Chocolate! *Choc-oh-lat*!" The king had become crazed, irate that I wasn't giving into his demands to magically make his chocolate appear.

"Boy! I have no chocolate!"

The king settled down and shrugged his shoulders. "Give me money!"

"*Money*? You want money?"

"Yes, money!"

"Heck no!"

"Give me money."

"I *got* no money."

" 'I *got* no money,' " the king mocked me.

Just then, an ANA soldier zipped over to us. The king's eyes filled with fear, and he jumped down from the bricks to outrun the Afghan soldier, whom was smacking the king's shins with his baton. The crowd of children moved away from the soldier, knowing they'd get hit if they were in his way.

A little girl stood her ground against the soldier, crying into her hands as the soldier raised his baton. The soldier whipped his baton towards the girl, and with impressive dexterity, halted his hand just before the baton clonked her. The girl, realizing she hadn't gotten hit, glanced up and saw that the soldier was only trying to scare her into moving away. Her sister emerged from the crowd, took her hand, and the two of them disappeared into the crowd.

I hung around the crowd awhile longer, loving every minute I got to spend with the kids. Despite the language barrier, it was as if we understood each other. At one point, while I tried talking with one of the kids, I rotated 360° and found I had gotten surrounded by a mass of children, all of my escape routes now blocked. Afraid some child would try to grab at it, I hugged my rifle and just hoped that none of the kids went for my pouches that had loads of ammo. It was a good thing that I had been warned before the mission to button up all my pouches and tie them down to prevent the children from taking my stuff.

I squeezed through the sea of children to return to the main group of soldiers, whom were still tossing bags of rice off the truck to give to the parents of the children. I heard a small voice behind me, so I turned around and found a child tugging on my pant leg. I got on my knees and tried talking with him. He couldn't have been older than five years.

"Please," he said.

"Is there something you need?" I asked, as if he could understand me. "Something you need?"

"Please," he repeated. "For me."

He pointed to the ground. I didn't understand.

"Please. See. For me."

I shook my head, frustrated with the language barrier.

"Give me, please."

He bent down and touched his feet. He was wearing flip-flops that had a hole in its sole; he would've almost been better off walking around barefoot.

"Please."

I bit my lips, remorseful that I was unable to help him. We didn't have any more shoes to give away.

"Sorry," I said. "No shoes today. I'm sorry."

"Please," he repeated. "Shoe? Please shoe. For me."

"No shoe. All out. Next time, give shoe. Okay?"

"No shoe?" he inquired.

"No shoe," I confirmed.

The boy nodded his head in acceptance, and ambled away in disappointment as the rocks scratched his calloused feet.

The child had seen me as a symbol of provision; he had approached me in the hopes that I would be able to provide him with something that my country's children have tons of. When I was a kid, I must've had a half-dozen different shoes. For this poor child, I couldn't even provide one pair.

Not long after, our group of soldiers packed up and returned to our humvees. As we sat in the vehicles waiting for clearance to start moving back to base, children started banging their hands against our windows, mischievously smiling all-the-while. They even tried opening the doors (to no avail, as they were combat-locked). When we started driving away, the children backed up and waved goodbye to us.

◊

Alright, I wanted to save what I'm about to say for last, but I'm bursting at the seams with this great news: *I will be coming home early from Afghanistan*.

At the beginning of the year, the Army told us that we would be back in our homes by midnight of September 29, 2009. Now, it's been cut down even shorter than that. I don't know how "early" I'll be leaving, I just know that it's earlier than previously thought. Yet, the funny thing is, the Army hasn't told me this at all. In fact, quite the opposite! I've heard rumors that we were being extended from day one, and some even said we'd be extended through January 2010. The Army is confidently telling me that I won't be going home early.

So how can I be so sure about this?

Well, I was lying in bed a few days after Christmas, trying to get to sleep when I was startled to full alertness. No, there wasn't a rocket or an alarm that roused me; my heart just started racing on its own, as if I could sense someone had slipped into my room.

I scanned the dark room and saw nothing. But I did *hear* something.

"You..."

That silent voice was back.

"You will be home early..."

Early? I'll be home early? From Afghanistan?

"You will be home early..."

Okay...

"Tell everyone..."

What? No, not again. I can't go through that again. I was so hurt last time. Don't make me do it.

"Tell everyone..."

I don't want to do this. Please don't make me do this! I believe You, but don't make me tell everyone again.

"Tell everyone..."

I can't do that. I can't. Don't put me in this position again.

"Tell everyone..."

I'll tell Joanna. And I'll tell my parents. But that's it this time. Nobody else needs to know.

"Tell everyone..."

Please, no. Please.

"Tell everyone..."

Please!

"Tell everyone..."

Fine! You know what? Just... fine. I'll do it.

I listened for a minute more, and when I didn't hear anything else, I closed my eyes and tried to settle my heart. The joke was on the voice; I wasn't actually planning on telling anyone, I just said I would so I could get some peace and quiet.

And I did feel peace – for a brief moment. That is, until my eyes shot open when I remembered a verse I had read an hour earlier. Grabbing my Bible and my flashlight, I returned to the passage I just finished reading.

"When you make a vow to God, do not delay in fulfilling it. He has no pleasure in fools; fulfill your vow. It is better not to make a vow than to make a vow and not fulfill it. Do not let your mouth lead you into sin. And do not protest to the temple messenger, 'My vow was a mistake.' "[13]

Ohh, nooo... I'm screwed!

I threw the Bible across my bed and smacked my head. I was so frustrated; I felt like I had been tricked!

But despite my feelings, I can't ignore the facts: God commanded me to do something, and I promised I'd follow through.

When I tell others about this, I know they're gonna groan, "here he goes again with his God ramblings." But then I think about when God told me to tell everyone that I would marry you (even though I hadn't met you yet), and I think about how accurate that's looking, despite residing in a country choked by separation and death. And then I think about the recent episode where God told me I'd be home early for Thanksgiving pass, and what came of that.

So, my hands are tied. I hastily promised I would tell everyone, and so I must. But, I do find comfort in one thing: I actually *believe* what I'm saying. I find no excitement in announcing it, but I do believe I'll be home early.

---

[13] Ecclesiastes 5:4-6

I wouldn't blame you if you didn't, though. It's not an easy thing to swallow (even CH Fardpot tells me I'm a boob for believing this). But, consider this my way of giving you advance notice that you'll see me before you thought you would, and you can expect me to be back in school with you next semester. I've already gone ahead and registered for classes and am in the process of securing a room on campus. Our anthem used to be "Wake Me Up When September Ends," but not anymore.

I have one prayer request right now: please pray for George Bush as he leaves office in a few days, and meanwhile please pray for Barack Obama as he takes on one of the most stressful duties anyone could fathom. Whether we like Bush or Obama is beside the point; please pray for them to be given wisdom regardless. "I urge, then, first of all, that requests, prayers, intercession and thanksgiving be made for everyone – for kings and all those in authority, that we may live peaceful and quiet lives in all godliness and holiness."[14]

Thank you, God bless, and have faith in what I'm saying!

Love,

A Boy Named Danger

---

[14] 1 Timothy 2:1-2

Danger gives an Afghan child a sucker during the humanitarian mission, January 2009

.: 5 :.

The Bridge is Out!

February 2006

I had returned back to school from telling my family and hometown pals my news; friends were hard to come by these days, but fortunately I had one in a man named James Amos.

James was in his late-20s, a scrawny-bodied but strong-spirited college student who shared my common beliefs about Jesus, though my journey to Christ wasn't nearly as dramatic as his. I had simply been raised in the church, and after struggling with doubts in high school, I researched the person of Jesus of Nazareth and logically concluded that He is, indeed, the Christ. Meanwhile, James had had a rough life riddled with depression and had almost hanged himself when he was a teenager. Several years and many regrettable life decisions later, James was approached by an elderly man on a college campus and explained the forgiveness that Jesus of Nazareth offered through His life and resurrection. Right there on the quad, James fell to his knees, accepting that following Christ was the purpose behind life. Since then, he had gone back to school full-time and was in his final year of acquiring his undergraduate degree, next planning on earning a Masters of Divinity and ultimately desiring to become a pastor.

Lucky for me, not only did I have a friend in James, but I had someone who believed my crazy story and wanted to help guide me.

We ate together at a burger joint one day to discuss what was going on in my life. Pouring the contents of a package of ketchup on a bun, James asked me, "So buddy, do you get why it's important for Christians to bring the message of the Gospel to non-Christians?"

I knew there were a million ways to answer this question, but James had a point he was trying to make.

"Imagine you're driving along a road when you see a construction worker waving his arms, asking you to pull over. You roll down your window and he informs you that, just up ahead, a bridge has collapsed, and if you continue on your way, you'll fall into a ravine below and instantly die. You thank the man for passing that information onto you, but before you leave, the man tells you that he needs your help, that he can't single-handedly stop every car from driving off the cliff.

"You put your car into park, turn your hazard lights on, and begin sprinting back from where you came, flagging down every car you come across to let them know about the bridge before it's too late. But, the first time you flag a car over, the man rolls down his window and gets indignant with you.

" 'How do you know the bridge is out?' he asks. 'Did you see for yourself that the bridge is out?' You shake your head no, and the man scolds you, 'It's impolite to force your beliefs on other people.' The man drives off to his impending doom.

"You stop another car, and the female driver inside insists, 'You should keep your opinions to yourself. It's close-minded of you to think that you know more about this road than I do.' And she drives off.

"Another driver stops and rebukes you, 'Listen, we're all just trying to get to the same destination, don't tell me which roads I need to take to get there.' You shout out after him as he drives towards the collapsed bridge, 'But your path will send you to your death!'

"You become discouraged. You're just trying to help these people based on your beliefs, but they keep spitting your efforts back in your face. But, are you going to stop offering people a chance at salvation just because most of the people you run into scoff at you?

"As Christians, we get scoffed at a lot because people think we shouldn't discuss our beliefs. 'It's rude,' they say. But if you're really a Christian, the thought of someone driving their car off a cliff into the depths of hell should crush your heart, moving you to want to warn them about the collapsed bridge they're speeding towards.

"I say this because, if you really are set on spreading the Gospel of Jesus, you're going to have people spit on you. But remember, there are also people out there that care to hear what you think. The Apostle Paul knew he was crossing over into dangerous territory by indiscriminately preaching to all, but he also knew that some would accept the Gospel of Christ as a result. And if you're a Christian, how can you not value that over anything else?

"We're not told that we need to convince anyone that Jesus is Christ. Instead, we're told that we should just tell people the story of Jesus Christ, merely planting a seed so God can send someone to water it. Maybe you get to help water that seed, maybe not; but God will ultimately be the one to make it grow.[15] It's just up to us to get people to listen to the story and make sure they understand it, as well as the implications of it if it's true. But you know what's one of the biggest reasons people reject Jesus?"

It was another question that could've had several responses, so I simply sipped my milkshake, waiting for James to fill me in with his thought process.

"Most religions are..." He stopped mid-sentence, noticing I was grimacing. "What's wrong, buddy?"

"Uh, *mint*, man. It's mint."

"So?"

"I *hate* mint. I ordered vanilla. Mint is my least favorite ice cream flavor."

---

[15] Mark 4:1-20, 26-32. Also, 1 Corinthians 3:6-7.

"So go and ask them to get you a vanilla. Do you have the receipt still?"

"Yeah, but it's okay. I don't wanna."

"You'd rather drink your least favorite flavor instead of just asking for the actual milkshake you paid for?"

"It's okay, let's not worry about it. I don't want to make a big deal out of it."

"You sure? They won't mind, believe me."

"I'm sure, James. Come on now. You were about to explain something."

"Okay. Anyway," James continued, "you know what's one of the biggest reasons people reject Jesus? Most religions are centered around 'doing,' not 'believing.' When people finally buy into the plausibility of the Gospel of Jesus, what's the first thing they ask?"

I knew the answer this time, from both personal experience and because the Apostle Paul was faced with this question in the Bible.[16]

" 'What do you *do* to become a Christian?' " I responded.

"Exactly," said James, still not chewing into his burger just yet. "It's in our human nature to want to do something to achieve results. For instance, devotees of Judaism focus on adherence to Mosaic laws. Muslims are focused on following Mohammad's teachings and abiding by Sharia, or Islamic law. Our Christian brothers and sisters who ascribe to Catholicism often get wrapped up in trusting in their good works instead of trusting in Jesus' finished work on the cross. Buddhists are focused on 'doing' inaction, if there's such a concept. Even most atheists believe in 'doing,' as in doing the right thing

[16] Acts 16:30-31

according to their own moral code. That's what makes our beliefs different. Others emphasize doing what they believe in, while we emphasize believing in what Jesus already did. And when someone truly believes in what Jesus already did, it will move them to carry out good works as a result."

I had already known everything James was saying, but I was appreciative hearing him put it the way he was.

"So," he continued while holding his burger, as if he was going to get a breath in to actually take a bite, "when someone asks, 'what do you do to become a Christian,' it's simple. You just..."

"...point them to Jesus," I took over to give him a chance to eat. "You explain that there's nothing left to do except believe in Jesus, that according to the Bible, 'whoever believes in Him shall not perish but have eternal life.'[17] No one can earn salvation through doing, but instead can accept God's grace of salvation through faith. You become a Christian by simply believing that epitomic truth, and strengthen your faith by praying and reading the Scriptures and gathering with other Christians to worship God and discuss godly matters."

James enthusiastically nodded in agreement, his mouth full of his burger that had been growing cold. We let silence fill the air for a moment as I slurped my unappetizing shake.

"So, let me get this straight," James said as he continued chowing into his meal, abruptly changing the subject. "This Joanna girl, you didn't really know her? And then, God told you that you'd marry her? And she believed it and everything? But then God also said that He wanted you to tell everyone you know about this story, not minding if you get ridiculed for it?"

"Right, that's about the gist of it so far."

---

[17] John 3:16

He looked at me intently.

"You're supposed to tell everyone, whether you think they'll believe you or not?"

"Right."

"You're supposed to tell everyone, even if they *hate* you for it?"

I nodded. I knew James was trying to make a point, but I wasn't getting it.

"You need to tell everyone, *even if you get persecuted for it*?"

I blankly stared at him.

"I don't get what you're doing, James."

He smiled at me.

"Doesn't this whole thing parallel the Christian message, buddy? Think about it! Jesus came to earth to be perfect, died in our place as a criminal on the cross, rose to conquer our sins, and now we, as Christians, have the ultimate job of telling this story to everyone, whether people will believe us or not. It's the same formula: something amazing and unexplainable and irrational happened in your life, and now God says that He not only wants you to believe it, but He also wants you to share this message with others. You might never see how it affects other people, just like how we might never see how our explanation of the Gospel can radically change someone's life, but we are charged with this duty anyway."

James just blew my mind; how could I have not seen this? He was right: I was obedient in telling everyone about my own wild story; why did I lack courage in sharing the Gospel?

As I pondered these things, James changed the subject again.

"So, what's the deal with this 'Danger' thing? I hear that's your name now."

I just laughed; he was right, a few people were starting to call me Danger. I'd been joking with some friends about how fun it would be if someone's middle name was actually Danger, and since then, they started calling me by that name.

"You know James, I'm not really sure what to say about it. Yeah, a few people have taken to the name, calling me Danger now."

"Well, if you're planning on going into East St. Louis, the name might be fitting. Do you know that city's history? Do you understand why it's so dangerous?"

I shook my head as I sipped from my craptastic shake.

"This is good for you to know, because it wasn't always the broken city that it is today. Once upon a time, East St. Louis was a thriving district. And I mean *thriving*. In the late '50s, it was even named an All-America City. That might sound like gibberish to you…"

"And it does."

"…but what that means is they were recognized for having an outstanding community; a community of cohesion and productivity. It was a great place to move to and raise a family. Business was booming and the economy was great. It was a regional hotspot; just like you go to hang out in St. Louis now, people used to go to East St. Louis.

"But the city always had an affliction: it bubbled with racial tension. There was always an even mixture of blacks and whites in the city, and they tiptoed around this metaphysical powder keg in the middle of the city, afraid of accidentally igniting it.

"For awhile, it was just quiet tension with a few hate crimes here or there across the decades. But the day Martin Luther King, Jr. was shot, the powder keg lit. The city's lull burst into flames and violent mobs rose from the ashes. Riots broke out and blacks unleashed their pent-up anger on whites; whites, who were largely the business owners in the city. Soon, an exile of whites snowballed, sucking the tax base right out of town.

"With factories closed and whites no longer helping support the city, many blacks lost their jobs and found themselves living in poverty in what had become the very definition of a ghetto. To make ends meet, arsonists set buildings aflame in an attempt to recoup some money through insurance entitlements. If you go there today, you'd think a fire swept through the city."

"And it did," I began to understand, "one house at a time, torching their sticks from the blown barrel's blaze."

"Exactly," James continued. "Today, less than a third of the population remains. The city doesn't even have enough money to replace street signs. Burglars steal the signs so that visitors will get lost, making it easier to mug and rob them. There are a few white people that live in the city now, but the racial tension is as high as ever.

"People might call East St. Louis 'godforsaken' or attach some other hopeless term to it, but you have to remember, people still live there. East St. Louis is home to some. God does not forsake, and therefore the people there are worth being reached out to. Do you understand what I'm saying?"

I nodded my head, my hands covering my lips in contemplation.

"I'm not trying to tell you that you shouldn't go into the city," James continued. "After all, God loves the people there and you very well may be used to touch someone's life. But you have to understand what I'm telling you. You're a peace-loving guy; I mean, you hate confrontation so much that you refuse to ask for the vanilla-flavored shake you actually ordered. This trait may work against you. This city is not safe, and the fact that you're white could cause you problems. East St. Louis isn't just dangerous in theory; it's statistically one of the most dangerous cities in America, if not the most dangerous. East St. Louis is one of the top murder capitals in the country, and its rape rate doesn't trail far behind. This isn't a game; this is your life, buddy."

Again, I nodded without saying a word.

"It's important you don't get pompous about your situation. You know where I stand; I believe what you've told me. But don't get a spiritual arrogance about yourself. You've been given a gift from God; that doesn't mean you know God any better than anyone else."

I nodded my head, wiping mint confection from my mouth with my napkin.

"Your name may be Danger, and you might not be able to die…"

I was hanging on his every word.

"…but you can still be paralyzed."

.: 5 :.

I'm Gonna Be (7,000 Miles)

4 February 2009

Hey hun,

It's a weird stretch we're in right now: I'm no longer seeing Afghanistan as foreign, though I'm still not seasoned. I feel like I've been here forever, but in reality, I still have several months to go. When I look back at when I enlisted, I never envisioned being deployed, but I have to consider how much the National Guard has changed in the last decade. When I signed the government contract, I was told that I would be working about 38 days a year. But in the first nine months of 2008, I was on duty about 70 days of the year (and that doesn't include any days of the deployment), and in 2009, I've only had four days off the entire year so far (ignoring the fact that I'm in Afghanistan and "time off" doesn't entail seeing my family). The "Weekend Warrior" has become a thing of the past, as far as I'm concerned.

When I think about it, if I *had* to be anywhere in Afghanistan, I'm glad I am where I am. It's a place with such a rich culture that other places within the country don't necessarily have. For instance, I stand in the same place where the Mongols once ruled, and one of Alexander the Great's castles is on a nearby hilltop. Concerning the darker side of the country's history, the devastating effects of the Russian invasion are all around, and the locals here can talk for days about it. Not to mention, every morning I get to wake up to the sun hitting snow-capped mountains with beautiful splendor. I look at the mountains and imagine a tourist snowboarding it, and I realize that if that image ever becomes a reality, then we've accomplished our mission.

We have a bazaar located on FOB Lightning that's open on weekends; it flourishes with American consumers looking for Afghan souvenirs. The shop owners sell items like locally-made wooden carvings, marble chess sets,

Foakley's,[18] high-quality diamonds and stones, luxury rugs, Russian hats leftover from the 1980s invasion, Afghan scarves, and assorted other trinkets at reasonable prices. Probably the best-selling shops are those that sell black-market DVDs of pirated movies and TV shows; I thought I'd share a verbatim description on the back of a Family Guy DVD box:

> Peter (protagonist) is always a lovely Shasha says his family. His wife is addicted to a baby son, the mischievous fun of the day, she envisaged how to control what she-year-old son, the one year old The son of a Trick or Treat ghost is born, he would come up with many ways to let his parents angry surprising things.

Well, I'm sold!

As far as the overall mission, I feel it's going well in most aspects. The Afghan military is progressively getting up to par, and this country is becoming a place that terrorists fear. In fact, there's hearsay that northeast of here along the Pakistan border, a district displays the decapitated heads of bereft Taliban on tall spikes, their glazed eyes frozen in place, warning their compatriots with their pallid lips, "Come, dear friends, and you will also be martyrs." As barbaric as that is, that's the kind of brute retaliation that may be necessary to scare the Taliban into abeyance.

While the Afghan military is progressing, there is one aspect of the American training that isn't going as well as hoped: the medical side. The process to become an Afghan doctor isn't very selective; any American with just an Associate's Degree would be more qualified than most of the Afghan medical student candidates. One American doctor who is mentoring the Afghan doctors told me a story about a patient that was suffering from appendicitis. The Afghan doctor cut open the stomach and heart area of the patient, taking out all of the patient's innards and setting it on his chest. The doctor then proceeded to massage the heart. The American doctor immediately stopped him and corrected the mistakes, setting his organs

---

[18] **Foakley's**: counterfeit sunglasses that are nearly identical to Oakley brand sunglasses, except much lower in price and quality.

back inside his body cavity and cutting out his appendix, saving the patient's life.

I realize that sounds like there isn't any progress being made, but you'd be surprised to hear that it used to be a lot worse than that. Another American doctor who's a colonel told me that he believes in 15 to 20 years, Afghanistan will be up to American standards. He believes America has done all she can to help the Afghans in the medical realm, and that the only way they'll learn at this point is through "evolutionary progress," as he described it. In time, they'll learn what to do and what not to do through trial and error, life and death. He pointed out, after all, that that's the way advanced medical practices arrived to the point they're at today. In theory, America could slightly expedite the Afghans' learning process by continuing to teach them ourselves, but it would take a couple decades to bring them totally up to par, and it's doubtful the American government (or its people) want to be holding Afghanistan's hand that long.

This whole mission reminds me of a video game I used to play called Pikmin. (Yeah, leave it to me to resort to a Nintendo analogy.) In the game, you're an astronaut named Captain Olimar who travels to another planet and meets all these puny creatures called Pikmin. Olimar leads them into battle and helps them kill the other species that threaten their daily existence. By the time Olimar leaves the planet in the end, the Pikmin have learned to fend for themselves. It's funny, but I realize how similar America is to Captain Olimar, and that our Pikmin need us less and less. We're not quite at the end of the "game" yet, but we're getting close. And I'm not just saying that to feign optimism; I really believe we're close to where Afghanistan needs to be.

The local Pikmin here are interesting, to be sure. In fact, I'm closer to the Terps than I am with any Americans on the FOB, and my camaraderie does not go unreciprocated. "Danger, you're our best friend," they've told me.

One time, Rambo Three even expressed, "You are a eunuch for us."

"A *eunuch*?" I responded in bewilderment. "Are you sure you're using the right word?"

"Yes Danger, you are *eunuch*! We've been friends with other soldiers, but you are one eunuch we've met."

"I'm not a eunuch, guys."

"Yes you are. You're just special like that, Khatar, our brofer. Many others have come before you, but you are one-of-a-kind. No one is like you."

"Are you telling me... are you saying that I'm *unique*?"

"Yes, Danger, you are very eunuch to us. There is none like Danger."

Relieved that I finally understood what he was saying, I accepted his compliment. And looking back on our time together, I realize why they've drawn so close to me. I often bring them their favorite energy drinks from the DFAC (as they're not allowed to enter ours unless accompanied by a U.S. soldier), and I've dropped off a few care packages in their hut when our chapel has been overflowing with boxes of candy and canned goods. When I bring them such gifts, they usually wolf down all the food within hours. One time, I failed to adequately screen what I was giving them, and a Terp ate a can of mini-sausages after I affirmed to them that were no pig products in the care package. After we realized the can had had pork in it, I felt awful, but the Muslim was quick to forgive me, pardoning my oversight because of how much value he puts on our friendship.

Besides offering them gifts of food and energy drinks, our relationships have flourished beyond superficiality. I spend most of my free time with them, and everything we do is such a blast: we browse the bazaar with one other, we play cricket together, we compete on the ANA obstacle course against each other, we have part-American / part-Afghan dance parties in their hut, and they discuss their Muslim religion as I discuss my Christian faith. Many of them have even gone to church with me, and at least half of them requested Bibles to read. I'm not welcome in their mosque because I'm not Muslim, so I haven't had the chance to go to their worship time, although I see them pray throughout the day. I'll just be sitting in their hut with them, and then they bust out a Muslim prayer rug and pray wherever we're at. They also tell me stories of when the Taliban ruled when they were pre-teens, and how the Terps would be physically abused by the Taliban. It helps me understand why they like me so much, and I feel blessed to be a part of something that their country appreciates and needs.

I'm sure you're wondering about my other friend, SGT Bandee, who's now been on his share of missions. Recently, he wrote me a rundown of some of the things he faced on his operations:

> Our inexperience was oozing on our first combat mission, as we got lost along our way and strayed from our green road to a black road. For over a half-hour, we tried figuring out how to get out of the situation we'd put ourselves in. At one point, we cornered ourselves into a dead end and didn't have enough space to even turn around. That's when we got ambushed. No, not ambushed by the Taliban, but by little kids pounding on our humvees' windows asking for chocolate and candy. We knew that we were sitting ducks for the Taliban, and there was no telling how close we were to getting hit by a terrorist. One could've easily climbed any nearby building and shot at us, knowing we had few recourses available. Eventually, we literally drove in reverse through the town to backtrack the route we had traveled. We were able to find the green road again, allowing ourselves to breathe a little easier as we tried completing our excursion.
>
> Along the way, I took the time to appreciate the kids of the country. The kids give soldiers "thumbs-up," and when a convoy passes through Afghanistan towns, the kids run out to the edge of the streets like American kids do for the ice cream man. I look out to the kids and see them use their hands to wave at me, and my hands return the gesture. They use their eyes to look at me in sheer intrigue, and my eyes replicate that intrigue. Their hearts go out to me because they know I'm in a dangerous spot, but not before my heart aches for them for the same reason. And as all that happens in a split moment, we drive on.

On the route, I look out my window and see the remains of several cars blown up by IEDs. There's one field in which there are around 15 blown-up vehicles, abandoned and alone, never to be used again. And as I'm in the vehicle thinking these things, we continually bump over potholes that feel like the precursor to an explosion, making me believe that I'm about to be launched out of my seat and added amongst this field of death. That is, until a quick moment passes and I realize that I'm still on the road, not being thrown from the humvee.

Our humvee's Blue Force Tracker reports that three vehicles that are about an hour or two behind us, taking the same exact route we just did, are caught up in a TIC. In times like that, I think to myself, "that could have been me just now," and I recognize that if it *had been* me just then, that I would need to be a true soldier and fight alongside my fellow soldiers and possibly do something I would never wanna do: kill another human being.

We continue into a dangerous district named Saydabad. We're told that we should expect to be fired upon. I pull out an extra carton of ammo and open its case, ready to feed it to the gunner in case he runs out of ammo in the anticipated scuffle. Fortunately, it's freezing right now. In fact, I'm shivering and my toes are going so numb that I have to wiggle them to fend off frostbite. These arctic conditions disable me. I have no desire to move, yet moving is what will keep me warm. I have a love-hate relationship with the weather, because as it conquers me, it also conquers the Taliban. And on this particular trip through Saydabad, nobody dies today because it's so dastardly cold.

Today, I ask that you pray for the troops as a whole. As Bandee just said, it's frigid here, and I agree with him that the cold is an awesome thing right now. But in no time, things are going to start heating up, and it'll be common for us to hear about our fellow soldiers going home early in coffins.

The cold has protected us a great deal, but the winter is thawing and the blood of spring is right around the corner. As for Bandee, the next time he goes through Saydabad, I doubt he's going to be as lucky as he was this time – and he knows it, too. So, may God be with all of our troops as we enter the long stretch of warmth ahead.

Thank you. And God bless you.

Love,

Sergeant Olimar

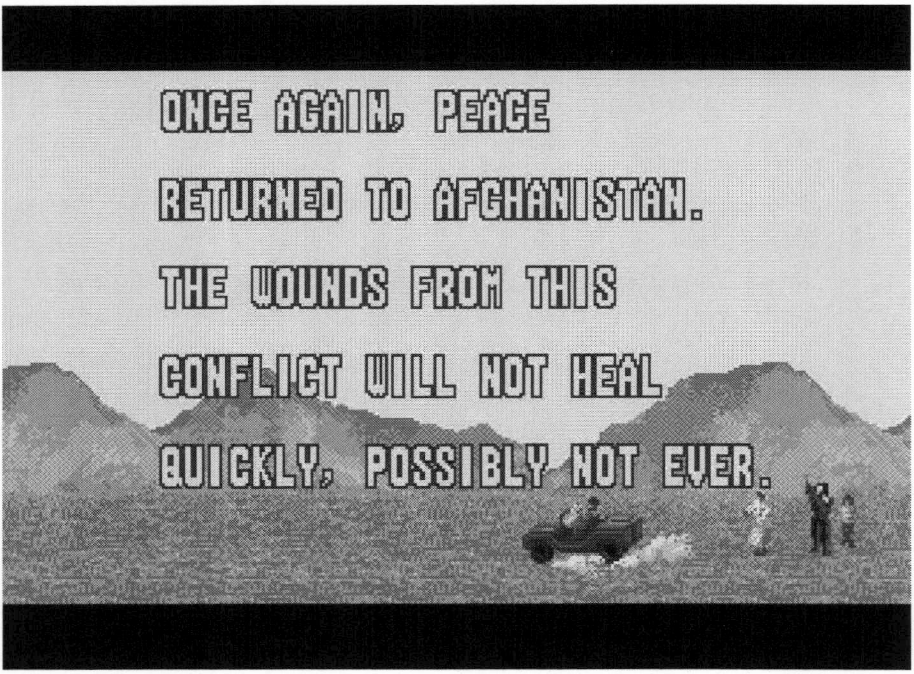

A screenshot of the ending sequence from <u>Rambo III</u>, a 1990 Sega Genesis video game (adapted from the 1988 movie of the same name) that highlights the lasting damage of the 1980s Russian invasion of Afghanistan

.: 6 :.

A Cold Fire

March 2006

I sat in my car, which had grown arctic since I turned it off a few minutes ago. I stared ahead at the bright casino lights, the last standing reminder that East St. Louis was once a prosperous city. I briefly prayed for the ministry I was about to conduct, not knowing exactly what I was supposed to be doing here in East St. Louis, but knowing I was called nonetheless.

I plodded away from the casino towards the run-down industrial area and quickly found myself hobbling around a deserted trail. I was looking for anyone that God wanted me to talk to, ignoring the fact that I wouldn't even know what to say to that someone when God helped me find them.

As I treaded a gravel trail, a car sped around a corner in the distance and zoomed towards me, flashing their brights at me.

Oh, shoot, my mind cried out. *Someone's chasing me!*

I turned around to run the other way, but found a second car had sprung up and parked behind me, preventing me from going anywhere. I ping-ponged my eyes between the parked car and the one speeding my way to devise an escape plan, but realizing I was surrounded, I held my hands up in surrender as the car zoomed towards me.

Oh, gosh. Don't run me over!

Screeching brakes and billowing dust filled the air as the car stopped just short of me. A different set of lights was now flashing in my face: patrol lights. I still stood with my arms raised as heat from the car's hood crept up my shirt. Two sets of bright lights exposed me like a lightning bolt exposes the night sky, and my breath was turning red to blue to red to blue as the patrol lights flashed on me.

I could barely see, but was able to decipher the silhouette of a man in uniform approaching me.

"This is private property, kid. What are you doing, roaming around here?" the cop grunted.

"I'm, uh… evangelizing, sir," I responded, my arms still reaching for the moon. The cop glanced up at my outstretched hands, one of which was holding a Bible.

"Evangelizing? Do you know where you are?"

"Yes sir, East St. Louis."

"Have you heard of this place before?"

"Yes sir," I lowered my arms. "I was told to come here."

"Who told you to come here?"

"The Lord did, sir."

"The *Lord?*"

"Yes, sir."

The cop was frustrated, obviously worried about my well-being. He asked to see my ID, and I showed him my military ID and driver's license. He quickly jotted down notes for his police report, and then turned to speak to me again.

"Do you know what time it is?"

"Yes, sir, it's midnight."

"12:45. You shouldn't be here right now. You're a white boy, wandering alone in a black neighborhood. If you stay here, you'll be stabbed and shot tonight. You *will* die tonight."

"The Lord told me I can't die tonight, sir. I'm supposed to reach out to people here."

"Kid, the only people you'll find around here are either high or drunk."

"There's someone here for me to talk to, sir."

"Well, there's no one right here," the cop raised his voice. "These buildings here are privately owned, and you can't trespass here."

"Sir, then how do I get to the heart of East St. Louis?"

The officer looked at me for a moment, internally debating if he should give me the information I was requesting.

"You take a left at the stop sign down that way," he sighed, "and keep going past the gas stations. I wouldn't suggest it though," he shook his head as if he was ashamed for divulging his knowledge. "You can't wander around here, especially this late, and especially alone, and especially being white, and expect to survive."

"Thank you, sir."

"You know what?" he blustered, finally washing his hands of the situation, "if you want to die in East St. Louis tonight, then that's fine, that's on you."

The cop rode off, surely expecting to have to shovel me off the streets in a few hours.

I got back in my car and drove to the heart of the city, following the officer's directions.

As I rolled through the true East St. Louis, I became even more nervous. The city looked like it had a tornado come through, or at least a small battle. There were collapsed buildings, gas stations abandoned and rusting, and drug deals happening right on the streets. The dull hum of distant sirens whirred over the city. To think that this was the atmosphere that some children were being raised in!

I stepped out of my car and onto the ashes of the All-America City, getting a dual whiff of kitchen trash and sulfur. I crept behind a gas station and heard a noise come from a nearby cluster of barren trees. I twisted my neck to peer in and saw a garbage can burning with flames, providing warmth to two men.

"Keeping warm?" I approached the fire.

They didn't hear me, so I repeated myself.

"Keeping warm?"

The two men looked at me, then laughed.

"What the fuck is this nigga' doing out here?"

"I was wondering if you guys wanted to talk..." I became sheepish. "...if you wanted to talk about God... or something."

The men stopped moving for a second, studied my face to see if I was serious, and one of them replied, "Yeah, sure. We'll talk about God," punching each word as he spoke.

The men introduced themselves as Kenny and Percy. They were bundled up in dirty clothes, and they both smelled pungent. Percy was so inebriated that he couldn't even stand upright. Kenny was a calm fellow and had alcohol stained in his beard.

"Have a seat," Kenny motioned towards a plastic crate. "I believe in God, but Percy don't."

"Why don't you believe in God, Percy?" I asked, trying to get my butt comfortable on the crate.

Percy replied, "I was almost a fucking ordained minister! But you know what? Adultery is a sin, right? Well, Jesus was born in a manger."

"Right..." I tried to follow.

"His mom was Mary! And she was married to Joseph!"

"Right..."

"But God raped her! He inseminated her, jackass! Adultery is a sin! I believe in a higher power, but I won't call him God, asshole! Hey asshole, what's your mom's name?"

Afraid to give my mother's identity away, I told him, "Diane… Diane Sawyer."

Percy followed up by taking the conversation in another direction, "You don't like cussing much, do you?"

"I never cuss."

"Why not?"

As if he would manage to remember when his alcohol-encased mind thawed back into sobriety, I entertained his question, "It's not Christ-like. Part of having self-control is being able to control your tongue, even in moments of anger."

"Now, I've been here all my life," Percy said, once again unable to keep his attention on one topic. "I was in the military…"

"Really, Percy? I'm in the Army National Guard."

"You fucking liar! Show me your paperwork!"

I pulled out my ID and showed Percy. Kenny snatched the ID, and after taking one glance at it, pushed it back into my chest and accused me, "You lied."

"I lied?" I objected.

"Your name's not Sawyer. Your ID has your name. You lied. You're holding a Bible in your hand, and you lied to me. You're supposed to be a man of God?"

I was more naked than a hairless cat.

"I'm sorry… I won't lie again…"

"Fucking Christian hypocrite," he muttered under his breath. "How do I know that you won't lie? You see what I'm saying? Now that you've lied about that, I can't believe anything else you have to say. If you're lying about *your name*, how can I believe anything you have to say about *God*?"

Percy piped in, "You're a homeless, aren't you? You got no home. You ran away. You're 18 years old, and you ran away."

"No, I'm 19," I contested. "I go to college."

TCHUU! TCHUU!

A pair of gunshots rang throughout the neighborhood, no more than a couple blocks away.

"College?" Kenny chirped. "What you there for?"

"Psychology."

"Psychiatry!" Percy protested. "Why the shit-stained-cock you doing psychiatry? You can't do psychiatry! You're the one who's crazy!"

"Crazy?" I questioned.

"Yeah! You're fucking nuts!" Percy asserted. "You a little white boy, and you come walking up to people you don't know in a nigger neighborhood."

"God sent me."

Percy added, "Fuck, no God! That's not a Bible in your hand!"

"Yes it is," I disputed.

"No! Bibles are leather and black-covered," noting that the Bible I held in my hand was a beige paperback copy.

Kenny laughed, "Don't mind Percy. He's drunk. I'll be right back, I'm going to get some wood."

Kenny strolled away as I looked over at Percy whose head was bobbing around as his neck strained to support it. I turned my head to see Kenny's figure disappearing in the distance, and decided to run after him.

"I'll come with you," I said as I caught up with him.

He ignored me and continued walking as if I wasn't there with him.

"I'm going to be honest with you, Kenny," I said as I followed him down the street. "I thought you were going to kill me or something by now."

"Ha! You fucking white boy!" Kenny chortled. "For the past eight years, I've come to drink in that same spot every night. Why the hell do you think you'd be worth killing, knowing that would ruin my spot? You're not worth it."

"Is that why we're walking then? So you can take me somewhere else to kill me?"

"You said you were sent from God."

"Yeah."

"Then why you worried?"

I thought about it for a second, shrugged my shoulders, and responded, "I'm not."

We picked up some wood and carried it back to the burning garbage can, where Percy had thrown my plastic seat in the fire. The fire was furiously burning, spewing toxic fumes from the plastic.

"I got fucking cold," Percy tittered.

As I crouched on the ground to find a spot in the dirt, a beastly woman listening to a pocket-radio approached Kenny's drinking hole.

"What is this?" she asked, referring to me as a "this."

"He's aight," Kenny said.

"What's your name?" I asked.

As if it was all one sentence, she responded, "Why the hell do you want to know my name, it's Renée."

Kenny said, "He came to talk to us about God, but we can't trust him. The Bible says not to trust any man. And he already lied to us."

Renée's jaw dropped as she studied my face, her bloodshot eyes glaring into my rueful ones. "Come *here*. I *want* to *talk* to *you*."

I looked at Kenny for assurance. He had a quirky smile, as if he was playing a practical joke and was having trouble keeping a straight face while it played out. Kenny said, "Go ahead, she won't hurt you or nothing."

Like a puppy who knew he was about to be punished for misbehaving, I slinked over to Renée. She inched her menacing face to mine and began barking at me, freezing me in sheer terror.

"What the fuck! You *liar*! You're a liar! How'd you get here? You're lying to us! You ain't nothing but a fucking liar! No good liar! And you say you're a *man of God*? You fucking *liar*! We can't trust you! You're probably an undercover cop! Why are you here? Who you looking for? Liar!" The whiskey from her lips splat on my face, prompting me to wince.

"I'm just here to talk, I swear!" I sputtered.

I looked at Kenny for him to pull back the leash on this dog, but he just looked at me straight-faced and said, "See where lying gets you?"

After she finished tiring herself out with her rant, Renée backed away and retreated behind a dumpster. Trying not to seem too afraid, I kept watching for her out of my peripherals like a mistreated child nervously keeps an eye on his abusive dad. Kenny picked up on my trepidation.

"She won't hurt you," Kenny said. "And Percy is too drunk to make sense."

"You jackass! God raped Mary!" Percy babbled. "Hey, asshole, you wanna fight? I'll fucking knock you out!"

"No thanks, Percy," I replied, validating his nonsense.

"Let me see that Bible," Percy said.

"You can have it," I told Percy. "But only if you promise not to throw it in the fire."

"No! I would never burn a book! I want to read this book of lies! This ain't no Bible anyway!"

"Do you want one?" I asked Kenny.

"Nah, I can't read or write," admitted Kenny, who later told me he only had a third-grade education.

"You sure?" I asked.

"You know what, why do you come here, saying you're a man of God, and... okay, say I forget about the lie altogether. But you also said 'I swear' earlier when you were talking to Renée, and the Bible says not to do that. See what I'm saying?"

Kenny was right, and I knew it. Off the top of my head, I recalled verses in Matthew chapters 5 and 23 which spoke to Kenny's point.

Percy raised his hand with the Bible and prepared to throw it in the fire.

"Percy! You said you wouldn't burn it!" I protested.

He tossed the Bible, but it bounced off the garbage can and landed on the ground.

"Percy! *No!*"

I lunged for the Bible, but Percy grabbed it first. Uninterested in provoking an aggressive drunk man, I let him hold onto it. Keeping my concentration on the Bible, my mind raced to conjure up a way to save it as if it was a scared little animal in the hands of a sadist.

"Percy," Kenny pleaded, "don't burn that. I'll keep it if you won't."

As if Kenny's petition was a challenge, Percy slung the Bible towards the fire.

I went to grab it in mid-air, but Percy pitched it so fast, I came up empty-handed. The Bible landed in the flames and burnt up, adding to our physical warmth, but smoldering my spiritual heat.

"Percy, dammit!" Kenny yelled at his friend, then looked at me in disgust. "See? See what happens when you give a Bible to someone who doesn't believe in God? Now why would you give him a Bible?"

I sat in shocked silence, distraught at what just transpired.

"It wasn't a Bible anyway," slurred Percy.

Kenny could see the look of disappointment on my face, and then asked me, "What's the difference? How is what he just did any worse than you lying while holding that Bible? You both sinned against it."

We allowed more silence to fill the air for a few seconds.

"Kenny, are you homeless?" I asked.

"Fuck, he's homeless!" yelled Percy.

Kenny zeroed in on my eyes, ignoring Percy.

"I'm not homeless," Kenny said, shaking his head.

"He's lying," muttered Percy.

"I *got* a *home*," Kenny raised his voice in Percy's direction.

I just nodded, realizing I wouldn't be able to tell either way, nor did it matter.

"Why did you stop going to church?" I asked Kenny, changing the subject.

TCHUU! TCHUU!

A series of gunshots rang again, sounding just as close as the first.

"See, I would go to church and hear a sermon. But then just a few hours later, I would see that preacher smoking a blunt or holding onto some ho," Kenny explained. "I mean, we have these 'Christian' holidays like Mardi Gras, and people go around loving Jesus, but have no problem flashing their titties or pussies like it's nothing."

I was disgusted for Kenny, too, and had no excuse for Christian hypocrisy. As I mulled over what he said, Kenny let me know something that was on his mind.

"When you done talking to us here, it's best for you to leave," Kenny stated matter-of-factly. "You just happened to stumble upon a couple of good niggers. You got lucky. But after this, you need to leave. Otherwise you'll be killed."

I knew that wasn't true, but I didn't feel like telling him that I couldn't die, in fear that maybe he would test how true that statement was.

Renée stumbled back over to me and gave me an inebriated hug, whispering in my ear.

"I'm sorry about what I said before," she apologized as if she had done something unforgiveable to me. "I am *so* sorry. *So sorry.* I'm *so* sorry."

Renée wobbled off into the night, and after Percy realized she was leaving, he jogged to catch up to her. I had a feeling that Kenny wanted to get some sleep now that both his friends were gone.

"Kenny, before I go, do you want a ride to your house?"

"Naw, man. I wanna walk. I'm coo," he responded, not even looking at me.

"You sure? It'd be no problem."

"I said *I'm coo,* dawg. I wanna walk."

I extended my hand out to Kenny, who turned his head to stare at it.

"Kenny, I'm gonna be back, okay man?"

He shifted his attention from my hand to my eyes.

"I promise it," I continued. "I'll be back in a couple weeks, and I'll have a Bible just for you."

Kenny grabbed my hand and shook it.

"Coo."

◊

I reflected on the entire night as I drove back to my warm dorm room. I was pretty sure Percy wouldn't remember a thing about the two-and-a-half-hour talk at all, and I didn't feel like I did anything for Renée or Kenny, either. A part of me felt like my night was in vain until I remembered that I had come to plant the seeds tonight. Just because I felt like I didn't help them at all doesn't mean it wouldn't have a positive impact down the road.

I couldn't know for sure either way. But one thing I was certain of: my little white lie killed every piece of credibility I may have otherwise had; Kenny and I had instantly been divided by a wall built by dishonesty. Right then and there, I promised myself that I would stop lying altogether.

That was a lie in itself, though. It wouldn't be the last time I'd do it to protect my family.

.: 9 :.

Tearful Interjection
11 February 2009

I need to talk to you.

As a kid in high school, I wanted to travel the world and get away from Zion, as far away as I could, so I could experience life without the biases of a hometown. So, I did everything I could to make that happen. I enlisted in the Army and I enrolled in a school that was as far from home as possible that still would be covered by my tuition assistance. And, wow, Joanna, I've traveled; I couldn't have anticipated going to all the places I've been to. I've traveled all over America and overseas, and I'm now writing to you from halfway across the world, essentially the farthest place I could possibly be from home. I know as I write to you, it's as if I'm writing purely from my emotions, but I can assure you it's more than that; I've traveled all over the world and have discovered a "truth," not an "emotion." Because, when I'm on my deathbed, will my travels be there to comfort me? When I look back on my career, am I going to say to myself, "Boy, I wish I had spent more time making money?"

My travels won't comfort me at my deathbed; my family will. I'll have wished that I spent more time with them and less time trying to make money. I've searched long and hard for something more important that this world offers than family, and have come up empty. I'm not saying my travels have been in vain, simply misprioritized (which is not actually a word, so that's why it sounds funny to you).

I've long wanted to move out to Los Angeles in an attempt to accomplish my dream of being a film actor, and I know we've planned on heading out there together after graduation to settle down and raise our kids. But now, when I'm done with my tour, I just want to stay home. I'm not saying I won't check out the rest of the world, I'm just saying that I won't check out the rest of the world at the expense of becoming detached from family. If God calls me to move thousands of miles away from my family, then of course that's what I'll do, but I'm done making those kinds of decisions for the pure sake of my selfish ambitions. I want to see my little cousins grow up in front of my eyes, and I want to be there when a crisis hits our Chicagoland family, and I want to be there to watch my parents live and die before my own eyes, and I want to assist my extended family in any way I can.

I just have a simple plea today. Love God, love your family, and everything else will fall into place. I tell you this because I believe I've learned it the "hard way," and don't want you to follow those footsteps. They're unnecessary. It takes time for some to realize who their "family" is, but they exist, no doubt. This is true even for the families who have lost a beloved member, as there are still a lot of people standing beside them, and they will continue to stand next to each other until one of them falls. I've been fortunate in that I've never doubted who my family is. Many calamities are coming our way; being away from our family doesn't have to be one of them.

Today, I experienced a heartbreak and am finding difficulty accepting it. I just found out that an old buddy from my unit, First Lieutenant (1LT) Jared Southworth, was killed two days ago in the Nad-E Ali district of Helmand Province. Jared and another soldier, Staff Sergeant (SSG) Jason Burkholder, were assisting in the defusing and disposal of a bomb when a second, more hidden bomb exploded. A 27 year-old man who left four kids and a widow, he no longer has the opportunity to experience his family, and my heart goes out to him and his for that. He was a fellow brother in Christ, and I don't doubt that he's with God now, but I know his family is deeply missing him. It hurts to know that. And for what reason am I not in the place of Jared? Why did God choose to allow me to live, yet others to die?

I know God wanted me to live today, and for that I thank Him, and I tell you, please be encouraged, because God has some precious things in store for you, as He does for me. And that's why I'm alive to write you, and that's why you're alive to read this.

But, *if* it had been me instead of Jared, *if* it was God's will that I died, I know what would be heavy on my mind in my last moments. As I lay dying, my last request would be to get family by my side. *You* would be my last thought.

I may still be a “kid” in many regards, but what I’m telling you is no joke. I know this was worth you hearing, which is why I got out of bed at midnight to write to you.

I love you very much,

Your Heartbroken Boyfriend

.: 7 :.

A Sorry Little Liar

March 2006

I drove into town again and parked in the same place I had parked before, feeling a lot less nervous this time. I was hoping that Kenny would trust me now that I made good on my promise that I'd return to give him a Bible.

I went to the place where I had met the trio a few weeks ago, but only found a smoldering fire in a barrel and broken glass bottles on the ground. None of the streetlights were on and it was a new moon, so it was pitch black; I'd never been anywhere this dim before, and couldn't imagine what it would be like to live in a place that gets so dark at night.

I allowed my eyes to adjust enough to decipher a shadowy figure standing on a nearby hill.

"Kenny?" I called.

"Yeah, who's that?" asked the figure.

"It's me. Do you remember me from a few weeks ago?"

"Not offhand, no…"

I approached closer, and realized I didn't know this man at all.

"Oh, I'm sorry. I thought you were Kenny…"

"I'm Ken."

"Oh, do you know Kenny or Percy?"

"Yeah, I haven't seen them tonight though."

Ken threw some branches and leaves into the barrel, reigniting the fire to give it a little more life.

"Hey, is Kenny homeless?" I asked.

"Kenny? Oh, yeah. Yeah, man. He's homeless."

An awkward silence filled the air. I knew Ken wanted to know what I was doing on his turf at midnight.

"Ken, would you care to talk about God with me? I'm interested in hearing your thoughts. "

"Naw, man. Normally I'd be cool, but I shouldn't be talking about God in my current state of mind."

In one hand, he held up a joint to show me what he meant. The other arm was tucked away in his jacket.

"You want a hit while you're here?"

"No thanks, Ken. What happened to your arm?"

"Shish. Bad situation, man. I was working – I work on roofs for a living – I was working, and I got hurt on the job, broke my arm. They ended up laying me off because they knew I wouldn't be healthy again for several months."

The fire started crackling, masking the silence that would've otherwise reminded me how inept I was at trying to relate to Ken.

"You asked if I know God," Ken tried reviving the conversation. "My answer is that I know who God is, but I don't really *know* God, you know?"

It was a perfect opening for me to talk about Jesus; to share the Christian message as Christ commanded His followers to do. But I got too nervous, not knowing what to say, so I took the easy way out.

"I brought a Bible. Would you like one?"

"Yeah, man! I'd love to have a Bible! You'd really give one to me? For nothing at all?"

Rather than trying to meet him where he was at in his faith life, I just threw a Bible at Ken. I didn't recognize it then, but I was being a typical calloused Christian, the kind that Kenny had been grumbling about last time I was standing here, someone who construes Christ's command more as a checkbox rather than an opportunity to explain how Jesus offers hope and transforms lives, creating a lasting impact.

As we hung out around the fire, a figure approached us. Remembering how upset Renée was about me invading her hangout, I began fidgeting in my place and just hoped that this person wasn't angry about my presence.

"Hey, how do you do?" the figure asked. "My name is June. What brings you out here tonight?"

June extended his hand and shook mine.

"I wanted to bring Kenny this Bible that I promised him a couple weeks ago. But he's not here, so I was just talking to Ken here about God."

"You're here in the Name of the Lord?" June hooted. "Good for you! I'm pleased to meet you. I consider myself a man of God, very close to Christ Jesus. I'm happy I ran into you tonight; it's good to see people spreading God's word."

Maybe June was giving me too much credit, but I appreciated his politeness and encouragement. He continued his praise of me.

"You know, most people would be too afraid to come to these parts, proclaiming God's word. But you know better. You know God is going to be with you when you come to places like East St. Louis, and any danger areas."

"So, you don't think I'll die if I go around in God's Name in dangerous areas like this?"

"It's not a matter of me thinking it. It's a matter of me knowing. God will keep you safe."

Though his point was countered by the fact that countless saints have been killed for their faith in the past, I admired June's confidence. I had just experienced something that I hadn't had in awhile: *encouragement*.

"Hey," June continued, "what did you say your name was? I didn't catch it."

"Oh," I realized I hadn't rendered the courtesy of introducing myself. "Me? My name's Na..."

I stopped mid-sentence to think, June cocking his head like a confused puppy who almost heard a word he understands.

"What did you say it was?" June politely asked. "I didn't hear what you said."

Standing around the again-dimming fire, I began to think about the name that was starting to spread. *Danger*. What a strange thing to be called. What had started just as a fun nickname was now starting to stick by more-than-a-few-people. And, ever since I started believing I couldn't die, I found myself becoming more fearless with each passing day, making the name all-the-more appropriate.

June continued to look at me, probably wondering how such a simple question had induced such contemplation.

"I... I am Danger," I blurted out.

"You are Danger?"

"Yes. I am Danger."

"It's nice to meet you, Danger."

After a few more minutes hanging around the fire, I prayed with Ken and June and then went back to my dorm room.

I never ended up seeing Kenny again. He would always remember me as a liar. Which I guess is okay, because it was the truth.

.: L :.

Party Like It's 1388!

21 March 2009

Top o' the morning to ya, milady!

I hope you're well; I'm doing alright, and I remind myself that each day that I endure here is one day closer to being home. I think of you often and drive myself insane wondering what you might be doing and wishing I could be there doing whatever it is with you. I find myself speculating if you had a good or bad day, who you happened to run into today, what you ate for dinner, where you're at, if you're thinking about me. Yet, I also realize that if I'm wondering these things where I'm at, then how much more you're wondering them where you're at.

The 33rd Brigade has been getting hit hard lately. In the southern city of Kandahar (which is in the province adjacent to where 1LT Southworth was killed), four more soldiers were blown up by an IED, two of which were from the Illinois Guard. 2008 was the deadliest year for soldiers in Afghanistan, with eight soldiers having died by the end of February. In January and February of this year alone, 29 soldiers have died; an increase of over 350%.

It's not just the south that's been prone to SIGACTs. Our friend SGT Bandee also found himself in the middle of a hotspot recently. Bandee had a 4-day trip turn into an 8-day nightmare as he found himself stuck on the eastern border of Afghanistan with no transportation back to base. I'll share with you his words as he reported to me:

> I got to Camp Clark via Chinook and found out right away that because of its temperate climate and location (next to Khowst City, just 22 miles from the Pakistan border), Clark is an active area with a bunch of Taliban activity. The last time I had been there was over New Year's; I spent 2009's first stroke of midnight sleeping on a cot with nary a concern of any Taliban attacking. But since that last visit, a rocket blasted Clark's DFAC and another destroyed a newly

constructed building. For Clark, it's abnormal for a week to go by without some kind of significant activity.

One particular day I was there, I learned that some casualties were being brought into camp for medical attention. I bolted over to the makeshift hospital to offer my assistance, finding a contractor lying on a bed with gashes around his eye, threatening to permanently pilfer his vision.

"What happened?" I asked one of the soldiers standing around.

"Sergeant, are you part of the medical team?"

"No," I responded, "I'm part of the ministry team."

"Oh, thanks for coming out, sergeant. Let's talk outside," he said as he put his arm on my shoulder, leading me out the door. "It was an IED. Two contractors were caught in the blast."

"Where's the other one?" I asked as a thundercloud started beading down trickles of rain.

"He didn't need medical attention..."

"Well, at least there's some good news."

"...he needed mortuary affairs."

KPUUUH!

A large explosion rocked Camp Clark as I ducked and hid my head with my hands. Rain started pouring as an atmosphere of chaos encompassed the FOB.

"Don't worry, that's a controlled det," the soldier told me. "They found an IED this morning and scheduled to detonate it around now. We should clear out of here, though; the medevac[19] copter is gonna be here in a minute to take the casualty to a more-equipped hospital in Salerno."

The contractor not only survived, but his eyesight was also salvaged.

Bandee arrived back to our home base just in time to get slated to tread the KG Pass. The first time he went over the pass was in December when there was no imminent threat, but this recent return to the mountainside was just five days after a convoy was blown up.

I attended the mission brief before the crew set off; it had a most bleak tone. Captain (CPT) Zollar, a hardened war veteran who has survived several Iraq deployments and usually exudes fearlessness, told the mission team that even *his* backfur stands on end when he travels over the KG.

After he spoke, one of our intel analysts reiterated CPT Zollar's anxieties by telling the soldiers that they needed to be prepared to "bite the bullet" on this convoy. SGT Bandee had a solemn morning as he prepared to go out on the mission:

> I'll never forget March 13, 2009... Friday the 13th. As I tied my boots that morning, I spoke aloud to myself, "This is the most dangerous day of my life."
>
> Not even 30 minutes into the 3+ hour convoy, we were flagged down by an American contractor who wanted to tell us that earlier that morning, he and some other contractors were shot at by insurgents. He told us that if we proceeded, we would surely be fired upon. At that point, a soldier told me over our radio headsets, "Sergeant, if you really believe in God, now's the time to start praying." Though he couldn't

---

[19] **medevac**: the emergency transportation of casualties to a hospital, usually by helicopter; literally, "medical evacuation."

see me, I nodded my head and replied, "Trust me. I've been."

As our convoy climbed the KG Pass, the terrain was all-too-familiar. I looked outside the window and saw we were a mere few feet away from falling down thousands of feet.

After hours of driving on the jarring mountain, we heard a notification over our radio that we were expecting and dreading all at the same time: we had arrived at "the bridge." It was the bridge where the convoy had been attacked less than a week ago.

We drove onto the bridge, and shards of glass and shrapnel from the recent IED explosion were distributed among the rocky land. I could see the ghosts of what happened five days earlier: there had been a humvee traveling over the bridge which was met with a large explosion. The vehicle started on fire and the soldiers inside began burning alive. A medic ran to the fiery carnage and carried one slightly-charred U.S. soldier to safety, and then returned to the burning vehicle. There were two more soldiers inside: one was already toast, the other was nearing that crisp fate. Had it not been for the medic who grabbed the dying soldier and treated his extensive injuries, there would have been two killed-in-actions (KIAs) reported, not just the one. The medic treated the soldier on the spot, ignoring the shrapnel that had ripped into his own leg. That burnt soldier is alive today because of the medic, though still in a coma at Brooke Army Medical Center in San Antonio and isn't expected to survive the year.[20]

As our vehicle drove over this death spot, replacing these ghosts with our own presence, I snapped back into reality

[20] The critically-injured soldier died in an American hospital in June 2009.

and grinded my teeth as we trucked over the bridge, anticipating a large explosion.

But no explosion came that day.

If you're curious as to why places like Camp Clark and Helmand and Kandahar are more active than other areas in Afghanistan, it has to do with the accessibility that Taliban guerillas have. You have to understand, Talibs are nomadic in an effort to avoid being traced, and they often live in tents on mountains for a few days, then drift to their next location after they launch an attack. Living high in the mountains in tents becomes problematic for them because of the harsh conditions, so the preferred spots are warmer locations.

But that begs the question, *Why Afghanistan? Why are the Taliban going to such lengths to try to take over such a fruitless country?* It's a legitimate question, and the answer lies in the politics, not the resources. After all, Afghanistan doesn't offer much: its agriculture doesn't produce any rare crops, it's too unsafe to be a tourist attraction, and the food isn't exactly worth the trip over.

The real problem abides within the fact that the Taliban, which is now believed to be grossly located in Pakistan, hates America. Plain and simple. They don't like American values, and they don't like the freedom of religion (and specifically freedom of Judaism and Christianity) in America. And so, wherever America goes, the Taliban will be there to challenge her. The Taliban fear that Afghanistan will someday become democratic like America, which would generate even more anti-Talib feelings in their areas of operation. For the Taliban to remain strong, they'll have to stop America now, otherwise their opposition may become too overwhelming for them. And if the Talibs are to be successful, they need to kill as many coalition forces as they can to convince the citizens of the United States and our allied countries that the war on terror is a "lost cause." Thus, that is why there's a war raging throughout Afghanistan.

In the past month, a multitude of reports from media and politicians alike have come out saying that the situation in Afghanistan is deteriorating and that we're losing the war. Believe what you may, but from this soldier's perspective, that information is fallacious in every sense of the word. For the people who are saying that we're struggling to maintain stability here, I don't know where they're getting their information, but they're certainly not sitting in on the same meetings I've been, nor are they seeing the progress that's developing here. The Afghan National Army has been successfully conducting military operations and defeating the Taliban, though you'd have to flip to page 12 of your newspaper to see that, as opposed to the front page headlines that only highlight the struggles. Perhaps the media feel our efforts are crumbling because of the sacrifices that have been incurred already, but if that's the logic, then our involvement in World War II was a failed effort as well.

I'm not the only one who shares these sentiments. The other day, Rambo Three stressed to me that Afghanistan has had a lot of progress since America was asked to help eradicate the Taliban. He told me that, before America came to Afghanistan's aid, a frequent occurrence was that Afghan children and adults alike would go and pray at the mosque, and then on their way back home, the Taliban would accuse them of not praying and threaten to beat them if they didn't return to the mosque and render Allah his due respect. Just five years ago, Rambo Three was living in Pakistan; his family felt it was much too risky to live in Afghanistan under the Talib regime. But after the American forces drove away the Taliban, his family finally felt it was safe enough to live here again and they've since moved back to their beloved land.

Though Afghanistan is far from becoming a land of Utopia, the locals take much more pleasure in the condition it's in now. Furthermore, the educational difference between generations is astounding: the Afghan National Army soldiers lived in a generation in which the Taliban ruled the country, and many of them consequently still can't write their own name. Yet, today's Afghan generations who've lived in this country since the Taliban exile not only have high school educations, but most of them aspire for college educations, dreaming of getting an education at an American university.

I'm sure there are skeptics who would hear this opinion and brush it off, rendering my experience here as meaningless. That's fine. Nobody has to take me at my word. But from what I've seen firsthand and from what I hear in daily reports on the situation in Afghanistan, we're not panicking. Please don't believe the media and politicians that give you this skewed perspective; it's almost as if some of them *want* us to lose, so they have a story to sell or so they can smugly wag their finger at those who started this war, saying "I told you this was a bad idea." I'm all for objectivity, and so I wouldn't mind these reports if we *were* actually struggling, but because they're channeling fear and despair by way of molesting the truth for their own selfish purposes, those propagating these reports are recklessly sponsoring the same endgame as the Taliban.

That's not to say there haven't been sacrifices. The Army recently announced that the suicide rate for servicemen and women is higher than it's ever been in its history. This phenomenon of increased suicides is one of the military's biggest concerns, and as such, Big Army has come out with a mandate that every soldier, whether in the United States or in a combat zone, must attend a suicide prevention brief[21] by a trained professional. Of course, this is easier said than done because there aren't many soldiers who are trained in suicide prevention, not to mention that many soldiers are on far-reaching bases in the middle of nowhere. But, just because it's a difficult task doesn't mean this suicide prevention business can go ignored, and so those who are trained have been charged with traveling to even the smallest bases.

So who are these certified suicide prevention specialists that've been tasked to travel to these outlying bases? That's right, the ministry teams.

While I've been conducting the suicide prevention briefs on our home base of FOB Lightning, SGT Bandee has been traveling to remote locations to

---

[21] **suicide prevention brief**: a military presentation that outlines the increasing suicide problem and provides the proper protocol for how to deal with fellow soldiers who display suicidal symptoms, as well as offers resources for those who are secretly contemplating suicide.

conduct these suicide prevention briefs. Not one to waste an opportunity for adventure, Bandee has been volunteering to go on combat missions at each of the locations he's visiting.

The first place Bandee volunteered to travel to was a little COP in Bermel, Afghanistan. Bermel is less than 30 miles south of where NFL star Pat Tillman was killed, and only four miles from the Pakistan border. You can see Pakistan mountains in the near distance, and Taliban activity is a daily event on the border. While there, SGT Bandee ended up in "downtown" Bermel to conduct a dismounted combat patrol, which is where you go outside the wire[22] and patrol the nearby area on foot, searching for any Taliban activity. Or, as Bandee puts it:

> I scanned the village's rooftops in search of threats while another soldier and an interpreter asked the locals if they knew anything about the Taliban activity in the area. We were one three-man team of many; our task was to ask the locals if they knew anything about the caches of weapons being hidden under woodpiles just outside the town, and while the locals' eyes expressed full knowledge of the situation, their lips belied complete ignorance.
>
> Even though we figured it would be a vain effort, we continued asking locals about the woodpiles in hopes that one good Taliban-hater would fess up and spill any information he had. But, it was apparent that these locals weren't like the locals I've met elsewhere: these Afghans' stern glares emphasized their disdain for us. After all, terrorism breeds economical gain for Afghan terrorists in the same way that gangster crime breeds economical gain

---

[22] **"outside the wire,"** a term used to refer to any location outside the safety of a base. Most bases are padded with barbed wire around its barriers, so anything not within the perimeters is literally outside the wire.

for American mafias, so by eradicating the Taliban, we were collaterally eradicating this community of one of the sources of income for their families.

We began talking to one local who was complaining that American forces had shot his truck two days ago, leaving a bullethole in his passenger-side door. We went to check out the truck to see if the local was telling the truth. However, it was apparent that he had formulated a fib: the bullethole was too large to be from a 5.56mm round, yet would be too small if it had been from one of our heavier weapon machinery. As we explained to the local that we were certain it wasn't our doing, transmissions were intercepted over our radio systems; the phrase "Allahu Akbar"[23] was being repeated by Afghans. Our team leaders swiftly notified everyone via radio that the mission was going to end early, and we retreated towards our COP.

After we rallied together, our objective of returning to the COP was interrupted by a loud noise.

kpuuuh! kpuuuh!

Two large explosions were heard (and felt) throughout the village. After I found cover behind a building wall with another soldier, I asked aloud, "What was that?"

kpuuuh! kpuuuh!

The soldier I was with didn't say anything, but continued patrolling again after a few moments. I figured he was told through his radio headset (an asset I didn't have) that it was outgoing fire. Apart from training simulations, I had never

---

[23] **Allāhu Akbar**: Arabic phrase that roughly means "Allah is greater" in English. Jihadists will often repeat this phrase during or just prior to an attack, so whenever a coalition soldier hears this expression, they recognize it as a battle cry and must react accordingly.

heard outgoing nor incoming fire before, so I wasn't sure of the difference.

As we hiked towards the COP, we were met with the woodpiles that we'd been asking the locals about. We casually investigated them with our eyes, finding nothing suspicious about them. There were hundreds of woodpiles; there was no telling which of them might be hiding weapons. I got on the ground and inspected the piles with my naked eye, but the wood was too dense to reveal anything, even if there were weapons stored underneath.

As we passed the woodpiles and entered the outskirts of the town, we were met with a car zooming towards us. An ANA soldier flailed his hands up and screamed for the car to stop while an American soldier echoed those demands by pointing his rifle at the driver. I couldn't raise my weapon at the car as there were five friendly forces in front of me, and I didn't want to risk flagging any of them. The car jerked to an immediate halt and the driver got out, promptly getting searched. He was clean, so we continued on with our mission. Shortly thereafter, we were catching our breath behind the COP's front gates, completing our mission.

Later that day, we had a Terp translate the intercepted transmissions. As suspected, it was a conversation among Talibs:

> "The truck is going right now with wood. Take the rockets and hide it under the wood."
>
> "Bring it to the mountain. After you set everything, contact me."
>
> "We are ready to attack. I am the enemy of your enemy. God-willing, you will kill a lot of Americans. Amen."
>
> "Allah is greater! Allah is greater!" [At this point in the conversation, rockets were being fired.]

> "Oh, you missed. Look in the binoculars." [Gunshots were then accompanied with the recurring phrase,] "Allah is greater! Allah is greater!"

Later in the report, there was strong indication that at least one of the members of this excursion was a corrupt member of either the ANA or ANP. At the same time that these transmissions were going on, a COP a few miles northeast of us had been attacked; it turns out the transmissions were coming from the offenders of that COP, not Bermel's.

The following day, we went out on another dismounted combat patrol to the same location, using a different route. I again eyeballed the woodpiles as we patrolled, but all I found was the decaying carcass of a stray dog.

When I arrived to the marketplace of the town, I witnessed an Afghan scurry out of the mosque in the center of town and then lie down right beside it, concealing himself under a blanket. He blended in well with the terrain, and had I not watched him hide himself, I wouldn't have ever noticed him in his camouflaged state.

I alerted other soldiers of the incident, and then an ANA soldier approached the man while a dozen other soldiers (including myself) stood by, keeping our fingers on our triggers. The man under the blanket revealed himself, claiming that he had just finished a night job and was trying to catch some sleep before his next shift.

Unlike the previous day's patrol, this mission ended on our own terms. We returned to our base not long after.

Bandee figured any and all excitement was over with at this point, but...

...the next day, I was standing in line for chow, casually thinking about what I had to get done and planning my afternoon around these tasks. But as it turns out, some Taliban members were nearby (just behind a dirt mound in Bermel known as "Spaghetti Hill"), and they *also* had plans for this afternoon.

Whiiizzzzzz... ***kpuuuh!***

An explosion penetrated the COP and I instinctively cringed in place. I looked at the flabbergasted expressions of the 20 or so soldiers that were with me, and knowing that they'd never heard an explosion as they had arrived to Afghanistan only two weeks prior, I investigated just enough to find out if it was incoming rather than outgoing; in other words, if it was, indeed, an assault on the COP.

I saw veteran soldiers running around in alarm and recognized that we were under attack. Not only had a rocket been launched towards our little COP, but it landed within our gates, no more than 150 feet from me.

I returned to the soldiers I had been standing with and stammered, "Buh...bunkers! Go...get to your bunkers!" The bewildered soldiers stared at me, as if I was testing them. I repeated myself with more command, "*Get to your bunkers*!" The reality then set in for all of the soldiers as the emergency sirens went off, and they scattered to get to their bunkers. I went into mine, and as I sat there in the concrete bunker that at least gave me a sense of safety, one final rocket exploded just outside the COP. Not wanting to get caught or give away their position, the terrorists fled before anyone could chase them down and respond to their shenanigans.

When I reflect on SGT Bandee's stories, I'm astonished by how unique his situation is. Many soldiers come to combat zones and are assigned to do the same thing over and over and over and over and over and over and over and over and over and over and over and over and over and over and over and over and over and over and over and over – paperwork soldiers get lodged in their office, tower guard soldiers routinely guard towers, combat arms soldiers stay on a rotation covering the same ground every few days, and medical soldiers assess injuries day-in and day-out. Sure, there'll be a few variations to their work from day to day, but in many ways, it's like reliving the same day again and again. But, not with Bandee. While most soldiers are stuck being Bill Murray's character in Groundhog Day, Bandee has gotten to be Bill Murray's character in Stripes. He's gotten to hop from base to base, blend in with the other soldiers, and do what they do for a limited time before moving on to a new mission. I can't even imagine the amazing experiences he'll get to endure before it's over.

Even more amazing to me is that Bandee has yet to get in a situation where he has to use his rifle, but that's simply the case. All the same, it seems fitting that Bandee experienced a "fireworks show" today; after all, it is the Islamic New Year. Starting today, the year is 1388 in Muslim culture, and when I think about the unpaved roads, the state of technology, the standard of education, and the principles of hygiene, it truly does feel like I'm living over 600 years in the past.

That being said, my prayer request this week is about a timeless topic and comes with a story, so bear with me. Lately, my Muslim friends, the interpreters, have been asking a lot about my faith. To them, Jesus is not the Son of God, but simply a great prophet. I'm of the opinion that just calling Jesus a "good man" or "respected prophet" isn't much better than calling Him a "mythological hero" or "absolute lunatic"; I believe one of Satan's greatest tricks was fooling the world into thinking that you don't have to accept Jesus as your sole Savior to be considered a follower of Christ. Yet the reality is that, to reject Jesus, you don't need to completely debase Him; you just need to make Him less than He is. Believing in a half-truth is the same as believing in a half-lie, and a half-lie is still a lie.

Because the Bible is considered one of their four holy books in Islam, these Terps are naturally interested in learning about the Biblical perspective of Jesus.

"Well, my friends, the difference between my Christian faith and your Muslim faith," I explained, "is that Islam regards Jesus as a prophet. In my faith, Jesus is so much more. I believe Jesus is the sole reason humans have a shot at going to God's Kingdom."

"Because without the Jesus, you wouldn't know how to live according to God's rules?" Rambo Three sought clarification.

"Well, yes, Jesus came and showed us the way. But it goes beyond that: Jesus came to *be* the way. It wasn't just about Jesus' teaching; it was about His *living*."

"You mean because the Jesus was such a good man?" one of the five of them asked.

"Well, it's more than just that, too," I responded. All five of them seemed to have trouble following what I was saying and I realized that, if I was going to properly explain the significance of Jesus, I'd have to give them the big picture.

"Danger, please explain us about the Jesus. We want to know what you think of the Jesus."

I sat down in front of them.

"You want the whole story?"

They all nodded their heads, sitting upright and looking as excited as a group of kids who were promised they'd get to hear their favorite bedtime story if they were well-behaved.

"Alright then. In the beginning..."

"Ohhhh..." they groaned in displeasure and rolled to their sides, making me snort in amusement, acknowledging how elongated this story was already shaping up to be.

"It's okay, it's okay," I leaned back and put my hands on my waist.

"Danger, we don't want to sit here until the doomsday!"

"You have my word," I grinned as they snickered, "it's going to move quicker than it sounds."

I suppressed my laughter as I tried again.

"In the beginning, mankind and God were very much in harmony. There was no disconnect between them at first. But shortly after God created man, man betrayed God and disobeyed His command to not eat fruit from a tree, a tree known as the Tree of Knowledge."

"Why did man disobey God?"

"Well, it can be argued man did it for several reasons. I think the best way to sum it up is man disobeyed God because man didn't trust God. Man valued having knowledge of good and evil over obedience to God. And as a result, sin and pain came into the world, and man and God were separated from each other.

"That's where the problem is, my friends. God is the epitome of love, but He is also the epitome of justice. One who has committed even the *least* of sins isn't worthy to be in His presence – unless that sin gets punished. For justice to be upheld, every sin deserves punishment.

"So God sent the prophet Moses to God's people to give them laws (which outlined God's moral standard), but the people repeatedly broke those laws. God didn't want His people to be eternally separated from Him, however, so He had always planned a solution to the sin problem: God allowed His people to 'pass' their sins onto animals, and then His people were to sacrifice these animals. The sins that stained these peoples' souls would be destroyed by this substitute sacrifice instead.

"The problem with this system is it still produces quite a divide between God and man. God didn't want it to stay like this; He didn't want sins to be forgiven by constant sacrifices. And so, God sent Himself to earth in the form of a man, Jesus Christ. Jesus lived the perfect life, and then became a sacrifice for *all* mankind."

"So," the Muslims tried making sense of what I had said so far, "because the Jesus lived the perfect life, He lifted the curse that was on the world?"

"His life wasn't the only thing necessary. His blood was needed, too."

"His... *blood*?" asked one confused Muslim, who had always been taught that Jesus wasn't killed. Instead, he understood that Jesus was spared by Allah by being ascended into heaven after Judas Iscariot betrayed Him. Then, Allah made Judas look like Jesus in appearance, tricking the people into crucifying Judas instead of Jesus.

"Yes, His blood. Jesus didn't deserve to die, but if mankind was to be redeemed, a perfect sacrifice was needed."

"Jesus..." they began to understand my viewpoint, "only He could be the perfect sacrifice."

"Yes."

"What happened to the Jesus?"

"He was handed over to mankind to be brutally slaughtered, like an ancient Hebrew animal sacrifice."

Silence filled the air. Any remnants of the uproarious laughter from a moment ago were now replaced with sullen stillness.

"Jesus..." Rambo Three began to reason, "He had to *die* for us?"

"He didn't *have to* do it for us. But He did, because He loves us. Jesus knew that *someone* had to pay the punishment for our sins; He knew that if He didn't do it, then *we* would have to suffer the pains of hell. Unlike other martyrs, Jesus was killed for who He was, not just for what He taught. He died so we can live."

"Danger, my friend and brofer," another Muslim furrowed his eyebrows and protested, "this is a terrible religion! That's so... sad."

"Well, you didn't let me finish the story," I smiled. "Jesus rose from the dead three days later, conquering death once and for all. He appeared to 500 witnesses and then ascended to be with God. Through the Resurrection of Christ, mankind can be saved from sin."

"So sin doesn't exist anymore?" one Muslim reasoned.

"That's not quite how it works," I explained my perspective. "After all, sin still existed even after God's people sacrificed animals in their place. The only way to be free from sin is to pass our sins onto the blood of Jesus."

"So," Rambo Three piped in, "because the Jesus paid for mankind, now mankind doesn't have to pay?"

"Right," I clarified, "the only caveat being that we have to believe and trust in Christ's sacrifice rather than trust in our own abilities to achieve salvation. We need to be humble. We need to *accept* what Christ did for us, otherwise we're still guilty and will pay for our sins in the next life."

"Accept it?" Rambo Three asked.

"Right, accept it," I said. "If someone hands you a gift, and you take that gift and just stare at it and reject it, can you really benefit from it? Of course not; there's no use for an unopened gift. *But*, if you take that gift, open it, and receive it, then you can use the gift's contents as it was intended to be used."

"If this is true," another Terp thought about its implications for him as a Muslim, "then this means the Jesus wasn't *a* prophet, but *the* prophet."

"I believe it goes beyond that, my friend. In my view, Jesus wasn't just *a* prophet or even *the* prophet. He was the *Christ*, the *Messiah*, the *Lord of all*. No mere prophet can offer themselves up as a substitute for punishment."

What I was telling them wasn't easy. Without saying his name directly, I had just told my Muslim friends that their most lauded prophet didn't have the power to save them. And while not rejecting their own faith, my friends comprehended the significance of Jesus through my Christian perspective.

"Tell me Danger, my brofer," one Muslim backtracked after a moment of contemplation, "they put the Jesus on a cross and He just died? Were they sad to kill Him? Did they at least treat Him with respect, the way of humanity?"

"Yeah, my sweet Danger, dearest Khatar!" another Muslim chirped. "Tell us more about how He died."

"I got a movie that shows how Christians think He died," I told them. "Do you want to see it?"

After an enthusiastic response, I brought over a filmed depiction of the death of Jesus and watched it with them. My friends grimaced in pain as they watched the movie, distressed that mankind is capable of killing God's Son.

While watching, they would grab their hair in an act of helplessness, wishing they could jump into the story and help Jesus through His trials. "Oh, it's not the way of humanity!" one Terp anguished during the flogging. As Jesus was whipped, some of the Muslims couldn't help but cry. When Jesus finally gasped His last, my friends breathed in relief that He was no longer in such misery.

The past couple of days have been an emotional time for these Terps, and that's where my prayer request comes in, Joanna. My friends are going through some heavy spiritual warfare, a literal jihad.[24] I ask you this week to pray for them as they wrestle with the concept of Jesus against their notion of Mohammad. Please pray for God to guide them to understand Him better in this critical period in their lives.

Before I sign-off, I want to share something with you. The following is a piece written by an Illinois National Guardsman who's already on his way back home to be with his wife and daughter:

> A strange thing…
>
> When I think about what surrounds me, the institutional corruption, the random violence, the fear and desperation, I feel the reasons why I am here more and more sharply. As we grow in our soldier's skills, surviving by finding the hidden dangers, seeing the secret motives and the shifting politics… we grow a set of skills that is unique and powerful in this situation.

---

[24] **jihad,** literally meaning "personal struggle."

We also see what you cannot see in the States, you are surrounded by the love of Christ and faith in freedom and humanity, like a fish you think water is a "puff of air" because it is always there, you do not notice it… we who are out of the water look back and see the world we love surrounded by enemies, poison and envy that wants to fall on you like a storm of ruin.

We who joined with vague notions of protecting our country see how desperate the peril, how hungry the enemy and how frail the security we have is. So the more I love you, all the more I feel I must keep fighting for you. The more I love and long for home, the more right I feel here on the front line, standing between you and the seething madness that wants to suck the life and love out of our land.

Does that mean I cannot go home? I hope not, because I want this just to be the postponement of the joy of life, not the sacrifice of mine. If it costs me my life to protect our land and people, then that is a small thing, I just hope that fate lets me return to the promised land and remind people just how great our land is.

War is a young man's game, and I am getting an old man's head… it is a strange thing. I just hope that I am not changed so that I cannot take joy in the land inside the wire when I make it home. I want to be with you all again and let my gun sit in the rack and float on my back in a tube down a lazy river…

The soldier who penned this is SGT Scott Stream of Mattoon, Illinois. He was unfortunate enough to be present at that explosion that occurred in Kandahar that killed four soldiers earlier this month, including two Illinois National Guardsmen. And, as I said, he is already on his way back to America.

His mode of transportation is a flag-draped coffin.

Love,

Your Fish-out-of-Water

FOB Lightning in Gardez, Afghanistan, just after sunrise

.: 8 :.

Drowning in the Truth

August 2007

As she looked off to the side, I studied her face to get a feel for her mood before I opened my mouth. Her tawny hair dangled over her face until she ran her fingers through to set it behind her ears, revealing her eyes; they were blue as an ocean, and just as calm, too. I knew that what I was about to say would shatter her tranquility.

"Joanna, I need to tell you something."

Her face swiveled towards me, making her hair flutter as if it had been hit by her eye's ocean breeze. Joanna knew that tone, the one that prepared her for big news. Then she began to grin and asked, "Why are you smiling?"

It was my nervous smile. I don't get nervous often, so she wasn't used to seeing it.

"No reason, I'm just… just smiling, I suppose."

She grinned even more, "Nuh uh! Spill it! Spill the beans! You have something to say."

She was right, but not in the sense she was anticipating.

"Joanna, I'm smiling because I don't know how to say this."

She kept grinning, but I could see she was getting a little more nervous. I felt so awful for what I was about to verbalize. After all we had been through, it was time to have this talk. At this point, we'd been dating a year-and-a-half, and she had even transferred to my college in the St. Louis area, becoming a fellow Cougar once again. She had been going to school with me for three semesters now, and our relationship was perfect as it was, having just spent the best summer of our lives together. It broke my heart to say what I was about to say; I felt like I was ruining everything.

"Then just say it," she demanded. Her face crimped as her eyes traveled all over my face, trying to read it in agony. I needed to just spit it out.

"Okay. You know how everyone always tells you how lucky you are that you have a boyfriend in the National Guard who hasn't ever been deployed before?"

Her wandering eyes froze. She knew. I didn't need to say anything else, but I did anyway.

"It's time."

She looked at me as if she didn't understand, but she knew exactly what I was saying. We stared at each other for awhile, and her eyes filled with tears as she accepted what I was telling her. She dug her face into my shoulder, and I encompassed her head with my hands, gently stroking her hair.

"We both knew this day was coming. We're ready for this, Joanna. We'll make it through this. It's a temporary test that will strengthen our relationship for the rest of our life together. It's all temporary."

The ocean that was calm a moment ago now was leaking down her face.

"Your transfer..." she reflected. "You were in a communications battalion, and you transferred to an infantry unit. You're going over there in a *combat arms* unit! You're not safe. You're gonna be in so much... danger."

The ocean raged harder and harder, a squall of typhoon-like proportions flooding the floor.

I didn't know how to reply; she was right. I had transferred to an infantry unit in Marion, Illinois because I knew it was my best chance at being promoted. Sure enough, after I transferred and proved my worth, I was promoted from Specialist (SPC) to Sergeant shortly after I turned 20 years old. But now, my self-serving ambitions would force a year-long separation from the one girl I never wanted to spend another minute away from.

I rubbed Joanna's back as she covered the tempest in her eyes with her fingers, using them like a dam. Yet tears continued pouring through the cracks until the dam collapsed under the pressure, allowing a tidal wave to gush out.

We both struggled to breathe, drowning in an ocean of truth. If only there was some way to soften the blow. If only there was some way to calm the ocean again. If only there was some way to trick her into thinking this wasn't happening.

God be with me.

.: 8 :.

Like a Penguin in the Desert

8 April 2009

Hey there kiddo,

The ministry teams across Afghanistan are still in "suicide prevention mode," and our deadline to reach every soldier is looming. After Bandee found a chopper to take him out of Bermel, he went straight to a FOB in Orgun-East. After administering his suicide prevention briefs, Bandee volunteered to help with any missions the Orgun-E teams had, knowing they were undermanned. And so, Bandee ended up becoming the gunner for a combat mission.

Gunning, in my opinion, is the deadliest position any soldier could have on a mission. If an IED goes off, the gunner is the first to get hit by the blast or be launched several yards away. They're the first to get fired upon, as well as the first (and often only) to return fire. If the enemy shoots a rocket-propelled grenade (RPG), the gunners are the ones who suffer serious injuries from the shrapnel. Not to mention, gunners have fewer restraints holding them in the vehicle than the rest of the passengers and, as such, they don't usually walk away from rollovers. This is the position that Bandee was needed to fill on this day: to be the gunner. While his team never experienced any combat that day, his story continues when...

> ...the following day, I went out on another combat patrol with a different team, parking just a couple miles away from FOB Orgun-E.
>
> We had parked at the base of a mountain in an area known to the locals as Pirkothi. We wasted no time in climbing the mountain, which turned out to be a demanding task, especially with all of our gear on. By the time we climbed up half the mountain, we received a radio report from the soldiers on ground that they had found a dead body in one of the cars they searched, forcing us into an alerted

standstill. But after we found out that the vehicle had authorization to be transporting the body, we continued ascending.

After we wheezed our way to the peak, we sat on some rocks to catch our breath. That is, until we saw the silhouettes of two people on the mountain across from us staring our way. We leapt into action, and one soldier who had a scope on his rifle zoomed in on the figures ahead to examine what was going on. Upon inspection, we realized that they weren't people at all, but two rocks that were eerily shaped identically to that of a couple of humans.

We relaxed a little bit, just sitting on the rocks at the top of the mountain, looking out in awe at the splendor of Afghanistan. However, our little moment was cut short as rain started tapping on us.

While one may think that rain would enhance the serenity of the moment, when you're at war, it's quite the opposite. When it rains, grounded helicopters are not authorized to lift off because of the limited visibility that bad weather brings. So, if rockets joined the rain in dropping on our helmets, we wouldn't have been able to medevac any casualties to safety. The rain, as serene as it may be in normal circumstances, instead signified great vulnerability in the middle of the warzone.

We tumbled down the mountain, slipping down the slick mountainside until we reached the bottom. After that, we returned to our vehicles and completed our mission, traveling back to Orgun-E with no complications.

Bandee eventually traveled from Orgun-E to FOB Salerno, a place he's visited before. However, while he was there, he ran into a situation he'd never faced before:

As I sat in my tent, trying to relax after a tiring day, a screeching sound pierced the night air.

WoooooooooooooOooOooOoOoOOOOO...... ***KPUUUH!***

It didn't take an ordnance expert to realize we were getting bombed, but I found myself a little perplexed as the rocket explosion had a couple nuances that I'd never come across before: it was louder than usual and felt like a mini-earthquake. The four of us in the tent exchanged glances that asked, "Was that incoming or outgoing?"

I told them, "I'm pretty sure that was incoming."

KPUUUH!

Another explosion hit without warning, rattling the entire FOB and sounding like it was but a few hundred feet away from the tent. Reasoning that we should get into a bunker, I put on my boots, sluggishly tying the laces into a knot when I heard the foreign sound of a whistle in the distance.

WoooOooOooOoOoOOO...

My heart dropped as I realized what the distinct sound belonged to. Our FOB was not only under attack, but it was being fired at with *mortars*, not just rockets...[25] and that mortar's whistle indicated it was heading in my general area. I became energetically numb as I cowered in place, waiting to find out if it was my turn to become the newest Purple Heart recipient.

---

[25] **mortars vs. rockets**: A rocket has better accuracy than a mortar, but often isn't as powerful. A mortar, on the other hand, can do much more damage, but has a greater margin of error to miss its target than a rocket. A rocket can be compared to a slower version of an explosive high-caliber bullet, while a mortar can be thought of as a modern-day cannon.

...*OOOO*...... ***KPUUUH!***

The third explosion sounded (and felt) like the mortar had exploded but a few feet outside our tent, so my lackadaisical moseying to the bunker turned into a game of "last one in the bunker is a rotten (and cracked) egg." I slipped on my body armor and sprinted to the bunker, my protective vest flapping against my chest because I didn't even take the time to Velcro it together. I sat in the bunker and wondered to myself if this was going to be an ongoing battle throughout the night. We'd already been hit by three; how many mortars were they going to pound us with?

I stayed in the bunker for a couple minutes and, realizing that the attacks had stopped, left the bunker and headed westward, which is where I heard the three explosions come from. Sporadic bright lights flashed in the sky, and I couldn't tell if they were flashes of rainless lightning or flashes of malicious bombs.

As I trotted towards the mortars to investigate where they hit, I was met with several soldiers scurrying away from the direction of the explosions, clueing me in as to where they landed.

I made sure the soldiers were unharmed as I brushed past them, bustling my way to the airfield. I looked up to the sky, and though there was no moon out and therefore no illumination, I could decipher a large black cloud of smoke hovering over the airfield. The only way I could see that there was smoke amidst the darkness was because the countless stars in the sky were veiled by a fog that was slightly blacker than the nightfall.

After I reached the last chopper deep in the airfield, I recognized that the mortars hadn't hit close enough to damage any of the aircraft, and *certainly* hadn't hit close enough to injure anyone. I retreated back to my tent under the flashing sky, knowing that any potential damage

couldn't be fully assessed until dawn shed her light on the situation.

Unfortunately for Bandee, he lost his assault bag during his travels, and so he's been spending chilly nights without his sleeping bag and extra uniforms. Imagine going to sleep in a 75° tent and waking up a few hours later to realize the temperature had dropped to a brisk 40, and you have nothing to cover you.

What an interesting exchange, Bandee and me. We have the same rank, pay, and job description, yet Bandee is dealing with the more rigorous elements of war and sometimes having to do it on few hours of sleep and minimal food rations, while I spend warm nights in my hut and get a full night's sleep, and I have the comfort of being able to wake up and know that hired chefs at the DFAC have prepared a complete breakfast for me. I sit in an office all day and am considered what is known as a "fobbit," someone who never leaves outside the wire. Meanwhile, here's an equal chaplain assistant, and he's out tangoing with death on a regular basis. I wrote a poem about this enigma:

I really wish that I was SGT Nicholas Bandee,
And I have good reason as to why.
My name is supposed to be Danger,
But the only one who's earned such a namesake is he.
As a penguin has wings but never takes flight,
Neither has my training adequately been put to the test.
Deep in my heart, I wonder if Bandee will ever make it home,
Eager to rush into violence and chaos,
Eager to prove he's not the soldier everyone thinks he is.

As for FOB Lightning, the only combat we've experienced is that of the weather. There was one day in particular that it felt like a hurricane was ripping across our FOB. It began as rain, then turned to mild hail, then progressed to bitterly large hail, and the wind shook our entire chapel as items crashed to the ground. For awhile, it was too heavy to even travel to the bathroom just a few hundred feet away. I'm told that this is what's considered "mountain weather," something I've never experienced before.

Speaking of new experiences, I got to do something that I was told I would never have an opportunity to do: speak to an Afghan woman. This week, Rambo Three was on the phone with his girlfriend and he had me talk to her, despite my limited fluency with Dari. I picked up the phone and attempted to ask, "How are you?" The other end of the phone drew silent as the interpreters around me erupted in laughter. Apparently, I need to brush up on my Dari, because instead of saying "How are you?", I slipped out "You are a terrorist."[26] Fortunately, Muslims are a forgiving people.

Lately, I've been contemplating how much I admire the Afghans here. In America, many people reject Christianity because Jesus' message is misconstrued as a means to breed hatred. People often feel they've been wronged by Christians, and though that may be accurate, it saddens me to see people turn away from Jesus just because of His obnoxious followers. But there's been so much more severe religious oppression here in Afghanistan than Americans could ever imagine, yet Afghans don't blame Mohammad for his followers' actions, and instead blame the ones responsible: the extremists. Instead of turning away from Mohammad, the Afghans continue to embrace their prophet. I know that if Americans were oppressed by Muslims, the Muslim population would certainly decline in America, just like the Christian population has been dropping as Americans feel victimized by Christ-followers. Instead, the Muslims' faith is rock-steady and they're just as apt to follow their prophet's teachings, whether they have radicals tainting their religion or not. I envy the faithfulness of the Muslim people amidst a time it would be easy for them to reject Islam. I just wish so-called Christians could have half the faith in Jesus that these Muslims have in Mohammad.

---

[26] In Dari: "You are a terrorist," pronounced TOOR-ist-UH. "How are you," pronounced CHA-toor-IST-ee.

Rambo Three and I were recently conversing about such matters; he asked me, “Danger, why do Christians put their Beebles on the ground?”

“Bibles on the ground? What do you mean?” I sought further elaboration.

“Many of you soldiers are Christians, and sometimes I see you guys carrying around your Beebles. But when you’re not using it, you’ll set your Beeble on the ground.”

I stared at him blankly, not seeing the problem.

“Danger, the ground is a place for unimportant things, not holy things.”

“Well,” I reasoned, “in the Christian tradition, it’s believed that the Lord God used to dwell behind a large veil in the holy temple in Jerusalem.”

“Danger, what’s ‘dwell?’ ”

“ ‘Dwell’ means inhabit, or live in. So, in this instance, God used to live in a special temple, and that place was so holy that only the holiest of priests could pay homage, and those visits would be few and far in-between. Those who weren’t deemed holy enough that tried to enter behind the veil would be struck down by God.”

Rambo Three seemed to understand everything up to this point, anticipating the rest of my story.

“But, when Jesus Christ died on the cross, this large veil was ripped from top to bottom.”

“Who ripped the veil, Danger? Did they die?”

“Well, any vandal who would try ripping the veil would only be able to get a small rip near the bottom at best. Nobody could reach anywhere near the top without a tall ladder. Not to mention, nobody dared try to rip the veil, for they knew the stories of people who had died because they got too close to God.”

“Who ripped the veil?” he repeated his question.

“The large rip is believed to be God’s doing, suggesting that now God roams all over the world because of Christ’s sacrifice. To Christians, this indicates that God now dwells, or lives, within His new temple on earth.”

“Where’s the new temple?”

“The new temple is the body of his creation.”

He still looked puzzled.

“Meaning, the new temple is *us*, mankind. God lives within us.”

He didn’t look any less confused.

“We are His temple...”

“No, I understand that,” Rambo Three interrupted. “But still, you don’t answer my question. Why do Christians put their Beebles on the ground where nasty feet and bacterial dirt and dead flies have dominion?”

“Well,” I chose my words carefully, not wanting to spur any more confusion, “Christians put Bibles on the ground because, unlike Muslims, we are less concerned about reverence towards our holy book because we believe our Lord dwells within us.”

He seemed less confused but more frustrated by my explanation. I could appreciate his annoyance, though, as I understood he was coming from a religion in which he is taught to keep his Qur’an and other holy books on the highest shelf in their rooms, kissing these books and asking for pardon when they accidentally drop one on the ground for even the most practical of reasons.

“Danger,” he repeated, “I get all that, but why do you put your Beebles on the ground?”

Silly Muslim! Okay, I need to spell this out in a way that can’t be misunderstood.

“In Christianity, we... well. If you think about Jesus, and how He said... or at least insinuated... Jesus, uh, tried to explain to the Pharisees, about the Holy

Temple... can I start over? Because we believe in God's presence, our Bibles..."

I looked into his eyes and realized he didn't understand a word I was saying. Even worse, neither did I. My attempts to verbalize my argument had decayed into incoherent rambling.

"The fact of the matter is," I conceded, "you have a valid point."

He did have a valid point, indeed. The Bible is our most revered Holy Book, a book that most Christians believe is the inerrant Word of God, a book that claims to alone have the full authority of God.[27] Why in the world would we ever put such a book on the ground? It's not uncommon for Christians to even use Bibles as footrests during church services! If we really believed what we say we do about the Bible, why would we do anything but carry it with both hands and at all times? And why did my lesson to further exalt Christ come from a Muslim who reveres Jesus as a prophet and nothing more?

Once again, it is the Muslim who puts this Christian's perspective back in order.

It's conversations like this that really make me admire these Afghans. My personal relationships with them make me wish this country would live up to its potential. And when I look at the countryside, I realize that the nation is full of underdeveloped possibilities. This place could become an amazing tourist attraction, but that thought seems almost unobtainable because there is so much work to be done. Besides the terrorism, there's much trouble with corruption from important leaders as well; the caliber of Governor Blagojevich's alleged antics are anything but unique in this country.[28]

---

[27] John 1:1

[28] **Rod Blagojevich,** the 40th Governor of Illinois, was found guilty of 17 charges of corruption after a series of investigations and trials took place from December 2008 to June 2011, culminating in a 14-year prison sentence.

When I was in America, I took so many privileges for granted, some liberties that are alien to the interpreters. For instance, they had no idea what a "roller coaster" was, and when I explained it, they were amazed to hear that I had actually been on one and lived to tell about it; they thought that it's impossible for a human to be flung upside-down in a seat and not fall out. I explained its basic physics, and they suffered a mental charlie horse. Yet with all the mountains here, an exotic theme park or grand roller coaster could draw a lot of tourist attention, if only it was a certainty that it wouldn't be blown up a week after it was completed. This is a country in which the thought of carnivals, malls, and waterparks are too foreign to comprehend.

At the same time, the country is being "westernized" by countless Afghanized versions of American TV shows. One favorite is "Afghanistan Star," the country's version of "American Idol." But believe it or not, even a contestant show like "Afghanistan Star" is run by politics – the winner of the show's most recent season was not regarded as the best singer, yet he won because he had strong political ties. Imagine an "American Idol" where Sanjaya Malakar wins the contest because he's friends with a senator.[29]

Even with all the problems in Afghanistan, it's still a comfortable place for its inhabitants, who are a simple people. They enjoy living a life that brings them closer to Allah, family, and friends. They eat together in fellowship, and treat each other (and outsiders like me) like royalty. The only hatred in their hearts is that of the theology of radical Muslims that give Islam a violent connotation. Though they know their country isn't perfect, they accept their homeland and love their country. When they're disappointed in their president, they're not ashamed of their country; when they're disappointed in their religious leaders, they're not ashamed of their prophet. Even though America is trying to help Afghanistan become a better

---

[29] **Sanjaya Malakar,** a sixth-season "American Idol" contestant who was constantly panned by many "Idol" fans, television critics, and especially show judge Simon Cowell. Cowell even went as far as to threaten to quit the show if Malakar ended up winning the competition. Malakar earned 7th place in the contest.

country, I believe that we could learn a wholesome lesson from this simple country, and in that way, Afghanistan would be able to help America.

I ask a prayer of you this week that I've asked before. Weapons and IEDs have increasingly been discovered outside my home FOB, indicating that the war has moved in around here, right on schedule. After all, it's gotten much warmer around here. So, my prayer request is again that you pray for the soldiers as things begin to heat up – both literally and figuratively – around Afghanistan. I'm tired of putting together memorial services for heroes that will never get to enjoy the fruits of their labor again. As for the rest of us, our "day" can come at any time, just as unexpectedly.

Along with that, I can't help but also ask that you pray for the Taliban. Christ charged us to pray for our enemies,[30] and right now I can't think of any human enemy that I dislike more than the Taliban.

In less than ten days, I'll be at the 50% mark of my deployment orders. But I know you'll be ready for me when I return earlier than what is thought to be "100%."

Have a God-blessed Easter weekend. I miss you, babe. You're the grenadine to my kiddie cocktail. Without you, I'd just be another sour tonic.

Love,

Your Fobbit

---

[30] Matthew 5:44

.: 9 :.

Early Morning Commute

October 2008

I sat on the coach bus as it violently vibrated from the engine that was situated under my seat. The pulsations weren't helping my nausea, which I think I got from standing in the way of the bus's sewer-scented fumes too long.

It had been just a few days since I slept alone in the armory after saying "goodbye" to my parents and Joanna. Our unit had stayed the week at our brigade headquarters, packing up and taking care of loose ends in our home state. But now we were getting on a bus to take us to a small private airport where we would get on a plane bound for Fort Bragg, North Carolina to begin intensive training to punch our ticket to fly into war.

Waiting to depart, I tried sparking conversation with the soldier sitting beside me.

"So, you ready?"

Without looking at me, the soldier incredulously replied, "Does it matter?"

I nodded and leaned my head against the window as I loudly exhaled and shut my eyes. On top of my nausea, I was fatigued, perhaps because of the emotional stress I endured during the week, but probably because of how early in the morning it was. I just wanted to get to the hangar as quickly as possible to start this grand adventure.

I figured the trek to the airport would be short and sweet. After all, it was still early and so we shouldn't have to deal with traffic. I would soon find out that I was right that we wouldn't have to deal with traffic, but it had nothing to do with it being early.

The bus began its five-mile trip. But right after it pulled out, it stalled to let a police car pass to its front. As soon as we started moving again, the cop turned his sirens and lights on, keeping pace with us to escort us down the road.

But it wasn't just one police car. Soon, we were being escorted by two police cars. And then three. And then four. And then we found ourselves surrounded by fire trucks, and then by ambulances.

I looked out the coach windows, overstimulated by the plethora of dazzling colors flashing; my jaw dropped to slurp in the flavorless rays of cherry, blue raspberry, coconut, and pineapple juice. I couldn't even count how many vehicles there were surrounding us. Not only was there no traffic (as cars weren't allowed on our road), but we were blowing through every stop light, red or not.

While we continued our trip as one large mass of sirens and prismatic lights, I found I was wrong that nobody would be out on the streets this morning. Instead, there were civilians lining the streets, hooting and hollering for us as we passed by. Children blew us kisses from the sidewalks. Elderly veterans held up signs that wished us well on our journey, affirming they would be praying for us. Morning drivers on intersecting roads put their cars in park, and stepping outside their vehicles, waved to us from afar. Policemen and firefighters lined the sides of the streets, and as our coach passed, they snapped to attention and saluted us.

If I didn't know better, I would've thought we had just won the Super Bowl. And not unlike this year's Super Bowl, the patriots were in attendance.

Who am I to be getting this star treatment? What have I done to deserve this? Does this make me a hero?

I pressed my forehead against the window, trying to take in the amazing display of nationalism I was witnessing. Tears began collecting on the bottom of my eye, but I tried preventing them from dripping down my cheek in front of all the other soldiers, though I imagined I wasn't the only one moved by this experience.

I'm no hero yet. I need to earn this praise. When I get over there, I need to do something that warrants this kind of accolade.

I remembered the goodbye I had with my best friend Matt just a few days ago. He gave me a hug and then cut to the chase, "I'm not gonna tell you not to be a hero. I know you're gonna do what you're gonna do. And when the time comes, I know you'll do what's gotta be done."

Everyone expects me to be a hero.

As we swept through the city's outskirts, a fire truck was parked off to the side with its ladder fully extended and at a 45° angle, hovering over the middle of the road. A large object was draped over the ladder. It was red. It was white. And it was blue. It had 50 stars and 13 stripes. And it was one of the largest of its kind.

When I get back from this deployment, I'll be a hero. Or I'll be dead. I won't go home without earning that title. I will be a hero to someone.

Leaving our civilian lives behind, we passed under the monstrous flag and through the gates of war.

.: 6 :.

AFGHANISTAN:
thoughts about it, the culture within it, and throwing rocks at it.

25 April 2009

Hello from the aching body of SGT Danger.

In recent months, I've been visiting the medics every now and then to check on my ever-weakening back. When I don my body armor, I feel the weight of this entire war on my back, and it's excruciating. On Easter morning, I woke up and the pain was more piercing than it's ever been. My lower back was aching, and my feet felt so heavy that I was almost limping noticeably. Pain originated at the bottom of my back and shot through my right hip and down the leg, stopped at the knee, but struck again just below my ankle. The ankle itself was numb, rendering it the least agonizing of my back pain. On that morning, I went to the doctor on the FOB and was diagnosed with a bulged disc, also known as a herniated disc, also known as a slipped disc, also known as a screwed-up back. The doctor gave me some painkillers, and that's helped so far, but it still hurts to lie down at night. I may be 22, but my body feels like it's 72.

On a more positive note, I'm alive. And as a Christian, I'm not particularly afraid of death because I have faith that I'll move on to be in the presence of Jesus Christ, but after talking with my Muslim friends, I realize that not every religion has an idealistic view of what happens after that last gasp.

Rambo Three told me a few days ago, "Danger, when you go back to the 'Merica, we're going to miss you."

"I'm gonna miss you, too," I responded. "But let's not worry about that right now. We still have lots of time together."

Then Rambo Three recited a poem to me, "When I die, see the sky. No cry; just *bye-bye*."

"Right, 'no cry'," I agreed. "I welcome the day I die."

Rambo Three was surprised by my comment; apparently I misconstrued his poem, which, to him, was more-or-less an overly-optimistic, unrealistic take on death. Instead of looking forward to the afterlife, Rambo Three expressed great fear towards dying, and after he explained his view of it, I can't blame him. When a Muslim dies, they believe that the walls around them will begin closing in, and eventually their body will be crushed. And, according to Rambo Three, as they're pinned against the walls, animals surround them and begin eating their bodies as punishment for their sins. While the Muslim is being punished in the spiritual world, families are immediately notified that their loved one has died, and they drop everything they're doing and travel to the funeral, which occurs just hours after their bodies have expired (keep in mind that Islamic countries don't have embalming fluids at their fingertips like we do in America).

Unlike other religions that see death as the soul's instantaneous graduation party from the body, Muslims believe their soul lingers around until after their funeral. As a deceased Muslim's body is lowered into the ground just hours after they've died, their head is tilted to look towards their holy land of Mecca, and the soul still trapped within the body begins screaming out for the family to hear them. The Muslim yells as loudly as he or she can without moving their physical body, "Please don't leave me! I'm right *here*! Don't go!" Yet, the families that are still alive in the physical world are unable to hear them. If someone were to hear their loved ones' screams, they would die instantly and join them in the afterlife. As for the animal race, they can perfectly hear the shrieking of the soul, yet they keep the cries they've heard to themselves, unable to communicate them to humans. Later, the soul departs to its judgment, and if the Muslim has more good works than bad, then they will enter paradise – you gotta feel pity for the Muslim who had 1,000,000 good works but 1,000,001 bad ones.

For the average Afghan, their life expectancy is 45 years, and though that seems like a young age, it's an improvement from recent years. However, that life expectancy average will mean nothing if the Islamic end of times arrives, because in that case, you'll die regardless of your age. Unlike the Jewish and Christian religions, if a Muslim is alive when the end of times arrives, he doesn't get to bypass the physical experience of death. However, just as the Christian view of the end times is great news for Christians and awful news for non-believers, Islam's end of times is great news for Muslims and awful news for non-followers of Muhammad.

So how exactly does the end of the world occur in Islam? Though there are a few variations depending on the specific Muslim sect you're looking at, it's generally accepted that the Mahdi, a crucial figure of Islam, will appear on earth in the last days, right after an angel blasts a trumpet to sound the arrival of the end times. Interestingly enough, the Mahdi will be bringing a powerful sidekick: Jesus of Nazareth, whom Muslims believe did not return to heaven (nor that he was crucified), but instead has been in some kind of a suspension since his death. After this Jesus reappears, he will come and destroy many evil-doers, including the anti-Christ, and will confirm Islam as the true religion. After 40 years, Jesus will die and be buried next to Muhammad. Then comes Allah, who will destroy all non-Islamic nations and people, and even all the angels in the spiritual world.

Don't fret just yet: a few signs will accompany the Mahdi in preparation for such devastation to the world, including the arrival of violence and plagues, the sun rising from the west, a star appearing in the east that shines as bright as the moon, Arabs taking back their land, what's vaguely described as a caller calling from heaven, Syria suffering a great war until it's destroyed, and death and fear afflicting the people in Iraq (and particularly Baghdad).

Interestingly, many similarities surface when comparing Christian eschatology[31] and Islam eschatology. Essentially, both faiths believe in cataclysmic activities occurring throughout the world as signs of the end times; another telltale sign is that Iran will grow as a super power. However, there's a stark difference between the two faiths at this point: while Muslims believe Iran will destroy an underprepared Israel, Christians believe the underdog Israel will defeat Iran and their allies. It's interesting to me that Christians and Muslims agree on many events that will unfold as the end times nears, except for that one *tiny* disparity in which Muslims believe

---

[31] **eschatology**: the study of the end times.

the Muslims will conquer everyone, while Christians believe Christ will prevail.

But Christ hasn't made His return appearance just yet, so let me bring you back to the present for a moment to talk about what's been happening now. I imagine you're wondering how our ministry portion is going here in Afghanistan.

SGT Bandee has had quite the discouraging month as our ministry teams have raced to reach every soldier with our suicide prevention briefs. Bandee intended on going to three fairly remote locations to minister to the troops that don't get many visitors: Zormat, Jaji, and Sarobi. Well, Bandee arrived on time to COP Zormat, a post so underdeveloped that you're not allowed to pee in the same bucket you poop in, because it makes burning the ordure much more difficult.

But Bandee quickly found that his efforts at this rudimentary post were in vain because 1) the troops he intended on visiting were out on a week-long mission, 2) there was a chaplain already present with the soldiers who were still at COP Zormat, and 3) the troops that *were* out on a mission *also* had a chaplain with them the whole time. And so, the command staff in Zormat made it clear to Bandee that his presence wasn't wanted, and ultimately, Bandee wasted four days getting stuck at the COP. Bandee cut his losses and headed back towards Gardez.

To get back, he had to convoy down a route affectionately known as "IED Alley." Bandee was able to make it without having to learn firsthand why that route is nicknamed as such. The convoy *did* take Bandee to Gardez – just not the same FOB within Gardez that he wanted to get to. The FOB he was trying to get back to was our FOB Lightning, but the one he ended up at was FOB Goode, which is less than a mile down the road from Lightning:

> I found myself waking up in Goode this morning, trying once again to find a means back to Lightning. I've had no luck today. There were no convoys that were able to take me, so I've spent most of my day at the helipad, approaching every chopper that lands here and persuading

the crew chief to fly a minute out of their way to drop me off at Lightning. Every chief denied my request.

I departed for the Entry Control Point (ECP), also known as the front gate. I looked across and, seeing my home FOB, I thought about just walking the mile back. But, preferring not to become a POW, nor wanting to feel the fury of an angry commander for jeopardizing my life, I decided not to walk out there by myself.

That being said, I still wanted to find a way across the road to get to my home FOB by any means necessary. As I was contemplating my potential solutions, I came across a local Afghan who was in his car leaving FOB Goode to go home. I theorized that I could probably coax him into providing me a ride to Lightning, get out of the car at Lightning's Afghan-manned ECP, and walk through the American-manned ECP like I had just been hanging out on the Afghan's side of the base. Surely this idea didn't pass the common sense test, but I was desperate to get onto my next mission.

I told the Afghan driver my predicament, and he had enough English to understand what I was saying and offered me a ride in his car. So, I crawled into his cab. It seemed like the idea would've worked had the team chief at the ECP not stopped me from riding off with a stranger. So now I'm hanging around the helipad again, waiting for a flight that's supposedly going to come in and take me to FOB Lightning, a FOB so close that I could burp and its tower guards would be able to smell the tacos I had for lunch.

Bandee did end up catching a flight back to Lightning late that night. The next morning, he was again on a helicopter, riding towards new adventures. He arrived in Jaji, Afghanistan, but found a similar situation that he ran into at Zormat: the soldiers were out on a mission and wouldn't be back before he left. And so, Bandee did a service for those that were present, then left the next day to Salerno.

Salerno is the same place where Bandee got mortared, and the reason he had to go back there was because it's a main hub for flights that go out to the distant bases, like Sarobi, which is where he was headed next. However, Bandee never made it to Sarobi; he got on a flight headed that way, but bad weather rolled in and the chopper wasn't ever able to land at the base. So, instead of meeting soldiers, he spent all day flying around eastern Afghanistan on a bird. The next flight to Sarobi wasn't slated for another six days, and so our base commander ordered him to abandon the mission and get back to FOB Lightning. The next day, he arrived back after a four-hour flight that took him over every terrain imaginable: rocky mountains, dry plains, desert sands, dusty brushes, and snowy tundra.

When he hopped off the chopper, Bandee looked less like a soldier and more like a crab who had been on the run from New England fishermen all day. Usually people don't get exhausted by simply sitting, but apparently that's not true if you take a day-long ride on a helicopter. Bandee was nauseous from the chopper's fart-flavored fumes and the constant turbulence. I can imagine how frustrated he is: instead of his original plan of going out on a 15-day gratifying assignment, he got sucked into a 9-day fruitless endeavor that left him traveling all over Afghanistan without actually getting to land and visit any of the 33rd Brigade troops at the bases.

The night he got back from his exasperating trip, a random laundry bag was found on a bench near our DFAC. It was packed to its full capacity, but tied tightly so you couldn't tell what was in it. Soldiers know that leaving bags unattended are huge no-no's in a war zone; often, when an item of uncertain origins is found on a base, the explosive ordnance disposal (EOD) team is called in to blow it up, just in case it might be a bomb that somehow infiltrated the base.

FOB Lightning didn't need EOD; instead, it has Bandee. After the bag went unclaimed for an hour, Bandee decided to end the concern that the mystery package was generating by hastening over to the bag, swiping its neck, tearing apart the knot that was holding it together, and dumping its contents all over the rocks on the ground.

"Well, it wasn't a bomb," Bandee affirmed while throwing the empty bag behind a bench. "But someone's gonna have to do laundry again."

Turns out, the laundry bag contained laundry. Go figure.

Oh, Bandee. Let me just say first that I like him. I really do. In fact, I'm gonna make sure you meet this Bandee guy when this deployment is over. But so often, he gets labeled as a "hero" and that he's brave for what he's doing. But for me, it's funny, thinking about this hero stuff. I look around, and I don't see heroes. I see a bunch of guys I eat dinner with and talk to. Yeah, they go out and do things that might get them killed, but they don't feel like heroes to me. We're us, not heroes. Heroes are things of stories, not our realities. Even if there was a soldier who saved a buddy's life while under enemy fire, I'd have a hard time accepting him as a "hero" if it was someone I knew, regardless of the circumstances of his valor. It just feels like here, no matter what we do, we can't be heroes. When we go home, people are going to call us "hero," no doubt. In fact, people called me a hero before I even stepped foot in Afghanistan, when I might, in fact, be a coward. How can I know? I haven't been tested. But the reason I say all this is because so many people speak of Bandee as being brave, as being a hero, and I don't see it at all. What has he done to earn the title of "hero"? I see him as a guy I share my life with; he has the same blood as me. Bandee's just someone that I share exactly the same thoughts with. He's not a hero; we're just exactly the same.

Let me shift gears for a moment. It was back in 2002 that one of my favorite movies was released: M. Night Shyamalan's Signs. But, as much as I love the movie, there's a scene in it that I've always thought was a waste of my attention. Every time I'd have to sit through this one part, I'd get annoyed, feeling like the director didn't care about my time. Here's the scene: Merrill Hess (played by Joaquin Phoenix) walks out of his brother's house and approaches the cornfield on the property. At this point in the movie, there had been several "signs" embedded in cornfields around the world (including his brother's), and many people were starting to believe that aliens had been the perpetrators, as crazy as it sounded. At dusk one night, Merrill looks out at one of the defaced cornfields. Staring at unseen dangers and the mystery of the unknown, he becomes agitated and chucks a rock as far into the cornfield as he can.

For a young viewer like me, I didn't quite understand the scene. It seemed a good waste of 50 seconds of my life. But now when I think about that part, I can't help but appreciate it, and feel like it's one of the most powerful scenes in the movie. I finally "get it." Merrill Hess is frustrated because he's in the middle of something he doesn't quite understand, yet he understands enough to know that it's a serious situation. He doesn't know exactly where the threat is, but he knows it's out there, somewhere, just watching him.

In the same way, I stand looking out across the gates that keep me "safe" as the sun retreats for the day, and I see the Gardez city lights ahead in the distance, only a few miles away. In just an hour's time, that sun will disappear and I'll find myself in a vulnerable time: nightfall, when the enemy can attack while remaining unseen.

As I look across my gates, I become frustrated, and I speak to the wind aloud, hoping it might carry my questions down to the threats that dwell in the city in the distance: "Where are you? I know you're out there, and I know you're thinking about attacking us tonight. Show yourself and fight like a man. Tell me, where are you?" The wind carries my anxieties down to the city, but doesn't return to give me a response. When I realize that there's nothing I can do about the enemy that's hunting me, I become agitated, yet all I can do is throw a rock on the soil just outside my gates.

Since I arrived to FOB Lightning, that enemy hasn't attacked our base, though I found out this week why that's the case. Just last year, this FOB was under attack nearly every week. In fact, there was a 14-day period where the FOB was attacked 12 times. But now, our last attack was in October 2008, just a couple months before I arrived here. It's believed that the same two Taliban were attacking the FOB throughout the course of the year. But, on one October night last autumn, a large explosion was heard outside the perimeter gates. When the QRF[32] investigated, they found what remained of one Talib and another that was severely injured: the two

---

[32] **QRF**, or **quick reaction force**: the team who is on-call to be first responders in the event of an attack on the base.

perpetrators had accidentally blown themselves up. The survivor was arrested, and now, there's somewhat of a peace in the immediate area.

I wish it was that easy all over, but it's not. Often, killing a Talib is similar to mowing down a mushroom on your lawn. Yeah, you killed that specific mushroom, but days later, you have a multitude of mushrooms growing right where you chopped the other one down. So, in this specific war, the question is this: how can we stop more Taliban from appearing after we mow one down?

In my fallible opinion, there are two recourses available:

The first strategy is to cut down the fungus at the roots. In this case, that's Pakistan. Most of the terrorists are being bred and arriving from Pakistan, and unless we launch an offensive against the Taliban in Pakistan, the Taliban in Afghanistan may never be eradicated. But, that's unappealing for several reasons: the time and money spent on such an offensive would take a toll on our country, and that's not to mention the sacrifice of American lives that would be expended on the war. But, if Pakistan *did* commit to fighting terror with us, the Taliban would have nowhere to go and it is my belief that they could become nearly extinct within one-to-two years. Al-Qaeda's Osama bin Laden would probably get caught or killed (as it's widely-believed he's hiding in a cave somewhere in Pakistan), the Taliban would lose hope and eventually disband, and there's a reasonable chance that al-Qaeda would follow suit and scatter in fear.

But, that only becomes a legitimate option if Pakistan decided to work together with us, which is unlikely. I don't know if the Pakistani government is trying to remain neutral (read: cowardly) on their stance on terrorism, ignorant (read: naïve) that their country is harboring terrorists, or actually tolerating (read: enabling) the terrorist presence in an attempt to keep their hands from getting dirty. Whatever the case may be, they've so far been unwilling to aid us in the effort. In theory, we could cross Pakistani lines to track down the Taliban there, but only if President Obama knew for sure we would swiftly win that fight. Otherwise, openly invading Pakistan isn't a reasonable choice. [33]

If that first idea is the pop-open-the-whitehead-and-let-the-pus-drain-out method, then the next one is steadily applying anti-acne cream on the zit: if America can educate the mullahs of the interpretation that non-radical Muslims uphold of the Qur'an and convince them of its merits, then the mullahs could, in turn, preach that same message to the peoples in the villages. As the mullahs are the most prominent religious figures in most villages, by having them preach tolerance, they would in turn prompt their people to become more tolerant. Again, the thought is not foolproof, and such a task is a lot more difficult than it looks on paper. For instance, I know I wouldn't be okay with my church preaching watered-down "nobody-goes-to-hell" Christianity, and I'm sure Muslims in Afghanistan wouldn't be overzealous to accept this new "westernized Islam" that's been injected into their land by godless American infidels.

So, it's a primitive plan already with its share of holes, I know, yet perhaps an alternative if the pimple starts to resurface. But theories are just theories, and you and I are stuck in reality, so let me redirect our attention that way, because I do have a prayer request for you.

I've spoken that I'll return from Afghanistan early, and what an amazing thought that is. I know you fondly remember when I got back for Thanksgiving pass a day early (I still hold that extra time dear in my heart). I'm sure you also remember how close I was to missing my flight that day, how close everything was to not happening. But, I did my best to remain steadfast in faith that day. In the same way, let's try to be steadfast in faith right now. Pray that your faith is increased, and that mine is, too. I don't doubt I'll get home early from this Afghanistan, but we need to foster our

---

[33] On May 2, 2011, Navy SEALs Team 6 reportedly infiltrated Abbottabad, Pakistan and killed Osama bin Laden, who was hiding in a housing compound, not a cave. The Pakistani government was criticized for harboring the terrorist leader, though they pleaded ignorance of ever knowing that he lived there.

faith, lest we care to see it dwindle over time. Pray for me and I'll pray for you.

Love,

Your Achy-Breaky Boyfriend

Bandee snaps a photo of the Afghan terrain below while riding around eastern Afghanistan aboard a Chinook, April 2009

.:10:.

Planes, Strains, and Automobiles

November 2008

It had been a long two months of pre-deployment training at Fort Bragg, North Carolina, and all the soldiers were excited: despite being told we wouldn't get any opportunities to see our families again until after our tour, we were all given 4-day passes to go home over Thanksgiving week. As if this thrill wasn't enough, we had just found out that we would probably be released a day earlier than anticipated, skyrocketing our enthusiasm and prompting everyone to find earlier flights home.

I began fantasizing about getting home a day early. It was so perfect: it would allow me an entire day more to spend with my family, and I would be able to watch an uninterrupted Green Bay Packers game; I hadn't been able to watch my Packers play since before the deployment began. Never had a single "day off" meant so much.

I had just gotten off the phone with my parents and Joanna to tell them we were told we could start booking earlier flights when my section sergeant burst my bubble. He told me that I had to go to what's known as the "in-processing station" to complete some paperwork the next day, and that I wouldn't be allowed to get on a flight until I had finished. While that seems simple enough, the problem was that the last time a group went through to do this in-processing paperwork, they arrived at 8:00 in the morning and didn't leave until late that night. The last flight to Chicago was scheduled to leave in the early afternoon, much earlier than I would be finished by.

The discouragement only piled higher when I got a phone call from my dad saying that he checked with the airline and every flight was booked, and there wasn't a chance of getting on standby. I hung up, downtrodden with my rotten luck.

As I tried brainstorming ideas to whip up a plan to get on a flight the next day, I realized something: there was *no way* that I could get on a flight. Even as persistent as I am, looking at the entirety of the situation, my hands were tied. This was a situation that was too big for me to handle. Recognizing my feebleness, I came up with a different plan: I started praying. Within minutes, a familiar still voice inflated my heart.

"You will be home early… you will be home tomorrow…"

My heart surged with faith, encouraged to finally hear something I wanted to hear. I called Joanna and my parents and told them to expect me home on that Monday, but they became worried about the grand disappointment I would feel if it didn't pan out.

For the next several hours, I kept calling the airline to see if I could get on standby, but each time I called, they told me that it was impossible. My family and CH Fardpot and several soldiers encouraged me to just give up, saying I can't expect to be home the next day. But I refused to hear it, only because I believed God refused to hear it.

The next morning, I still had no means to get home, yet I went to in-processing with just the clothes on my back, not bringing any additional uniforms "just in case" I was wrong and would have to sleep overnight at the airport. Instead, I left that morning, fully expecting to be at home that night.

◊

In-processing got off to a late start, which didn't help my cause. And whenever I had a free moment, I'd call the airline to see if they found an available seat, but they repeated that they had no flights for me. On one particular attempt, I called the airline; a single seat became available, but the last-minute change would cost hundreds of dollars that I didn't have. The airline representative asked me to fax in my deployment orders to see if they could use that to their advantage. I just so happened to have my orders on me, and so I got off the phone and began searching for a fax machine as if it was the pot of gold at the end of a rainbow. I did find one, and after petitioning to be allowed to use it for non-business-related matters, I faxed my orders.

When I got back on the phone with the airline rep, she confirmed that she received my orders, but in the time it took me to find that blessed fax machine, the one available seat got booked.

I had hit the final brick wall; there was nothing more I could do. Unless a seat magically popped up on the 12:40pm flight and the representative decided to go out of her way by calling to tell me, I wouldn't be on that early flight home. No bonus time with my family. No Monday Night Football. No miraculous happy ending.

Even though it looked like I wouldn't have my miracle flight, one piece of amazing did happen: in the eleventh hour, I finished the in-processing. I had tenaciously downsized an 11-hour day's worth of paperwork and medical examinations into a 3-hour gauntlet. I was given the green light to start my Thanksgiving pass, if only I could find a way home.

At this point, the one available (albeit booked) early flight was leaving in about an hour-and-a-half. After that flight left, the next one wouldn't be leaving until the following morning.

I contemplated my options as my cell phone rang.

Oh no! I groaned to myself as I realized it was my section sergeant calling. *The last thing I need is to be told that I forgot to do something and can't leave until it's done.*

Knowing I was obliged to answer the call, I picked up.

"Hey sergeant, it's SGT Geist. What's up?"

"SGT Geist, how close are you to finish in-processing?"

Here it was. He was about to give me a new task, grounding any chances I had of getting home early, as God had told me I would.

"Sergeant, I'm done with that. I just finished it."

"Great," he said. "I'm *en route* to your location. I'll pick you up in five minutes."

"Pick me up?" I inquired. Why did he need to pick me up? Was he going to shuttle me back to base for something?

"Yes, pick you up. You need a ride to the airport, don't you?"

Oh my gosh. I had completely forgotten that I didn't even have a ride to the airport, which was at least 30 minutes away. This was an oversight that would've cost me all my efforts: being completed with in-processing and having a flight would've meant nothing had I no transportation to the airport!

As I waited for my section sergeant, I wondered what I was going to do once I got to the airport. Just when I resolved that I would covertly duct-tape myself to the wing of a Chicago-bound airplane, my cell phone rang again. I didn't recognize the number.

"Hello?"

"Yes, Mr. Geist?"

"Yes, speaking."

"Mr. Geist, we found a seat on the 12:40pm flight to Chicago."

Not only did a seat magically pop up on the 12:40pm flight, but the representative decided to go out of her way by calling to tell me. I was bamboozled, but it didn't amount to much of a miracle just yet. Could I even afford the last-minute change?

"Well thank you, thank you very much. But, uh… how much is this going to run me?"

"Mr. Geist, we have waived all the extra fees for you. Would you like to book this seat?"

"Ma'am, you have no idea how much I would love that. Thank you. Thank you so much."

"Not a problem, Mr. Geist."

"No, ma'am. Really. Thank you. You have no idea how much this means. Thank you."

"No problem at all, Mr. Geist. You have a good one, okay?"

"You too, ma'am. You too. God bless you."

"God bless you, too." I could hear the smile in her voice.

Just as I ended the call, my section sergeant pulled up – I must've looked as stunned as a deer in headlights. Everything was coming together.

As we drove to the airport, I wasn't yet at a point where I could settle back and relax. After all, my flight was leaving in about an hour, and I was still a half-hour away from the airport. That would only give me 30 minutes to print my tickets, check my bags, get through security, and find my terminal.

Another soldier broke my musings when he announced, "I just got off the phone with another soldier and he said that it took him two hours to get through security."

Knowing my situation, an officer turned around and said to me, "You hear that, Geist? You're not gonna make it on this one."

I laughed under my breath.

"Trust me, sir. I'll be on that flight." After all I had been through, there was no way I wasn't going to be getting on that flight.

"You're wrong, Geist. Did you hear what he just said? You don't even have a chance. You'll have to get a flight for tomorrow."

"I'm not worried about it, sir."

We arrived to the airport with little over a half-hour before my flight left. I went to get my tickets; no problem there. I checked my bags; there were no complications. I got in line to go through security; I stepped right through. I found my terminal; it was 12:20pm.

And then I was soaring through the air on a 12:40pm outbound flight to Chicago.

On the flight, I was able to decompress and reflect on the day. I was reminded that "faith by itself, if it is not accompanied by action, is dead."[34] I was so grateful that my faith hadn't been dead; when I felt God tell me I'd be getting home early, I didn't sit on my butt waiting for a chopper to land behind my tent on Fort Bragg. Instead, I acted on the faith that I had to put the miracle into motion. Certainly, it wouldn't be the last time I'd have to act on my faith to achieve something God has promised.

After the flight landed in Chicago, I walked out of the airplane and into the arms of Joanna, who had managed to get past security with my dad to meet me as I got off my flight. We stood there in the airport embracing each other, tears rolling down our cheeks. My dad gave me a warm "welcome-home" hug, and then we got into the car and drove home.

Yes, I would be bound to dangerous Afghanistan in just a few weeks from this point. But for one special night, I was with family, and I was free.

That very evening, I walked into my warm home, a testament that God's promises are true and trustworthy.

---

[34] James 2:17

Danger and Joanna during the November 2008 Thanksgiving Pass

.:10:.

Hello Muddah, hello Fadduh, here I [still] am at Afghanada!

10 May 2009

Joanna, it's been an eventful two weeks. Let me get right to it.

First of all, let me just say that I can't wait to get back to college. When I first was a college student, I went because it was the "thing to do" and because the National Guard was willing to pay for it as long as I was still in the Army. But, now I've gathered a newfound appreciation for education and my opportunities to have it. This is mainly because of how much I see the Afghans strive to earn a coveted education that I take for granted. Most of the Afghans I've talked to have a lifelong goal of attending any university in America. To me, that seems so foreign. Isn't attending a university the very thing that I've always felt got in the way of my life? And here these Afghans are, gnashing their teeth to get into an American school.

It's no surprise that Afghans agree that America is educationally advanced compared to their own country. And in fact, America seems to be advanced in almost every aspect: economically, politically, intellectually, judicially, and militarily, to name a few. However, there's one thing in which Americans don't seem to excel: moral advancement. The Afghans find many of the crimes that Americans commit to be appalling. For instance, it's unheard of that an Afghan would kill his entire family after losing a job. Yet in America, news like this frequently hits headlines. While this may be a product of the fact that Afghanistan also has a less advanced free press system than America (and therefore awful events like these may take place over here but remain unreported by the media), one Afghan I talked to believes this is because Americans don't have a war on our land, nor have any of us ever experienced war on our own soil. Americans don't have much concept of what it means to be loyal to your country. The closest we've come to experiencing such a thing is September 11th, a time when all of America joined together for the length of a solid week, maybe two weeks at best. The Afghans have experienced terrorism every single day on their land since they were born. As a result, they're dedicated to bettering their country at all costs, being loyal to the land until death. Instead of killing each other, they've always had a collective enemy on their land (that currently being the Taliban), which drives them to want to be better people for their country.

Now, that's not to say that Afghans are perfect people, or that they don't struggle with some of the same things that Americans do. In fact, just this week I had an interpreter beg me to find him a porno magazine, trying to convince me that "it's the democratic thing to do." Furthermore, their religious law isn't sympathetic towards violations of their culture. The Afghans gave me some insight into their Islamic punishment system. For instance, a man who has sex with a woman outside of marriage receives 80 lashings. For women who lose their virginity before marriage, they're stoned until the rocks literally cover the stoner's view of the woman. And if you were to have intimate same-sex relations? A large wall would be pushed down onto you, and you would have to try and survive for 15 minutes. If you're alive after the 15 minutes, then you've renewed your right to live and someone will pull you out. So, while Afghans seem to try to uphold what they consider traditional values, it seems to come at the expense of vile and cruel punishments. And while I haven't firsthand seen or heard about these penalties happening to someone, it does make me better appreciate the justice system in America in the event that these punishments really do happen behind closed doors.[35]

Not wanting to inundate you with unsubstantiated gossip, let me turn your attention to the less-abstract SGT Bandee, whose lack of adventure last month has been rectified in full this week when he went out on a convoy with Colonel (COL) Staar, one of five regional commanders under Task Force Phoenix.

---

[35] Under Taliban rule, stoning was the accepted punishment for many crimes, but after the Taliban fell to American forces in 2001, stoning was no longer an acceptable means of punishment. However, stoning is still conducted in secret by those who uphold Sharia as the official law. In August 2010, 150 men in Afghanistan witnessed the Taliban-sponsored stoning of a couple guilty of committing adultery.

COL Staar is a commander who demands nothing less than excellence from his soldiers. Since the war on terror began, he's been in combat zones longer than he's been stateside and, as such, has been augmented into a staunch leader who displays admirable fortitude, carrying himself like the Airborne Ranger he is. He's the kind of officer who makes it seem like he doesn't need to conform to military standards because his body automatically does it for him: it's as if his hair naturally grows thick on top and tapered along the sides, meanwhile his boots shine themselves at his demand, and I'm convinced he was born wearing a camouflaged diaper to appear less vulnerable in front of his parents.

Not only was Bandee on the same mission with the commander, but was also assigned to the same vehicle as him. That's not to say Bandee was intimidated about having to conduct a mission with such a bigwig:

> Yesterday morning, as we were getting ready to leave on the convoy, it dawned on me that the mission I was about to go on was, in fact, another precarious mission. To get to where we were going, I would again have to get through IED Alley. Not to mention, the ante gets raised whenever you have a cheese riding with you. But it was another soldier who put the situation in perspective for me: "Hey, at least you're not going down Route Virginia!" That's when I realized that at least that was true: after all, Route Virginia was the most unstable route in the area at the moment. Not only had soldiers just gotten attacked on that route, but there were also two known pressure plate IEDs placed on the road somewhere, just waiting for a convoy to roll over them.
>
> Our convoy made it through IED Alley and to our destination with no complications, and I was already deciding what I'd do with my free time when we got back to Gardez. That is, of course, until COL Staar decreed we needed to make another stop at a small ANA base out in the middle of nowhere. But to get to this base in the middle of nowhere, we had to backtrack through IED Alley and shoot through... you

guessed it… Route Virginia. So, we trekked down the most dangerous road in Paktya Province as the sun set on the day.

Riding down IED Alley and Route Virginia (which are both unpaved) all in one day was one of the rockiest experiences of my life. The seat I was sitting on was directly above one of the rear wheels, and every bump sent me flying in the air, sometimes even hitting my helmet on the roof of the vehicle. If you've ever played "break the egg" on a trampoline, then you have an idea of how it felt to be in that vehicle (which is known as a Cougar). Except in the Cougar, when I flew in the air, I wasn't falling down towards a trampoline; instead it was a hard seat, and I was surrounded by bags and weapons that would hurtle onto me. When I'd get launched in the air, I didn't always land on my butt, if you catch my drift; COL Staar laughed at me as I cried out at one point, "I wish I had a vagina!" By the end of the trip, I learned how to react so quickly that, while in mid-flight, I'd extend my legs to stand and press my hands on the top of the ceiling so I could stabilize myself like I was the fulcrum to a bridge.

Near the end of Route Virginia, there was a dead Afghan covered with a plastic sheet, lying on top of a fresh grave off to the side of the rocky road. All banter that wasn't related to the mission hurried to a halt as a morbid mood filled our vehicle.

There was one good omen about our trip, though. As we were traveling, locals were out and about in the streets and marketplace, and children were playing to the side of the road. When out on a mission, this is always a good sign, because when the locals are conversely off the streets and staring at our convoy through their doorways, as if there's a parade about to pass in front of their house, it's usually because they're expecting to see a fireworks show. You never want to underestimate the knowledge of the locals in Afghanistan, who are often clued in when and where attacks are supposed to happen, but refuse to inform American troops out of fear that a Talib will find out they leaked the terrorists' plans. So, to see the locals fearlessly conducting business as usual, we had a good feeling that we would be safe today.

After offroading for a couple miles, we arrived to the ANA base with no complications, except for the fact that we didn't have enough sunlight to make it back to Gardez. So, we had to stay the night at this small ANA compound that consisted of a 10,000 square-foot area that was closed in by some HESCO barriers.[36] We were out in the middle of a field, sharing the space with an Afghan shepherd and his flock. We were completely exposed, and there were several mountains off in the distance that could easily be launchpads for mortars; we knew it was likely that we would be getting attacked during our stay. Regrettably, there were no buildings in this compound, nor any real facilities (i.e., flushing bathrooms, chow hall, nor lodging). We were either going to have to sleep in our vehicles or outside on the ground. There were some cots, but not enough for everybody. To remedy the likelihood of attack (or at least be ready in case it happened), we decided that everyone needed to pull guard shifts. Because there were so many of us, we would only have to pull one-hour shifts.

And with that, we had officially settled in The Middle of Nowhere, Afghanistan.

That night, I laid down my sleeping bag on the ground right near COL Staar, knowing that if we were attacked, I would dedicate myself to protecting his life, as there was no chaplain for me to take care of on this mission. I settled into my sleeping bag with my rifle and looked up at the stars above. I recognized that, today, I had been up and down

---

[36] **HESCO barrier**: mesh box that is filled with dirt and/or sand, and covered by heavy fabric to prevent small pieces of shrapnel and indirect fire from penetrating a stronghold.

some of the most threatening (and bumpy) roads in Afghanistan, I didn't have any shelter above me, I was susceptible to an attack, and here I was, lying on large rocks in place of my bed. At that moment, I acknowledged how miserable I felt. Not miserable for myself, but for everyone who wasn't going to fall asleep like I was, getting to spend my entire night watching God's craftsmanship above me. I felt miserable for everyone who has never experienced what I've been privileged to experience. And, I felt miserable that there were so few moments like this that I would get to enjoy in my life.

Even though it was cloudless and probably going to stay a dry night, I looked up to the sky and prayed that God ensure it didn't rain on us, and that He protect us from snakes and scorpions. Just before I shut my eyes, a shooting star shot through the sky. Cuddling my rifle, I smiled and closed my eyes, ready to defend this base in the case of a likely attack.

0300 hours rolled around, so I got out of bed, put on my boots, and carefully watched the cameras mounted in the Cougar for the next hour. I scanned for any suspicious activity, searching my zone for any possible Talibs. All I found were grazing camels. When my hour was up, I woke up my relief and crawled back into my sleeping bag.

The night had gotten very windy and therefore very cold, so I was cocooned in my sleeping bag when dawn broke a couple hours later. As the sun began skewering me like I was a pig-in-a-blanket, I felt something poking me.

What is that? I wondered. *Is that a scorpion? A snake?*

I peeked out of my sausage casing and saw a frightened puppy retreat from my emerging face. I couldn't help but giggle at the cute little guy. That is, until I realized the cute little guy had my boot in his mouth, and he had already carried it farther than an arm's length away.

I yelled at him, "Hey! Hey! Give that back!" Apparently, the pup spoke Dari, not English, because he wouldn't stop prancing around with my boot clenched in his baby teeth.

"Fine. If you're not coming to me, I'm coming to *you*!"

If my bag was a cocoon, then I had fluttered out as a groggy half-metamorphosed butterfly, clumsily chasing the mangy puppy while my feet scraped against the rocks. When I got close enough, the puppy got scared and dropped my boot from his mouth and scrambled into a bunker.

I hobbled back into my sleeping bag, this time not without nuzzling my boots. As I dozed off, the puppy emerged from the bunker and, realizing that I had hidden my boots from him, trotted over to COL Staar's pile of belongings, snooped around until he found the commander's boots, and dragged one of them into a ditch to chew on.

It was time to get up shortly after. I got out of my sleeping bag and headed to an area where I could take a leak, all-the-while getting my boots bitten by the puppy who didn't seem to understand that he couldn't steal my boots while they were on my feet.

I envied the puppy's energy; I felt as sore as an NFL quarterback who leads the league in sacks received. I wasn't sure if my aches were from the bumpy convoy or from sleeping on jagged rocks, though I imagine it was a combination of both. But, shortly after we all woke up and gathered our stolen belongings from the midnight thief, we were all ready to drive back down Route Virginia to get back to FOB Lightning.

Before we left the base on the convoy, we were heeded one warning: if anybody sees a motorcyclist driving parallel to our vehicles, we need to immediately call it in. Apparently, there was a recurrence of suicide bombers using this technique to pace coalition forces and blow them up at the opportune moment.

Route Virginia was a little bit different than it had been the day before: instead of children and locals bustling throughout the streets, today it was an eerie ghost town. We prepared ourselves for the worst.

If the lack of activity wasn't jolting enough, the few villagers that *were* in the area stopped what they were doing, mesmerized by our passing convoy as if we were a blessing of galloping unicorns.

To further raise anxieties, within minutes of our convoy, the very thing we were warned about appeared. An Afghan on a motorcycle was waiting for us off the road, and when we neared him, he began driving parallel to us. When we stopped, he would stop, and when we sped up, he'd speed up. The entire time, the cyclist kept his eyes on our Cougar, as if trying to figure out the timing of the vehicle's movement.

There was no question about it: we were in the proverbial crosshairs of the enemy, and he was in great position to blow us up at the timely moment. But, because of the rules of engagement, we couldn't do anything about it because we had no proof he was a member of the Taliban.

As we continued on our route, a soldier witnessed an Afghan watching us from an alley, and it was determined that there was a good chance the Afghan was a spotter in cohorts with the motorcyclist still riding beside us.

COL Staar radioed to me, "Sergeant, if an IED goes off, I want you to dismount and tackle the guy on the bike."

"Roger, sir."

There was an awkward silence; I don't think I gave him the response he was expecting, so he clarified.

"Sergeant, you know I was joking, right?"

"Roger, I know you were. But I wasn't."

COL Staar chuckled. "Yeah, I don't doubt you'd do it."

As we traveled on, we prepared ourselves for an explosion, if not from the motorcyclist, then at least from one of the two pressure plates that we had somehow avoided the day before. When we arrived to the outskirts of the town, where it would be most logical to blow us up, I breathed a deep breath in and prepared for the blast.

"Commander, he's right on us," the gunner reported through the headsets, interrupting my breath-holding.

"I know, gunner. Just keep an eye on him."

"But sir, he keeps inching towards us. Can I point my gun at him?"

"No, denied. Shout at him."

"I've already done that, s... sir! He's getting closer."

COL Staar didn't respond.

"Sir! He's really close!"

"I know, gunner. I see him, too."

"Sir, I need to fire a warning shot. He's right next..."

"Gunner! You are *not* to shoot unless he points a weapon at you, do you understand?"

"Sir, I understand, but he's..."

"*Listen to me*. I don't care what he's doing: unless he's pointing something at you, you do *not* fire, understand?"

Silence.

"Do you understand?"

More silence.

"Gunner?"

"Sir…?"

"What is it?"

"Sir… the motorcyclist… he… *what the shit*…"

"What is it, gunner?"

"Sir, he… *the guy*…"

"Spit it out!"

"He, uh, he… just left. He's gone."

"He's gone?"

"Yes, he's gone, sir. He slowed down and is turning around to go back the other way."

The motorcyclist faded away in our rearview mirrors. A couple hours later, we returned to FOB Lightning, unscathed.

After we got back, all the soldiers recounted what had just happened, trying to make sense out of why we hadn't gotten attacked. Many of them chalked it up to chance, that our jamming system on our Cougar prevented the explosion from occurring when the trigger man pressed the button. Or that maybe it was coincidence: the kids weren't out today because they were busy with chores inside; the Afghans gawking at us just moved into town and had never seen an American presence before; the motorcyclist was intrigued by our vehicle and just wanted to study it in action; the "spotter" perhaps was just a homeless man who lives in the dark alley; maybe we got lucky and just barely missed the pressure plates.

Could be. But as I lift my eyes, I have a different theory.

While Bandee was able to befriend and earn the trust of COL Staar on this trip, I, on the other hand, had the opposite effect on our commander this week.

Let me back up.

Since the day I arrived on FOB Lightning, we've shared our space with some of the native inhabitants of the land. I'm not talking about the Afghans, but rather the undomesticated dogs of Afghanistan. There are several ways for a dog to get onto a FOB, from trotting past the front gate undetected to finding a hole wide enough to squeeze their bodies through onto the base. For the most part, this goes unnoticed by commanders on most FOBs, yet is welcome by most of the soldiers. On our particular FOB, we have dogs that became best friends to the soldiers and contractors. A young contractor raised Breach since she was a puppy to the adult dog she grew to become. A grouchy contractor identifies with Ben because they both share the distinguished honor of being the oldest of each of their kind on the FOB. One soldier claims that his dog-friend, Security, knows all his secrets, and just finished the paperwork to adopt and transport her back to the United States. Soldiers go out on missions and look forward to coming back to these creatures who seem to somehow understand the stress that the soldiers go through.

But it's not rainbows and butterflies for everyone. A clause in General Petraeus's General Order Number One[37] states that no animals are allowed to become "mascots" or "pets" on any "territory or possession" of the United States of America. FOB Lightning, as well as every other base across the world that is run by the U.S., falls under this category. In fact, American bases on foreign land aren't considered foreign at all; the soil is considered American soil, despite the homeland being thousands of miles away.

---

[37] **General Order Number One**: a list of the most fundamental orders that U.S. soldiers are expected to abide by in combat zones. Compiled during the 2003 invasion of Iraq, it is mainly a set of rules and prohibitions that defines contraband and upholds military discipline.

From before I deployed, I was familiar with this clause in General Order One. I've feared that, someday, the beloved animals on this FOB would be eradicated because of the rule. In a few instances, I've woken up to the sound of barking well after midnight. Afraid that this would target the dogs for removal, I'd run outside my hut and call them over to have their backs scratched until they calmed down, hoping that the wrong person hadn't already been woken up. I thought that as long as I remained vigilant to stop these dogs from being nuisances, everyone might be able to live in peace on the FOB.

I was naïve.

Earlier this month, one of the bigwig commanders, Major General (MG) Garnett, marched through the FOB and noted the prohibited presence of dogs. As a result, COL Staar was reprimanded, gnarled at to "take care of the problem." COL Staar, in an attempt to get out of the dog house, ordered a swift removal of the canines. A small group of soldiers were elected to round up the pets.

When the soldiers pulled up a van and tried forcing them in, the dogs knew that whatever was going on wasn't good, so they each desperately fled from the soldiers they had come to love. But after a short struggle, every dog had been seized, put in the vehicle, and driven just outside the FOB, all attempts at escaping having proved futile.

Being the oldest, Ben had struggled the least and was naturally the first to be taken out of the vehicle. Confused, he looked up at the soldier who had taken him out of the van. The soldier cocked his pistol, raised it, and aimed right between Ben's eyes.

TCHUU!

Kicking Ben to the side as his blood drained from his skull, the soldier opened the van door again and tried grabbing the next in line. The dogs had heard the gunshot and huddled together, burrowing into one another for safety. The soldier grabbed Security next, pulling her nape until her toenails couldn't dig into the van carpet any further. Looking down at the cowering dog with her tail between her shaking legs, the soldier had an easy target.

TCHUU!

One-by-one, each dog was yanked from the van one second, lifeless under it the next.

Breach was the last, and having heard the gunshots coupled with the yelps of her dying friends, she attempted one last escape to avoid the same fate as her friends. When the van door opened, she made a break for it, but didn't get far.

TCHUU!

A bullet tore through her eye and she lay bleeding on the ground, twitching from the intense pain throughout her head. The soldier put the longtime pet in his crosshairs, and with one last bullet...

TCHUU!

...the FOB was purged of its problem. The soldiers took each of the dogs and tossed them down in a nearby ditch; a proper burial for a proper death.

◊

Members of the FOB were grief-stricken over the slaughter of the dogs, lamenting that their pets were such pure and innocent yet defenseless creatures. Some soldiers were so upset, it seemed as if a mutiny might be on the commander's hands.

I felt compelled to talk to COL Staar. At this point, he and I had a great working relationship, and when I'd walk into his office, he'd intently listen to me, knowing that I was his eyes and ears to alert him about morale issues that he was unaware of.

"COL Staar?" I knocked on his door as I poked my head in his office.

"Ah, SGT Geist!" COL Staar stood up and motioned his hand towards a suede chair perched in front of his desk. "How are you doing? Have a seat."

"COL Staar, I won't take up more time than I need to, but I wanted to talk to you about something. A lot of soldiers on the FOB are upset."

Immediately sitting back down, his eyebrows furrowed and he leaned in.

"SGT Geist, what are they upset about?"

"The dogs, sir."

"The dogs," he repeated, knowing exactly what I was referring to. "What are they saying about it?"

"They're upset with how the command handled it. Some of them want to report it to the Inspector General."[38]

"The IG? What do they think that'll do?" He raised his hands in the air. "We followed military protocol!"

"I understand, sir. I don't think going to the IG is the right method, either."

"What can we do, SGT Geist? Do you think it would help if I talked to them about it?"

"Yes, very much, sir. If you can just give them your point of view, what you had to go through, it might help most of them to understand. And perhaps then..."

"What would *they* have done?" he interrupted me, his hand covering his mouth. "What was I *supposed* to do?"

I sat in silence.

"People don't understand the tough decisions that I'm faced with on a daily basis." COL Staar's eyes began to turn red and swelled as tears collected. "I had *a General* breathing down my neck about the issue, telling me I had to solve the problem *immediately*. What could I do?" A tear fell on his desk. "Alright, thank you, SGT Geist. I'll go and have a FOB-wide meeting about

---

[38] **Inspector General**: an ally of subordinate soldiers in the military, intermediating between command officers and junior soldiers, particularly in regards to cases in which a specific soldier was wronged or his/her rights were unfairly restricted.

this so they understand. You've done good here today. Thank you." COL Staar stood up and began rummaging through his desk, expecting me to leave.

I remained seated. I couldn't get up. I wasn't done.

"Sir."

COL Staar plopped back down, understanding there was something on my mind.

"Sir, I am included."

"You are... are *included*? What do you mean, SGT Geist?"

"I am included. I'm not happy with what happened."

COL Staar realized he wasn't meeting with a friend, but the enemy. Perplexed, he stared at me.

"Sir, I don't want this to ever happen again."

"SGT Geist," he chuckled, "do you understand why this policy is in place? Here's what happens: once we start letting dogs and cats on our FOBs, we invite disease into our living spaces. Soldiers will get rabies. Do you know what it's like to get rabies, SGT Geist? It takes a soldier out of the fight *completely*."

"I understand, sir."

"This issue isn't organic to this FOB, you know. Thousands of dogs are killed every year in combat zones. This isn't something that just happens on FOB Lightning, this happens everywhere, including Iraq. Killing dogs is common practice, you realize."

I knew he was right about that. I had once talked to a friend in the Marines who was ordered to kill his platoon's pet puppy in Iraq.

"I understand, sir."

After an awkward moment, COL Staar exhaled, understanding that I hadn't come to debate the issue with him, but rather had come to give him a courtesy head's-up about my intentions so he wouldn't be blindsided.

"Sir, I have written a letter that I intend to send to my congressman."

COL Staar's eyes froze on me, unable to blink. As quickly as a piece of Fruit Stripe gum loses its flavor, I had lost my novelty with the commander.

"SGT Geist," he tensed up. "SGT Geist, that's not going to help."

"Sir, I have to do something. This policy is awful."

"Do you know what's going to happen if you send that letter? Here's what'll happen: you send that letter, the congressman responds by sending me a letter saying that he wants to know why I did what I did, and I'll reply explaining that I followed my General's orders. Nothing will come from it, all that will happen is you will create more work for me. No change will come."

I didn't know how to respond.

"SGT Geist, you're not pushing back against *my* policy, you understand. You're against General Order Number One, against General (GEN) Petraeus. You shouldn't be talking to your congressman about what I did. Instead, you should be going to the next level in your chain-of-command. You're talking to me now, so the next step is to talk to Brigadier General (BG) Jonah, the commander of Task Force Phoenix, using his open door policy."

I didn't even know how to get a meeting with the General; I was in way over my head.

"After that, you would need to go talk to MG Garnett. After that?" COL Staar began raising his voice, his gentle tears burned away by the fire in his eyes. "GEN McChrystal. And after *that*? GEN Petraeus."

I swallowed all the spit that had been collecting in my throat. My mouth was so dry now.

"You're not being smart, SGT Geist," he thundered. "You're thinking with your emotion."

I couldn't disagree with him more. I hadn't even known any of the dogs' names until after they were killed. I wasn't emotionally upset, I was morally upset. But I dared not speak.

"Step back and think about it logically. What are you going to say to him, SGT Geist? If you request an audience with BG Jonah, and you don't have a foolproof plan, he will *crush* you. You know that BG Jonah is from your brigade in Illinois; if you don't have a legitimate reason to be taking up his time, your military career will be *over*." He pointed at me, chiding even louder. "*Over*, SGT Geist. You'll have shit jobs the rest of your career, and you'll never be promoted. Do you hear me?"

"Sir, yes, I..."

"You wanna know what *I* think, SGT Geist? Here's what I think. You have circular logic. What you're saying doesn't make sense. So I have to ask myself, 'Why is SGT Geist doing this? Why is he causing all this trouble?' And you know what I think? I think that you're nothing more than an attention-seeker. You want to pursue this issue because you love yourself, and you want your name to be known. You want everyone in Afghanistan to be talking about you. But you know what? What you're doing is going to have the opposite effect of what you want. By publicizing this issue, you'll be bringing attention to the fact that many FOBs have pets within their gates. Commanders across the board are going to be ordered to seek and destroy every animal on their FOB. I can see it now, here are the headlines," he leaned back, slapping the air with each word, " 'SGT GEIST CAUSES DOGS TO DIE.' " He leaned back towards me. "You're going to be the *death* of those *dogs*! Do you want to be a *dog-killer*?"

I paused for a moment, gathering what I wanted to say next.

"Sir," I licked my lips, "one of the seven Army values is 'integrity: do what is right, legally and morally.' I need to follow my conscience. I don't mean to create more work for you, and I certainly don't mean to anger you." His face bore resemblance to hot sauce, showing I had failed at that much. "But I will use BG Jonah's open door policy to talk to him about this issue."

COL Staar's elbow was on his desk, his thumb and index fingers holding up his head.

"Sir, thank you for your time," I said. The commander nodded his head, excusing me from his office.

I lumbered back to the chapel and collapsed into one of the sanctuary chairs, breathing a sigh of relief that that was done. Not long after, the chapel phone rang. I picked it up.

"Geist, tell me what the hell is going on."

It was the head chaplain assistant of my brigade, the guy I have to report to every week on our ministry activities.

"Sergeant," I sought clarification, "what do you mean?"

"What's with this dog stuff? You want to talk with the *General*? Don't you know that you never fight a direct order unless it's illegal, immoral, or unethical?"

"Well, yes, sergeant, and that's..."

"Geist, CH Stanford is *furious* with you. He got a visit from one of the top chiefs of Task Force Phoenix asking why one of *his* chaplain assistants is misbehaving so badly."

Apparently, my decision to fight this fight had had a ripple effect up through the chain-of-command in a short period of time. The top leaders of Task Force Phoenix knew me by name. And unless you've been recommended for an award of valor, you usually don't want those top leaders to know you by name.

After my boss at brigade finished lambasting me and ended the phone call, I rubbed my eyes with my fingers, reflecting on my motivation for committing to die on this hill. "Speak up for those who cannot speak for themselves,"[39] I reminded myself. "Speak up for those who cannot speak for themselves."

I've burnt the bridge and there's no turning back at this point; I'll be meeting with BG Jonah in the near future. You can be sure that if I survive the encounter, you'll be hearing about it.

◊

In other news that doesn't have to do with the downward spiral of my military career, I know you're wondering when I'll be coming home. Well, let me relay to you what the military has relayed to me. Last month, we were told that our entire brigade would be home before August 29th. Last week, we were told that we would be transferring to Helmand or Kandahar on June 10th, but we would leave the country altogether in late July. Today, we were told that we'll transfer to western Afghanistan (Herat Province) on June 14th, and that we would leave the country altogether on September 9th. And within the last hour, that latest timeframe, too, has probably become obsolete. So, to answer the quandary as clearly as I can with the information I've been provided: I will be transferring to an undisclosed place in Afghanistan at an undisclosed time, and will leave the country altogether in the undisclosed future.

That being said, I know at least that I'll be leaving Afghanistan earlier than September 29th, as God told me in December. Believe me on that one.

◊

Recently, my friends, the Terps, were able to procure Bibles translated into the Dari language. They were excited to hold a Bible in their hands that was in their native tongue, yet they seemed troubled about them.

"What's wrong?" I asked them.

---

[39] Proverbs 31:8

"Khatar, Danger, dear brofer," Rambo Three explained, "we like reading this Beeble here in Gardez, but we want to take these home, too. We want to read it at home and share with family and friends."

"So, can't you throw them in your bag and take them there?"

"Danger, you don't understand. To get home, we pass five... no, six checkpoints where ANA soldiers search our stuff. If Beebles are finded on us, we'll be in the trouble."

"Okay, okay, I'm following now. What kind of trouble? What happens if you get caught with a Bible?"

"If we're lucky? Well, *Inshallah,*[40] we get throwed in jail."

"Oh, no. What if you're not lucky?"

They just shook their heads. That was answer enough.

"Alright, so let's brainstorm this."

" 'Brand-storm?' Danger, what's 'brand-storm?' "

"No, 'brainstorm.' Let's brainstorm this, let's think it out together."

We thought through our options, all of which seemed to result in a more-than-likely chance that they'd get caught. At times, I wanted to just throw my hands up and say, "It's not worth it." But if my friends were speeding towards a collapsed bridge, would I just throw my hands up and say, "It's not worth it"? These Muslims wanted to learn about Jesus at their leisure, and I was going to help them.

"I got an idea!" I announced.

"You 'have' an idea, Danger," corrected Rambo Three.

---

[40] **Inshallah**: Muslim expression of hope that is derivative of the Arabic "Insha'Allah," literally meaning "God-willing."

I smiled. "If you were to take one Bible at a time, do you think you could hide it easier?"

"Well, yes, Danger. With one Beeble, we could put it in a small compartment, or hide the Beeble in our laundry. And if we get catched with just one Beeble, we can remind the soldier that the Beeble is one of our holy books."

"And they wouldn't throw you in jail?" I asked with a raised eyebrow.

"And they wouldn't throw us in jail." The Terps now shared my smile. "Danger! We did it! We discovers our solution! Just take them one at per time!"

The little room ensued with jovial Dari banter, and though I couldn't understand most of what they were saying, I heard them yell out "Danger" while they began clapping their hands. Rambo Three put his hand on my shoulder, looking over at the heap of nearly 100 Bibles in their hut.

"But Danger, just one thing, my dear brofer and best friend. If we get catched, and they don't believe our story, what can we do? If we're in the trouble, how can we to tell you? How can we get your help?"

I soberly shook my head. "My friends, you *can't* get my help. I won't always be here. If you're going to smuggle these Bibles into your homes, you need to be willing to take the responsibility of whatever happens. If I can help, I will help you. But I won't always be able to."

"What do we do, Danger? I'm scared."

"Pray. You just need to pray. Tell Jesus you want to learn more about Him, and then just have faith that our plan will work."

They nodded, accepting that learning more about Jesus outweighed the risk of incarceration and death.

"Alright, sweet Danger. But there's one more question for you."

The Terp looked around to make sure the wrong person wasn't listening in, then asked his burning question.

"Danger... what do you *do* to become a Christian?"

◊

Pray for them, Joanna. Pray that they're protected as they seek Truth, and that they may find it.

Thanks Joanna. God bless you. I'll be seeing you *soon*!

Oh, and happy muddah's day!

Love,

SGT Geist today, maybe SPC Geist tomorrow

Bandee's boot gets attacked by a persistent puppy during his mission in the Middle of Nowhere, April 2009

.:14:.

Understanding the Rules of Engagement

20 May 2009

It was a warm afternoon in Buffalo Grove, Illinois, and Joanna carefully opened the presents that were on her lap. All eyes were on her - after all, it was *her* birthday party. And though her special soldier couldn't be present on this day, many other loved ones were, including Joanna's family, my family, Joanna's best friend Corrine who flew in from Arizona for the party, and my best friend Matt. In fact, it was Matt who orchestrated the gathering: months ago, he suggested that the group should throw Joanna a birthday party this year to cheer her up, to let her know that even though I wasn't with her, she wasn't forgotten.

Joanna finished opening the last present and got ready to thank everyone for the gifts, but not before Matt offered her a card, explaining that I had sent it to him to give to Joanna at her birthday party. Intrigued, Joanna read it.

> Joanna, I know I already gave you presents for your birthday, but I didn't want to leave you empty-handed at your party... which is why you need to report directly to the secret hiding spot. Love, the Boy Toy.

Joanna knew exactly what hiding spot the card was referring to. There was a small closet on the top floor in her house, just across from the guest bedroom, where I had hid countless presents before. So, Joanna marched herself upstairs to find a DVD waiting for her in the closet. It had explicit instructions to be immediately viewed, so Joanna popped it in for everyone to see.

It was a short video, the setting being that of the FOB Lightning chapel. Just a few seconds in, a uniformed man sporting a nametape that read "GEIST" hastened through the chapel door and halted in front of the camera, holding a sign up:

You have a surprise waiting for you in the spot we first met. Go get it before someone walks off with it! Bring everyone along.

Within minutes, an unplanned convoy was headed to Joyce Kilmer Elementary School. As cars stalled in the parking lot, confused thoughts were shared aloud.

"Why couldn't he have just told one person to fetch the surprise?"

"Isn't today a school day?"

"Why would he have told us to go to a playground?"

"Joanna, are you *sure* this is where you first met?"

All these questions were answered as the entourage followed Joanna to the playground, where she saw and immediately recognized what the surprise was: on one of the slides sat the bright silhouette of a soldier.

In disbelief, Joanna scrambled towards the silhouette, her legs wobbling with raw anxiety. The soldier slid down the slide, just as he had done with Joanna so many years ago on that same playground when they were children. At the base of the slide emerged this soldier, there to give a hug to a very weepy Joanna.

Joanna didn't utter a word and simply dug her fingers into the soldier's side and cried her tears on the soldier's shoulder. The soldier ran his fingers through her brazen hair and whispered in her ear, "I love you."

Everyone else remained frozen in shock. Suddenly, SGT Danger Geist was no longer in the middle of a war; instead, I was in the flesh and blood right before them. It seemed a fantasy, just a fairy tale too good to be true.

My mom bawled on my shoulders, and my dad squeezed me as tightly as he had on the night he left me at the armory. Nobody said a word, afraid to cheapen the experience with anything other than tides of joy.

After everyone processed that they weren't dreaming, I broke the silence.

"You're probably all wondering why I called you here today."

Laughter erupted on the playground (from a group of adults, for once, rather than an army of children).

"So, I have 15 days of leave," I continued. "I have to go back on June 3rd."

The "I have to go back" part was ignored, everyone instead focusing on the "I have leave" part. Before the deployment began, every soldier was told that nobody would be granted leave, yet for reasons that are above my pay grade, every soldier not only got a 4-day pass over Thanksgiving, but also were granted 15 days of mid-tour leave if they wanted it. So, "I have to go back on June 3rd" sounded more like I had said "I have to go back sometime next millennia."

Slowly, things began to make sense for those still seeking clarification.

"Come on," my mom swooned, "let's go back."

"Well," I stopped her persuasion, "I had also thought originally that this would be a good time to propose…"

Gasps flew, so I quickly quashed where their imagination was going.

"…*but*, there were a couple things that I had to take into account. One of them was that I had promised Joanna that, when I proposed, it would be in person. So, *that* was met. But the second thing I always promised her was that I would ask her dad first before I did such a thing."

Joanna's dad perked up when he heard that last assertion. At that moment, when I announced the stipulations for such a proposal, he knew something that the others didn't: I already *did* get his blessing during my 4-day Thanksgiving pass. And so, it came as no surprise to him when I looked into Joanna's eyes, got on one knee before her, and pulled a diamond ring out of my pocket and uttered the most vulnerable words in the human language.

"Will you marry me?"

Ogling the shining ring that was custom-crafted by an Afghan jeweler, Joanna's jaw dropped and, as if I had just posed the most barefaced question she's ever been asked, she answered me.

"Uh, *yeah*!"

I slipped the engagement ring onto the finger of my fiancée, and after picking myself up and gazing into her sea-breeze eyes, I pulled her in for a lasting hug as she frantically sobbed on my shoulder.

As if this excitement wasn't enough, the Kilmer school principal and teachers emerged from the recess doors to congratulate us on such a joyous event. But, they weren't just *any* school principal or teachers, they were *our* school principal and teachers from when we attended Kilmer. There was Kim the principal, Mrs. Snelson the 1st grade teacher, and even Mr. Ryan the gym teacher, looking just as fit as ever (though his hair indicated he had grown wiser). They had guided us so many years ago, and now were back to see us through on such a joyous occasion.

And so, in the sight of our loving family and loyal friends, in the sight of our first teachers and beloved principal, and, most importantly, in the sight of God, Joanna and I became a couple that was now engaged to be married in the near future to live a life of love and cheer.

I squeezed Joanna as if this would be the last time we'd ever see each other again. But in fact, this was only the beginning of a life in which we would see each other forever more.

Only, unlike every moment up to this point where I saw her as my girlfriend, I would soon be seeing Joanna as my wife, just as God planned all along.

.:12:.

Please return to your seats, the intermission has concluded.

22 June 2009

Welcome to Act II of this deployment. The characters have already been introduced, a few plot twists were thrown into the mix, and we're inching towards the curtain call. If you find yourself getting antsy already, don't worry, because I promise the Second Act will be remarkably shorter than the first. And that tune you hear? That not an overture; that's a crescendo building to the finale. And hear you me, the finale might just blow your mind, so please don't get in your car to leave.

For now, please settle back into your seat and silence your cell phone because the curtains are rising.

◊

I returned from mid-tour leave feeling refreshed, yet already looking forward to the moment I get back on the plane to Chicago. I left to go to war leaving my life behind, yet was so blessed to be thrust back into it for 15 days. I love that I got to spend so much time with you, eat meals again with my family, sit in an American theater once again, drive my car without worrying about the threat of IEDs, and know that any loud noises weren't intended to harm me. For the first time since long before the deployment, I didn't have to be in a life-or-death mindset. And words can't describe how it felt to physically hold you close to me, rather than shutting my eyes and trying to remember what that feels like.

Now that I'm back in Afghanistan, I intend on finishing my professional and personal missions here, and then I will return and make you, my fiancée, into my wife as we begin the rest of our life.

I digress. For the moment, I'm in Kabul, Afghanistan, where the air quality is more dangerous than the combat in the area. An ominous cloud of smoke looms over the capital, a result of excessive tire-burning throughout the city; the sky is the shade of dead man's lips, and just as wrinkled. At FOB Lightning, I always knew to try to stay indoors when it drizzled, as Gardez is conducive to acid rain. Yet when it rains in Kabul, I sprint to shelter as if the clouds are vomiting little specks of cancer on me. Call that drastic, but considering you can smell the carbon in the smog over a mile away from Kabul, I would rather be melodramatic at 22 than bed-ridden at 65.

When I left to go on leave nearly a month ago, I was told that I wouldn't be returning to Gardez. In fact, when I left, I had to vacate my room and ship all my stuff to Kabul, where I would report to after getting back from leave. And so, I left Gardez after saying goodbye to all of my Afghan friends, hoping and praying for the best for them.

Fast forward a month, and that's where Bandee and me are today. I'm back from leave and have reported to Camp Phoenix in Kabul. I was told that I needed to stick around for a few weeks here while some logistics are figured out, specifically where I'll be transferred to next, whether it be Kandahar, Helmand, or Herat. In the meantime, I've been helping the chapel staff with their daily business, from conducting memorial ceremonies to assisting the religious services. I detest staying at Camp Phoenix because the brass seem to forget we're in the middle of a war; many of the officers here are more concerned with whether or not I shaved today than when the last time was that I cleaned my weapons.

For instance, just the other day, Bandee was helping out another soldier by pulling his tower guard shift (a simple task where a soldier just sits at the top of a tower and scans for potential enemy activity and returns fire in the event of enemy attack). But when the SOG[41] checked in on him, Bandee wasn't wearing his helmet. The next morning, Bandee was summoned by the First Sergeant (1SG); she grilled him about his decision to not wear his Kevlar. Bandee explained that, having pulled tower security in other

---

[41] **SOG**, or **Sergeant of the Guard**: In this use, the term refers to a soldier who has been put in charge with overseeing the soldiers in guard towers during their shifts. The SOG is responsible for such duties as ensuring the tower guards have enough water and aren't disobeying any general orders. While a Sergeant or above generally fills this role, junior enlisted sometimes take on this role at the discretion of the command.

locations where a helmet isn't required, he didn't realize Camp Phoenix had a different protocol.

You figure Bandee would've been given a slap on the wrist or, if the First Sergeant was in a particularly sour mood, maybe some extra duties at worst. Well, that's not how things run at Camp Phoenix. Instead, SGT Bandee was ordered to wear his helmet wherever he went the rest of the day, roaming around the camp like he was some dimwitted Private still in basic training.

But, just because we're stuck in a place as juvenile as Camp Phoenix doesn't mean he hasn't been able to seek out his fair share of new antics to partake in. And so, the adventures of Bandee continue in Kabul:

> Since I've arrived, I've been able to go on missions of a different breed. They're considered Personnel Security Detail (PSD) missions, which is where we transport the bigwigs that are crucial to Task Force Phoenix. We all pack into up-armored sports-utility vehicles and floor it through the streets of Kabul while escorting the precious cargo. Though the missions aren't as intense as previous assignments, they offer a unique adrenaline.
>
> In these missions, our car would be side-by-side with the vehicle carrying our dignitary, and whenever there was a potential threat of an Afghan car approaching our entourage, our SUV would speed up and cut off any access point to our important personnel. Our whole mission is basically to take the hit if a VBIED approached our dignitary's car to blow it up. In order to accomplish this, we often took up two lanes of traffic, weaving back and forth between the streets in an attempt to ward off any overly zealous Afghan drivers from reaching our bigshot's car. For those that seemed to miss the memo, one of our passengers would flash a green laser into their car, which signifies to the Afghans that they need to back off. The laser has the power to temporarily blind humans, and in some rare

circumstances, can cause permanent blindness. When the green light didn't convey the message, our driver would hit the accelerator and nearly ram into the car of the pushy Afghan.

Certainly this annoys the Afghan people, but they can't understand how important this job is. At one point, I was instructed to roll down my window and point my 9mm pistol at the driver of an aggressive vehicle.

I drew my pistol and got ready to roll down the bullet-proof window, but by the time I did so, the driver backed off. The rest of the ride, I held the pistol in my hand with the tip of its barrel resting on the window's automatic controls, ready to open it and point it towards any impatient Afghans at a moment's notice.

It didn't excite me to have to do something like this. I could just imagine the situation: the car behind us was being driven by an Afghan who was late for work, and because money is so scarce in this country, this Afghan was doing everything he could to open his shop before he lost too much business. But every time he'd try speeding up, our car would swerve and almost force him off the road. Getting agitated, the Afghan would keep trying to get past us, but instead would be met with me waving a pistol at his face in an effort to convey that he needs to seriously reevaluate his efforts.

But, when you consider the ramifications of failing to protect a bigwig, no chances can be taken.

One early morning the following week, a group of 15 soldiers gathered at the Camp Phoenix flagpoles to get ready to drive out to the Ghar.

The Ghar is a mountain in Kabul that's as famous to Camp Phoenix as Kilimanjaro is to Africa. While every mountain in Afghanistan can technically be referred to as a Ghar, when you ask a Camp Phoenix soldier about *the* Ghar, there's only one that comes to mind.

Just as privileged people are usually the ones who can afford to climb Kilimanjaro, only soldiers invited by top officers get to ascend the Ghar. Though no functional purpose to it, high-ranking officers regularly climb it as a pastime.

On this particular morning, Bandee had been pulling more tower guard duty and was headed back to his hut to catch some shut-eye; he could sleep in as long as he wanted because he was given the entire day off.

On his way back, he passed the group of 15 soldiers gathering to drive out to the mountain and stopped for a moment to watch them leave. While standing there, the Task Force Phoenix Commander, BG Jonah, approached Bandee, who snapped to attention and saluted the General. BG Jonah had recognized Bandee from his participation protecting him in PSD missions.

"You wanna go on this mission?" BG Jonah returned Bandee's salute.

"Sir, yes I do, sir. Do you have room for me?" Bandee replied.

"We'll make room. Come on. You don't need anything but the clothes you're wearing."

Bandee packed himself in one of the SUVs and was off to the Ghar:

> We drove to the mountain in the same manner that we did on any other PSD mission, and this time, I was the green laser operator. I ended up having to lase the car behind us a few times, but was really more focused on the recreational mission ahead.
>
> When we arrived to the Ghar's base at 5:00 in the morning, I tilted my head to look for the summit, but there was no telling where it was from the bottom. The mountain itself is over 1,500 vertical feet high and clocks in at over 7,400 feet above sea level at its tallest point.

Despite the fact that I had been up since 11:00pm pulling tower guard duty, I thought this would be a simple climb. After all, we weren't required (or allowed) to wear any body armor like we had to on the mountain in Pirkothi. This task was too simple… or so I thought.

It seemed like a straightforward climb: just keep hiking upward. Truth be told, that's all it demanded at first. However, the higher you got, the steeper it became (as with any mountain). But about halfway up, the hike turned more into a full-blown rock climbing adventure: it was no longer about finding the proper footing, but about finding ledges and cracks in the rocks that would allow you to pull yourself up just a bit higher. And every time you reached what you would think was the "top," you'd find that you were fooled.

By 6:30 in the morning, I had negotiated the entire mountain and reached its peak. I was the first of the group on top of the mountain, and in a moment of solitude, I breathed in the mountain air and felt a closeness to *El Shaddhai*.[42] I looked down at Kabul and watched as the others arrived. I thought I had overcome the worst of the adventure; that is, climbing upward. I figured the descent would be much easier. I was dead wrong.

Just as I was the first one on top of the mountain, I began leading the way down after the rest of our party reached its summit.

But as I continued down, I began to realize that I wasn't finding a path anywhere. In fact, the entire terrain I was trekking over was unfamiliar and didn't look like it had much been traveled. There was no dirt or grass on this part

---

[42] **El Shaddhai**: Name used throughout the Old Testament to refer to God as the Almighty One; literally "God of the Mountain."

of the mountain, just jagged rocks that slid down the mountain whenever my feet would touch them.

I continued slipping and sliding down the mountain, unaware of the fact that there was nobody around me anymore. In fact, it was only when I looked down the mountain and couldn't spot our vehicles that I realized I was alone. Not just "alone" in the sense that nobody was immediately around me; I was "alone" in the sense that there was nobody else in sight or earshot. It was just silent. I was completely on my own.

It finally dawned on me: I had gone down the wrong side of the mountain... the side that would be used as target practice for the shooting ranges in just over an hour. I wondered to myself, if it took an hour-and-a-half to climb up the mountain on a well-established trail, how long would it take to descend on a path that wasn't meant to be traveled over?

Unlike Gardez, Kabul has a potent heat; I looked up and saw the sun spitting its rays at me. I knew I needed to hurry or else the miserable heat would stick me a lot closer to *El Shaddhai* than I had in mind.

I continued to dip down, regretting the path (or lack thereof) that I had chosen; whereas the dirt trail on the other side of the mountain offered some shade, I was right smack under the sun's wrath.

My head started pounding; I'd become dehydrated. I had already drunk a water bottle on the way up, and my second (and final) one had but a few pints left, albeit warm and unsatisfying.

My legs began trembling; the lack of water and rugged terrain was kicking my butt, and my sleep deprivation was starting to take its toll, too. But I kept inching forward, shuddering at the thought of being found unconscious on the side of a rock hours later.

I pulled out the last of my water, desperate for just a little swig. As the balmy water slid down my throat, I called upon *El Shaddhai* to give me the strength to get to the bottom. My face was beat red and hot to the touch; I was on the verge of heat stroke.

I took a few more steps, then collapsed to catch my breath. I hugged a rock like I was a child clutching a teddy bear, my heart pounding as if to escape from my chest. I had slipped into a less-than-lucid state of mind and deeply lamented going down the wrong side. I yearned to just lie down and allow myself to slip into unconsciousness, but I realized that every moment I wasted resting was one more moment under the scorching sun, which was only becoming more blistering with each passing minute.

I looked at my watch; there were about 30 minutes before soldiers would be shooting bullets in my direction unless I got to the right side of the mountain. I stumbled to my feet, refusing to relax again until I was at the base of the mountain. Of all the things I've been through in this war, I wasn't about to let some inanimate mountain be my demise.

I cleared my mind of all the things working against me and hurried towards the other side of the Ghar, getting back within sight of our parked vehicles. I could tell that there weren't many people at the Ghar's base… I wasn't going to be the first one down the mountain, but I certainly wasn't going to be the last.

My legs were screaming out for a break, but my body was screaming out for the water that was at the base of the mountain. Feeling like a drained runner who vastly underestimated his preparedness for a marathon, I continued stumbling forward against the will of my feet and reached the base of the mountain. I grabbed a water bottle and went into one of the SUVs, which had air conditioning running already.

As I anticipated, I wasn't the first one down the mountain, but I certainly wasn't the last.

While SGT Bandee once again found himself rubbing elbows with top officers like BG Jonah, the less-daring SGT Geist once again found himself ruffling feathers with top officers like BG Jonah. After all, there hasn't been any closure to the animal rights fight.

I found a silver lining in being temporarily stationed at Camp Phoenix: I was on the same base as BG Jonah, the next step in the chain-of-command after COL Staar. After cutting through some red tape and defying the desires of CH Stanford and several of the other top leaders, I finally was granted an opportunity to sit down with BG Jonah.

I sat outside the Brigadier General's office, waiting to walk the plank that could destroy any semblance of a military career I had left. As I sat there going over what I would say, I was met with a familiar face, that of Major (MAJ) Bane, an officer who had been one of the bigger proponents of my animal rights crusade back when we were still in Gardez. Back at FOB Lightning, there had been a small group of soldiers, some of them higher-ranked officers, who banded with me to challenge the dog policy. We committed to raise a stink about our outrage together, but when we were told we'd get in trouble for pursuing a resolution, everyone else dispersed and I was left to fight the issue alone.

MAJ Bane had recently gotten transferred to Kabul, and so when he saw a friend from Gardez patiently sitting in a seat in front of him, it took him aback.

"SGT Geist, what are you doing here?"

"Hey, sir. I'm meeting with the General in a few minutes."

His eyes widened.

"For *what*?"

"For the dogs, sir."

His mouth opened and he breathed heavily, "*Dude*... I thought that issue died a long time ago. You're... *wow*, SGT Geist. I hope you know what you're doing. You're barking up the wrong tree, pal."

I wasn't surprised he didn't want to stick his neck out on the line for this issue anymore. After all, he was a Major, and had a lot more to lose than a lowly Sergeant if this crusade went terribly wrong – or, in a sense, if this crusade went terribly right. But that's not to say I didn't feel my heart fall to my stomach while he admonished me.

Yet, feeling like I'm being looked down upon isn't abnormal these days; I've become the "loony animal rights" guy. Whenever someone mentions an animal while I'm around, all eyes turn to me to see if I approve of what's being said. When I get food in the DFAC, I feel like people check to see if I'm eating meat or not. This is a position that I never imagined being in. I'm just a normal guy, but in the eyes of those around me, I'm the animal rights extremist. "Don't dare make a joke about animals, or SGT Geist might call PETA on you!" But I suppose this comes with the territory, and I've accepted that role.

Which is why, a few moments after talking to MAJ Bane, I was sitting before the General in his office.

BG Jonah was a confident leader and looked as gentle as a grandpa – as long as that grandpa was a Nazi-knocking, Viet-Cong-killing, Talib-torturing machine. He's the kind of person you imagine would automatically make you wiser just by listening to his stories, as if you could actually absorb his experiences as they poured off his tongue.

I kept in mind that the man I was dealing with had at least five times the authority that COL Staar had. Except, unlike COL Staar, the General's influence would follow me back to Illinois.

BG Jonah shot a quick smile at me.

"SGT Geist, do you want some water?"

"No thanks, sir," I confidently replied. His offer was the equivalent courtesy as a boxer's handshake before a bout.

Then the bell rang.

"So, SGT Geist, you're upset because you can't have pets on your FOB?"

"No, sir. Actually, I can swallow the 'no dogs' policy. I don't necessarily agree with it, but I'm not here for that."

I cleared my throat.

"Go on, sergeant."

"What I *am* here to talk about is the method that has been used to remove the dogs, sir. Nowhere in the policy does it state that killing animals is a justified way of removing the dogs, especially when you consider that the dogs had been domesticated by the soldiers on the FOB itself. My problem is that the rule is never strictly enforced until someone reminds the command that it's a rule, in which case, it's too late to simply keep the dogs off of the FOB, and as a result, the dogs are executed. I believe that unless the proper procedures were initially undertaken to ensure that stray dogs didn't wander onto a FOB in the first place, the choice to kill them should not even be a legal option, unless the dogs contract rabies or become threatening."

Up until this point, we'd be dancing around the boxing ring, keeping our distance from each other as we sparred just to figure out our opponent's approach before we *really* went at it. To my surprise, BG Jonah didn't start with a flurry of power punches; instead, he went for the gentle grapple, something usually reserved for the end of the match after we both exhausted our best strategies.

"Sergeant, I think the problem may be that we just disagree on that point. This method has been utilized in combat zones for years. It's not pretty, but it's accepted, and it's legal."

"Sir, not to be contrary, but it's not legal. Article 134 of the Manual for Court-Martials prohibits animal cruelty, including 'any wild animal located on any public lands in the United States, its territories, or possessions.' "

I had just thrown the first punch: a right hook to the rib cage. But BG Jonah was no fool; he had undoubtedly prepared for every angle I might come at him from, just as I had prepared for his attacks. The only difference was he literally had a dossier on the topic in front of him, though not once during our tussle did he need to look through it.

"Killing dogs to prevent the spread of disease doesn't constitute animal cruelty, SGT Geist. Soldiers have to be a higher priority than stray animals. Do you want to know what's really important in this war?"

He held up the picture of a soldier who had just been killed in an IED blast.

"*This* is what's important. Not stray animals. Soldiers outside the wire are the higher priority."

He blocked my hook.

"I agree, sir. Soldiers are absolutely a higher priority. But I also believe this issue is worth attention, too. Soldier issues are brought to your attention every day; no one is willing to speak about this dog and cat issue, though. And, at the same time, I believe this *is* a soldier issue as well. I believe our methods have the potential to create more terrorists."

"How do you figure that?"

"Sir, our mission here is to 'win the hearts and minds of the Afghan people.' We didn't make any friends by killing these animals: they weren't American dogs; we killed Afghan dogs."

"I hear what you're saying, and please understand that I respect your decision to take up this fight. But the problem, SGT Geist, is there's no other solution to our problem."

"Sir, there is a solution. It's just easier to shoot the dogs and be done with it."

I kept eyeing the water; I wish I had accepted his offer several minutes ago.

"So what's your solution?" I had his full interest now.

"Sir, here's the solution. The military can fund two separate non-profit animal rescue shelters, one that is housed in Afghanistan and one in Iraq. I've met with the coordinator of the one in Afghanistan, and she says she'd be willing to partner with the military. Members of her staff are willing to travel to almost any FOB to save dogs or cats if they're about to be killed. The problem is that this group is underfunded and don't have the facilities to house more than a hundred animals at a time."

I got my first jab in, but he didn't flinch.

"SGT Geist, it's hard to negotiate a partnership plan when there's a *ban* on adopting or caring for stray animals in combat zones."

"Sir, I understand there's theoretically a ban, but its stipulations are vague and not enforced. One soldier on our base was about to send his pet, Security, to the United States just days before she was killed; this is not a unique situation. The fact that there's a slew of organizations allowed onto bases to get soldiers' adopted pets sent to the U.S. leaves the ban open to interpretation, at best. But all this is a moot point anyway: these rescue shelters aren't under the Central Command's provisions, anyway. Nobody would be breaking any rules."

He thought about the loophole for a minute, then backed off his strategy of simply citing policy.

"I see your point, SGT Geist. By the way, are you sure you don't want water?"

Rope break.

"Actually, yes, please." He poured me a glass of water and handed it to me.

"So sergeant, what about dogs and cats that don't want to be caught? I know it's not easy to get ahold of those animals, especially the feisty ones."

"Sir, I have step-by-step instructions right here on how to trap animals in temporary holding devices," I said as I handed him a piece of paper with detailed instructions on how to catch the wildest of dogs and cats. "These live trapping methods have already been implemented on military bases in America since 1996."

It was a punch to the chin, but I again didn't seem to have any effect on him. BG Jonah put on his glasses and examined my notes, his lips in accordance with the words on the page he faintly read aloud. Keeping my focus on his eyes, I sipped from my glass, so thankful that my corner man was water instead of tea.

BG Jonah let out a soft "Hmm," and then looked up at me again.

"The problem with your solution, as detailed and well-thought out as it is, is that the military doesn't have that kind of money to fund rescue shelters. If we start funding rescue shelters, what's next? Will we fund children with cancer? A worthy cause, to be sure, but not one that the military can throw its money at."

An easy jab to counter.

"Sir, currently, the military spends funding on soldiers whose sole job it is to travel around and euthanize dogs on FOBs. So when I hear the arguments that the military doesn't have the resources, or that the military doesn't have the manpower, I can't accept those as justifiable excuses. The military can spend just half of what it spends right now to kill dogs by implementing my plan and funding these rescue organizations."

BG Jonah scratched his temple as he thought about what I was saying, maybe to soothe where I had just landed an uppercut.

"Sir, not only is this plan economically beneficial, but soldiers won't have to kill their own dogs, thus increasing troop morale. The dogs that are picked up by the rescue shelter will either be adopted by soldiers who have befriended them, or they'll be sent to America's Veteran's Affairs (VA) hospitals where they can be used for therapeutic purposes for soldiers suffering from post-traumatic stress disorder (PTSD). The military claims it's concerned with helping soldiers with PTSD. Well, here's an opportunity for them to prove that they're concerned for soldiers who've been affected by events that transpired in a combat zone. Best of all, the military has to do almost nothing to help: they simply fund these non-profit shelters, and then the shelters will receive a call whenever a FOB has a problem."

BG Jonah nodded, probably understanding that I wasn't some glass jaw who was going to go down without a fight.

"You have a good course of action, SGT Geist, but you have to understand, I can't implement this plan countrywide. I only have control over Task Force Phoenix. So I need to hear from you, what can I do for you? What can I do for you that would make you pleased with our conversation?"

All along, this is the angle I wanted him to come at me from. It was time for the final blow; all or nothing, baby! With all my might, I blasted a haymaker right into his breadbasket.

"Sir, I want to meet with your boss, Major General Garnett."

BG Jonah took a deep, winded breath.

"I *can't* stop you from meeting with MG Garnett. He has an open door policy, like me." (Translated: "Go ahead and meet with him about this trivial issue. I'll tell CH Stanford to start planning your memorial ceremony while I'm at it.")

I shrugged off BG Jonah's hesitation.

"Sir, you have been most earnest in hearing my plea. I appreciate your time."

I shook hands with him, stepped outside his office, and breathed a sigh of relief. Though I left with a black eye and the match was technically a no-decision, it felt like a victory. I hadn't come for a knockout against the bruiser; I came to throw a few punches and prove I could hold my own, pushing my way closer to earning a bout with the heavyweight champion.

Two down, three to go. Next up was MG Garnett.

Over the following days, I didn't make any leeway in achieving a meeting with MG Garnett. As I contemplated my next course of action, I was approached by Command Sergeant Major (CSM) Grath, the highest-ranking enlisted soldier of Task Force Phoenix.

Though other soldiers of his military stature chastised me for taking up this fight, I was especially worried how my campaign to save feral animals had been perceived by CSM Grath because he's from the 33rd Brigade and therefore I would see him again after we returned to Illinois. Not to mention, he's an intimidating man: not only could he crush my military career with the amount of rank he has, but he also looks like he has the strength to effortlessly crush my manhood with a single kick to the groin. His face is always in a scowl, soundlessly affirming, "Yeah, and I'd do it, too."

But when CSM Grath approached me, he didn't meet me with a glare and a kick to the beanie-baby, but with a smile and a handshake.

"I like what you're doing, SGT Geist. Central Command shouldn't be killing dogs as a means to enforce General Order One; I've never agreed with that. I personally wish dogs were allowed on FOBs, but that's not my call. Anyway, know that because of your efforts, there will be no more orders to round up and kill any dogs under Task Force Phoenix. Congratulations."

Fireworks of excitement were bursting within me, but I tried not to let it show.

"Sergeant Major, thank you. I appreciate your encouragement."

"It's no problem. Have you had a rough go of it so far?"

"You could say that, Sergeant Major. I've found that the same people who urge you to stand up for what you believe in tell you to stand down when they don't like what it is you're standing for."

"That's to be expected, unfortunately. Is there anything I can do to help you?"

"Actually, Sergeant Major, there is. I've been trying to get a meeting with MG Garnett, but I've been given the run-around."

"What about CSM Foreman? Would that do? You know he's MG Garnett's right-hand man. If you talk to him, your chance at getting a meeting with

MG Garnett will be a lot more likely. Can I set up a meeting for you with CSM Foreman?"

"Sergeant Major, that'd be tremendous."

"Outstanding. I'll let you know what I find out."

CSM Grath kept true to his promise. In just a couple days, I'm scheduled to travel a few miles down the road from Camp Phoenix to meet CSM Foreman at his office.

◊

While it's fortunate I'm in Kabul, it doesn't change the fact that I've really begun to miss my "home" FOB in Gardez. And, more than anything about the east, I miss my Muslim friends. I still recall my last night that I spent in Gardez.

On that last night in the east, my Afghan friends threw a party for me in their hut as a final goodbye. It was exciting yet solemn, and telling my interpreters goodbye was difficult. Afraid that I'd leave with some unspoken tension towards them, each of the Terps hugged me and begged for forgiveness for any wrong they *might* have committed against me while we were together. But, not to completely put a damper on the party, there was also plenty of joking and dancing and celebration with my friends. Though, I did notice that one of the interpreters wasn't present, and as this would be my last opportunity to see him, I was a bit saddened and inquired of his whereabouts.

The response I got was one that I won't soon forget.

"Danger, he went home to see his family," Rambo Three lowered his voice amidst the celebration. "But, when he left, he didn't just take one or two Beebles. He taked a whole box of them! Danger, he didn't follow the plan. He taked a whole box and tried to get past all the checkpoints without getting catched."

"Oh, no... why'd he do that? Why didn't he just follow the plan?"

"He wanted to take them all at once; he just wanted to get them home. He trusted God would keep him safe."

"Tell me what happened to him, guys. Is he okay?"

"Well, Danger... he tried traveling home and making it past all the checkpoints."

"Come on! Tell me, is he okay?"

"Danger, he didn't get catched at any of the checkpoints."

"So... he's not in trouble?"

"Yes, he's fine! He made it home. He taked most of the Beebles, and what he didn't take, we taked home later."

"What? All the Bibles made it into your homes?" I looked around and realized that I didn't see any Bibles hanging around anymore.

"Yes Danger! It's done!"

Imagine that. A group of Muslims put their lives in jeopardy for a chance to know Jesus.

We began celebrating the great success, high-fiving and hugging each other, whilst Rambo Three cried out, "Danger, we thought it was Mission: Impossible, but it's actually Mission: Possible!"

I left their hut that night in Gardez feeling quite encouraged; I felt I had a made such a positive impact. During my time with them, not a single Muslim fell to their knees and proclaimed Jesus as their Savior, renouncing their Islam faith. But my intentions weren't ever to force a conversion; I merely wanted them to understand my viewpoint as I learned theirs. By smuggling the Dari Bibles into their homes, they had more-than-proved that they respected my viewpoint enough to at least explore it.

I couldn't have asked for a better "goodbye" from them.

So, it would seem that God has been protecting my interpreters in their quest to understand Jesus. But, what has God done in the realm of me coming home early? Well, I'll put it this way: I don't know how God is going to work it, but He'll work it. As of right now, I'm being told the same thing I have all along: don't expect to go home early because it's not going to happen. In fact, the other day, I sat down for lunch with a fellow chaplain assistant who began our lunchtime conversation by saying, "Well, we only have about 100 days left at this point." But I shook my head and said, "It'll be sooner than that." He responded with a slight laugh, "Well, my sources say that we're leaving in mid-September, and it's a pretty good source… he's the guy that's arranging all the transportation for our movement back home." I looked at my fellow soldier and responded with a smirk, "Yeah, but… I got a pretty good Source myself."

And as for you, Joanna, as far-fetched as it may seem, don't doubt it: I'll be coming home early. There will undeniably be a war come this September, but I won't be a part of it. God is moving, even when we can't see it.

◊

Joanna, please pray for those affected by the many deaths this month. Across the seas from you, tragedy is abound. In fact, we've lost eight soldiers under Task Force Phoenix this month, not to mention a slew of injuries. And with the troop surge that's supposedly on the horizon, these statistics won't start getting better any time soon. So, please keep requesting protection over all servicepersons abroad, but don't forget about the families of those who have already fallen.

You know, I hear that "freedom isn't free." It makes me wonder, what makes a cliché a cliché? Just a month ago, I was freely driving on the paved roads in America with my windows down, feeling a warm breeze glide across my face. But I couldn't help but wonder: how did I get this feeling? I mean, what made it possible for me to feel so free? Did I earn it? Absolutely not. The roads I drive on in America are paved with the ancient corpses of my ancestors, and the streetlights guiding me home are fueled by their blood. I didn't earn these roads of freedom. They did. I'm simply taking advantage of what the heroes of the past earned but will never get to use. And, that's when it dawns on me, the trite but inescapable truth that I'm always so eager to overlook: freedom isn't free.

Being in Afghanistan, the phrase doesn't seem as much a cliché anymore. I'm not saying that it's not one, I'm just saying you shouldn't bother telling me that it is. I already understand that it is. But after firsthand seeing and feeling the sacrifices that mold that single sentence into an overused cliché, I can't help but value it, even if it's cheesy. Ask anybody who has felt the shockwave of war if the phrase is merely a cheap cliché. Ask the family of 1LT Southworth, my friend who fell this past February. Or ask the widow of SSG Josh Melton; she's the wife of a soldier from my unit in Marion, Illinois who was killed last Friday. Or ask any soldier from my infantry unit in Marion who had to process the news that we lost yet another one of our own. Or ask me, the chaplain assistant who had to break the news to soldiers who hadn't yet heard. I'll never forget the conversation I had with one of the Marion-based soldiers who had been unaware of any casualties. Knowing he wouldn't appreciate any sugarcoating, I approached his bunk and broke the news.

"It's Melton. He's dead."

The soldier stared at me, trying to process what I just said.

"Wait, what? Melton's dead?"

"SSG Melton was killed today."

"Melton died? Like, it's confirmed? He's gone?"

"Yes, Melton died today."

"So... Melton's dead?"

He didn't want to believe what I was saying.

"Yes, Melton is dead," I repeated a fourth time. The soldier was fighting his tears. I searched for the appropriate words to comfort him, but what could I say? I was struggling to fight back my own tears. Besides, isn't that what's supposed to happen in war? Leaving your home at the appointed time, hoping none of your team is going to die, secretly knowing that some of them will, praying that it won't be you, eventually finding out who it is that doesn't make it, pretending that it doesn't bring you to tears, finally accepting that it's okay to cry, and thereafter carrying on your buddy's legacy: that's the soldier's cycle. It's inescapable, it's tragic, but it's reality.

Welcome to war, boys. Stamp your timesheet on the way out.

Love,

Someone Trying to Make It Out in One Peace

Two soldiers mourn over a picture of SSG Melton during one of several memorial services conducted during the month of June 2009

.:12:.

Fright Fest

October 2009

It had been about a month since my deployment ended and I was back in the States. But when I'd lie down to go to sleep, I found myself frequently revisiting Gardez and Kabul against my wishes. I can't help but feel that these nightmares were fueled by what happened on that hot, August night in Herat, Afghanistan. Not to mention, the stress I felt when my company commander definitively told me that I wouldn't be getting home early had crossed over into most of my dreams as well.

These dreams would cast a funk around me all day. At times, I'd lie down and my body would refuse to sleep, perhaps afraid that it would find itself trapped in Afghanistan again. I wish I was dreaming of Freddy Krueger; at least then I can fight back.

The latest installment of my nightmares involved me trying to find a flight home, but there was none available. I was stuck in some kind of a purgatorial state, endlessly circling the base in hopes that I'd be given a task to keep me busy until a flight came in.

I wandered over to a dazzling palace in the middle of the base; I realized it was the base commander's living quarters when I got a brief glimpse of him as he stood on a balcony overseeing his territory. I zoned in on his face; the colonel had a mug that could scare away cancer. It was scalded, and the burns were caked over with white powder to conceal his hideousness. He had the grandeur and wrinkles of Marlon Brando's Kurtz, with the lunacy and cosmetics of Heath Ledger's Joker. All the colonel's soldiers were identically concealed in white makeup, perhaps to help their commander feel better about himself.

The sinister colonel began descending his crystal stairs, petrifying nearby soldiers and making them scram. I was deeply afraid too, but I was more scared of being a coward, so I continued my planned routine of circling the base, trying to ignore the fact that my blood got colder with every step I took towards him.

Before I could get close to him, though, I was informed by one of his goons that a flight had come in to take me home, and that I was to immediately report to the aircraft on the other side of the base.

I dallied towards the terminal, but looking over my shoulder, I realized I had caught the colonel's attention, and not in a positive light. All his powder-faced cronies were looking at me with resentment, so I picked up the pace, understanding that I was not welcome in the colonel's graces.

I spotted a parked school bus on the side of a road, next to a ravine that had a 20 to 30 foot dropoff. I decided to spend a few minutes in the bus until those menacing eyes stopped gawking my way.

I scampered to the back of the bus and sat down in a seat, not realizing there were two soldiers in white makeup near the front. After exchanging glances with each other, they hustled towards the side of the bus, throwing all their weight against the side to try to tip the bus over.

"Stop!" I cried, looking out the window and peering at the ditch's dropoff below.

The two rammed themselves against the side again, this time tipping the bus past a 45° angle. The bus teetered for a moment, then began to roll over into the ditch.

Eieieieieieiei... ***puuuh!***

All three of us survived the rollover, but after I gathered myself, I found a pair of gun barrels shoved in my face. The henchmen began shooting at me, but I dodged their bullets and forced the guns out of their hands. Pointing their own weapons at them, I pulled the trigger.

CLICK. CLICK.

The guns wouldn't fire, so after tossing the pistols to the side, I crawled out of the back of the bus and escaped into the streets.

Several men were running my way, so I hid myself in a costume shop. I found I wasn't the only one harbored there; another fugitive was throwing on a sequined burka and then tried slipping through the streets, which were now in chaos. It wasn't long before the burka-clad man was knuckled down by a malicious mob.

Two men were inspecting the outside of the costume shop, so I slammed the door open in the face of one and pistol-whipped him until his face was covered in blood. Then, I pointed the gun at him and pulled the trigger.

CLICK.

No bullets were coming from this gun, either.

You can make this work, I told myself. *Take back control of the dream! You're in command, not these apparitions.*

I cocked the gun and tried pulling the trigger again.

TCHUU!

The bullet created a gaping wound in his chest.

Unfortunately for me, the other guy in the shop had set up a high-caliber weapon, but before he could fire, I stepped to the side of the weapon's long muzzle to assure I wouldn't be obliterated by its slug. My enemy now essentially weaponless, I shoved a gun to his head.

TCHUU!

Watching his blood splat to the ground confirmed that I was free to go at this point.

I stumbled away from the shop, realizing I was getting weaker with every step. I palmed my side, which was warm and damp: I had gotten shot and my adrenaline had masked the wound until now.

My initial reaction was that I should call Joanna because this could be the last time I'd get to talk to her, but I wanted to wait until I knew this ordeal was over with. The last thing she needed to hear amidst our conversation was a gunshot that was followed by silence.

I staggered to a nearby house to hide myself from my assailants. Expecting a safe haven, I instead stumbled upon a brood of dead bodies inside and realized I had naïvely walked right into a trap.

I turned around to escape after a group of men appeared in the house, but halted as a man pressed a gun against the left side of my chest. I was surrounded, weak, and out of options. I knew that I was going to die, just like in all the other dreams I'd been having. Some sort of inescapable combat always found me these days; it was like a cruel game that I was cursed to revisit.

I looked at the perpetrator who was about to shoot me, fell to the ground in submission, and hugged his legs as I cried all over him.

I wondered to myself, where was Bandee? Why wasn't he here to be strong for me this time, knowing exactly what to do in this combat situation and reacting appropriately? Where was my hero when I needed him the most?

Then I remembered Bandee was gone. He wasn't alive. Not just in my dream, but in reality. And I knew it well, too. When I'd wake up, he'd still be gone, leaving a coward like me in his place. It was as if when I went back to America, I left Bandee in the combat zone to die. Bandee was so strong in Afghanistan, but I was so weak at home. I didn't have any fight left in me. I was exhausted, powerless against these dreams that returned me to war.

I was done. I wanted to go home. I didn't want to fight anymore. I just wanted to be with Joanna one last time.

As I lay there weeping on the armed assailant's legs, having given up all hope that I'd ever return home, I heard a gunshot.

TCHUU!

And then another.

TCHUU!

And another.

TCHUU!

Loud bullets were being shot sequentially.

TCHUU! TCHUU! TCHUE! TCHEE! CHEE! HEE! REE! REE!

When I looked back up, the man was gone. Everyone was gone. Afghanistan was gone. I was looking at a bare ceiling in my room. But the blaring sound wasn't gone yet.

REE! REE! REE! REE! REE! REE! REE! REE! REE!

That's when I understood that the rhythmic noises weren't gunshots at all, but my phone's alarm clock. I was in my bed, and it was time to get up.

I grabbed my phone to turn off the alarm and found that I had a text from Joanna waiting for me.

"Hey hun, I'm ready to go whenever you are. Excited to see you! As always."

That's when I remembered I would get to see her later today. I was home now, though Bandee was still gone.

But I didn't need his protection. No one was going to try to kill me today.

◊

Since my return, Joanna would take me on dates to the locales we used to frequent before the deployment. I was trying to find a new normal, and Joanna was doing her part in helping me adjust.

One chilly evening, she took me to a Six Flags amusement park. It was Fright Fest season, my favorite time of year at the park. Unlike the regular season, the park during Fright Fest is transformed into a "scream park," full of employees dressed up as ghouls, while the park itself is decorated to fit a similar theme.

As we drew near the main gate, I could smell cotton candy and funnel cakes, and when thrill-seekers weren't heard screaming, the sound of carnival music filled the air. I'd missed this pastime for so long.

As we strolled through the sparsely-filled parking lot, I thought about how I had to explain what a "roller coaster" was to my Muslim friends. Remembering them put a smile on my face.

kpuuuh!

My smile was wiped away as I shut my eyes and cringed, ducking to avoid shrapnel that might be sent my way. I wasn't sure if the explosion was that of a rocket or a mortar, but I didn't want to wait to find out. When I opened my eyes, I looked around to find a bunker to run to, but there was none. I was in the middle of nowhere with my chaplain, and all that surrounded me was brown, rocky terrain.

I was in Herat, and if I didn't act fast, we weren't going to have a happy ending today. But there was literally nothing to cover us, only dirt.

If another rocket or mortar was heading our direction, there was nothing we could do to prevent it, so I clenched my eyes as I felt the chaplain grasp my hand, squeezing the life out of it.

"Are you okay?"

I opened my eyes and turned towards my chaplain, only to find he wasn't there now. It was Joanna holding my hand.

I looked around and realized the blacktop parking lot was back; Herat wasn't anywhere to be found. I focused ahead and saw a set of propane torches near the main gate.

kpuuuh! kpu-kpuuh!

One of the propane torches was malfunctioning, setting off large explosions that emitted a sound not unlike that of a Taliban-launched RPG. But unlike a Taliban-launched RPG, it lacked the whizzing sound that preceded its loud booms.

It's okay. You've got this, Danger. It's not hostile.

"Yeah," I took a deep breath. "I'm fine. Let's go face the frights."

.:13:.

Still Fighting the Fight – but which one?

16 July 2009

My boots floated across the jagged rocks and, without even knocking, I burst into the hut and announced my presence.

"Natersade! Khatar injast!"

The Terps' eyes widened as they started shouting in words I couldn't understand for the most part.

"Dah-la fee-oh-ee shuri *Khataaaaaaar*! It's *Dangeeeeer*!"

I was ambushed by a gaggle of Afghans, getting picked up and paraded around the hut like I was a Cricket World Cup trophy.

Rambo Three cried out, "Danger, you're a piss off ma hurt," which I knew meant "piece of my heart" for people who have thick Dari accents.

Yes, I'm back in Gardez. During my stay in Kabul, it was decided that I would be one of five soldiers from the 33rd Brigade staying in eastern Afghanistan, while everyone else moved out to Herat in western Afghanistan, or Kandahar or Helmand in southern Afghanistan. As a result, I've been granted more time with my friends. We thought we would never see one another again; instead, it turns out we have some time left together.

But they're not the only ones who were excited to talk to me.

Just before I went on leave, I had packed away an infrared American flag patch that goes on my right shoulder; a required part of the uniform. When I realized I had packed it away, I began asking other soldiers if they happened to have any extras, but none of them did. But there was this older man, a government contractor, who approached me while holding the patch that I needed for my uniform. The man, Mr. Maurie, was in mourning of the loss of Ben, his FOB dog. He had heard about my crusade and that I was trying to get an opportunity to speak with GEN Petraeus about the issue. The old man handed the patch to me, rasping, "Tell General Petraeus we want our dogs back."

Don't think I left the capital without finishing that fight.

◊

I stood outside of CSM Foreman's office in Kabul listening to the Sergeant Major's aide.

"SGT Geist, I'm going to let you go inside in just a second. But listen to me, make sure you render all proper military customs and courtesies while you're in there. Understand? Alright, go ahead."

I stepped into CSM Foreman's office, and upon reaching his desk, snapped to parade rest.

"CSM Foreman, SGT Geist." CSM Foreman was a taller fellow, a lighter-skinned black man with a bit of a belly and sharp brown eyes. He stood up from his desk and, towering over me, offered his hand.

"Relax, kid," he said as I shook his hand. "Have a seat, young sergeant. Where you from?"

"Sergeant Major," I addressed him as I sat down, "I'm from Zion, Illinois, which is a suburb north of Chicago."

"You ever been to Disneyworld?"

I was caught offguard by such an arbitrary question.

"Yes, Sergeant Major. I went once as a child, and then again shortly before this deployment."

"Isn't it an amazing place? I just got back from leave, and that's where I took my family."

"It's a blast, Sergeant Major. I can't wait to take my own kids some day."

"You have kids, SGT Geist?" He leaned in towards me.

"Well, no, Sergeant Major. I recently got engaged, and hope to have kids down the road."

CSM Foreman had a great big smile on his face.

"How about that! Congratulations on your engagement."

All my previous meetings had felt fix-your-tie formal, but CSM Foreman was much more unbutton-that-coat informal, allowing me to breathe much easier.

"Now, SGT Geist, let's talk about what you came here for. What's the issue? It's been a *long* time since any soldier has used my open door policy. I love it."

"Sergeant Major, I'm not sure if you're familiar, but recently there was a feral dog problem on my FOB, FOB Lightning in Gardez." He began nodding. I couldn't tell if he was aware of the situation or if he was just listening. "MG Garnett came through the FOB and told our commander to get rid of the dogs. The dogs were all executed. This happens frequently across..."

"Now," he interrupted me with an inquisitive face, "why'd they kill the dogs?"

I smiled. This was going well.

"Good question, Sergeant Major. That's why I'm here."

"Nobody needs to be killing dogs. That's not ethical."

"Sergeant Major, I'm prepared to offer a solution so the killing of dogs doesn't need to occur."

CSM Foreman chortled, "You're here to offer *a* solution? SGT Geist, there are a *bunch* of solutions to this problem. The only time I would ever say that it's justified to kill a dog on a FOB..."

He became solemn.

"...and I don't even like the thought of this, but if it had to be done, I'd understand it... is if the dog was foaming at the mouth, and there was no doubt it had rabies. But if we're just killing dogs as our first response, then we're being lazy."

This conversation was either going better than I could have ever dreamed, or he was just telling me what I wanted to hear so I'd stop pressing the issue with top leaders. I needed to find out which it was.

"Sergeant Major, I'm excited about the response I'm getting from you. Is there something specific you have in mind that we can try?"

"Now, there's a problem right there, SGT Geist. You asked what we can *try*. Do me a favor: ask me if I'll have dinner with you tomorrow night."

"Alright, then. Sergeant Major, will you have dinner with me tomorrow night?"

"I'll *try*."

I didn't know how to respond, so I just nervously fidgeted.

"SGT Geist, do you think I'll actually show up if I said that I'd *try* to be there?"

"No, Sergeant Major."

"Exactly. When someone says they'll *try*, they're just copping out. There's no commitment involved. So when you ask, 'what can we *try*,' my answer is that we're not going to *try* anything. We're going to *do*. You want to know what I'm going to do?"

"Absolutely, Sergeant Major."

"SSG Fredrich, come in here."

The aide hurried in to the room as CSM Foreman handed him a laminated bookmark, muttering inaudible instructions, then added in a normal volume, "Do you understand, SSG Fredrich? I want this done. Right now."

"Roger, Sergeant Major."

SSG Fredrich hurried out of the room.

"SGT Geist, this is what's going to happen. I'll talk to MG Garnett about sending a directive down to every commander under his authority, prohibiting the killing of animals as an initial solution to the feral dog and cat problem. Within the next 24 hours, I will send an email out to every Command Sergeant Major urging them not to kill dogs, and asking them to reply back with any non-lethal solutions they may have to the problem. I will include you as a recipient, and I want you to reply back with your best solution as well. We'll take the simplest, most effective solution and implement it. Also, I'll send an email to all the Command Sergeants Major at all training sites that are preparing to deploy to Afghanistan under my authority to let them know upfront that killing dogs on FOBs will not be tolerated when they reach Afghanistan."

SSG Fredrich hurried back into the office, handing CSM Foreman a pair of new laminated bookmarks.

"Thanks, Fredrich. SGT Geist, one of these is for you to keep. Read through it."

He handed me one of the bookmarks. It was a checklist of sorts, reading boldly at the top: "CSM Foreman's Newcomers Brief." I read through the checklist, finding a new bullet-point at the bottom: "Humane Removal of Dogs on FOBs."

"SGT Geist, whenever new commanders come into Afghanistan, they have to sit through what's known as a newcomers brief. I address Command Sergeants Major and Generals alike. Now that this is on my checklist of topics to talk about, you can rest assured that I will address this topic directly. Every commander coming into Afghanistan will know they're prohibited from killing dogs and cats on FOBs."

"Thanks, Sergeant Major. Thank you."

"You did the right thing, SGT Geist. Because of you, no dogs will be killed on any of the 288 FOBs across Afghanistan that fall under my command."

It seemed less like a statement and more like I was listening to a renowned poet rattling off prose from his *magnum opus*.

But that only made it harder to say what I had to say next.

"This is great, Sergeant Major. But..."

"But?"

He looked at me with incredulation, surprised that I wasn't satisfied with what he had already promised to do.

"But I don't just seek change on these 288 FOBs. I'm seeking change across the board, for all FOBs under Central Command."

He nodded and cleared his throat; I couldn't tell if I had hit a sore spot with him or if he was considering this next step.

"I understand. But can I give you some advice, young sergeant? You can't go and meet with GEN McChrystal or GEN Petraeus and just offer a solid theory. They'll chew you alive for that. You need to go and meet with them and offer a sound solution that's been *proven* to work. You've changed the policy under CSTC-A, my command. We'll be implementing solutions and see if they work. Let's take this one step at a time; let's see how these new solutions work. If and when they prove to be efficient, then let's meet with GEN McChrystal and GEN Petraeus. Okay?"

To my knowledge, neither of those Generals have an open door policy. Therefore, I didn't have the "right" to meet with them as I did with the commanders I've met with so far. So, what CSM Foreman was saying made a lot of sense. This was the closest thing to a resolution I would get while on this deployment.

"CSM Foreman, I understand. Thanks for your counsel. Let's see how these solutions fare."

◊

Over the course of my final days in Kabul, I collaborated all the ideas that leaders provided and wrote a Standing Operating Procedure (SOP) of how to humanely remove dogs from FOBs. I sent it to CSM Foreman, where it was well-received.

So, as soon as I returned to Gardez, I knew there was one person I had to see before anyone else.

"Mr. Maurie?" I announced as I stood before his desk.

"Hey there," he smiled back at me. "What can this old timer do for ya, son?"

"A couple months ago, you gave this to me." I pointed to the American flag on my right shoulder. "Since we last spoke, I've been doing everything I can to prevent other animals from being subjected to the same fate as your ol' dog, Ben. I've butted heads with the likes of COL Staar, BG Jonah, and even CSM Foreman. Now, the fight's over: no more dogs will be killed on this FOB."

Mr. Maurie concentrated on my eyes as if he was peering into my soul.

"I can't bring your friend back. But know that Ben's death was not in vain, and other animals across the country are now protected for his sacrifice. It was a sacrifice that none of those dogs asked for, but one they ultimately gave."

I ripped the American flag off my shoulder and waved it at him.

"In every meeting that paved the way for this victory, this patch sat on my right shoulder. It's served its purpose, and now I'm returning it to you."

With trembling hands, Mr. Maurie took the patch and studied it, then simply choked out, "Thank you."

◊

As much of a success that I believe my crusade was, spirits are not high in Afghanistan right now. The decision to transfer most of the 33rd Brigade soldiers out of the east has come with great criticism. The soldiers themselves are frustrated that they've been reassigned to a whole new area of Afghanistan when there are but two months left on our tour. Many soldiers arrived in the west only to find that there was no room for them: they had to set up their own tents when they arrived, and there were no missions for many of them.

To make matters worse, some soldiers have even been extended as a result of this transfer, while many of the soldiers from our brigade headquarters in Camp Phoenix have been getting sent home early to attend military career advancement classes. So, perhaps you can understand the frustration from the ground soldiers who have been in the east with me. Here these soldiers are, faithfully serving out their duties in the thick of the war, and their reward is an extension. Meanwhile, for the soldiers that found themselves in the safest spots in all of Afghanistan (i.e., Camp Phoenix), they're getting sent to America to attend courses that will result in a promotion because there's no room or reason to keep them in this country at this point. You see, the Georgia National Guard has already moved into Afghanistan to take over Task Force Phoenix, and there's just not enough room for everyone on Camp Phoenix. In fact, here in Gardez, besides CH Fardpot and SGT Bandee and myself, there are two other chaplains and two other chaplain assistants already here replacing us. Yet, we still aren't scheduled to come home until late September, despite the fact that our mission is complete. I was even told the other day that I, too, should anticipate being extended (a comment that I obviously shrugged off).

If this transfer sounds ridiculous to you, then you and I are on the same page. You know who else would agree? The family of SPC Christopher Talbert, a medic from my home unit in Marion. Talbert was one of the medics who conducted a physical exam on me because of my back problems. And as of last month, his mission was done: he had served his time in Salerno, Afghanistan, but was told that he would be a part of the transfer to head west. SPC Talbert arrived in western Afghanistan, assuming he would be a survivor of the deployment (as western Afghanistan is remarkably safer than eastern Afghanistan, especially when you consider that he had been serving in the hostile Province of Khowst).

But that's not how things played out for him. SPC Talbert was placed on a convoy on July 7th, and his vehicle happened to roll over an anti-tank mine, detonating it. The explosion shot up through the wheel and ripped through Talbert's seat, which was directly above the wheel. Talbert's body received the entire explosion – a catastrophic explosion[43] from a mine that was

---

[43] **catastrophic explosion**: in military use, refers to an explosion in which the victim of the attack was instantaneously killed with no hope of revival. Also referred to as "catastrophic kill."

designed to disable a *tank*. Thanks to Talbert though, the other five soldiers in the vehicle were unharmed because he took the brunt of the explosion. Had Talbert not been sitting where he was, there would've probably been two other dead soldiers and a critically injured gunner; Talbert's tragic death saved the lives of his fellow soldiers.

I wish I could be there for the guys dealing with this loss in Herat, whether I'd have a designated place to sleep or not. Though right now, I, too, am sharing the experience of living in a tent in the middle of a warzone. FOB Lightning is so overcrowded that many soldiers do not have a hard roof over their heads, and because I was believed to never be coming back here, my room was occupied by someone else within an hour of my departure to go on leave.

I don't mind living in a tent all that much, even if I have to share it with up to 15 soldiers. After all, I lived in a tent for over two months while in Fort Bragg. But, that's not to say it's convenient. Bugs constantly slither over me as I sleep, and the nights can get rather chilly. Yet, I realize things could definitely be worse – at least I have *some kind* of shelter. Though the tent is where I lay my head down at night, that's really all it's good for. It's not a comfortable place to hang out, and it would be rather unfortunate if a rocket landed on such a soft "roof," so I spend much of my free time now in the Terps' hut, where I now secure much of my personal gear because someone already sifted through my belongings in the tent and took my wallet while I was out on a mission.

I don't tell you this so you feel bad for me. Like I already said, I don't mind living in a tent so much. If you want to feel sorry for someone, pity those soldiers who were in Afghanistan back when the first bit of the war was launched, those soldiers who had to sleep where they spit, couldn't charge any electronics, and had no bunkers for refuge. Compared to those guys, I'm in a five-star hotel.

The reason I'm in Gardez at all is because CH Fardpot felt I would be better used here than in western Afghanistan, though I disagree with that disposition. Since I've been re-assigned to Gardez, I've only had two job responsibilities: 1) escort CH Fardpot to meetings with the mullahs and then do my best not to fall asleep during the sessions, and 2) send reports up the chain to notify COL Staar's staff whenever one of our teams leaves the wire to visit troops. I'm doing work that could be accomplished by a child not yet old enough to attend junior high, not the kind of work you'd expect to see from a seasoned NCO.[44]

Bandee is enduring his share of frustrations, too. Bandee thrives by going out and traveling the east, but now that's stopped for him, too. Because there are two new chaplain assistants here, Bandee is no longer allowed to go out and travel like he loves because he's told that his mission is complete, and he shouldn't be taking any chances at this point. When Bandee found out that one of the chaplain teams was going on a convoy over the KG Pass, he begged them to let him tag along, but his request was rejected. He feels like he's become that kid that nobody wants on their kickball team.

I can understand Bandee's sadness: it's bad enough for a guy like him to be denied participation in missions, but it makes it ten times worse to be denied participation in missions and instead have to sit on his butt all day, twiddling his thumbs, waiting to be told when he can go home. Bandee's got an itch for adrenaline that only adventure can scratch, but now the only battle he's going to face the rest of this tour is getting up each morning. And right now, that battle has been the hardest combat he's faced yet.

I feel exactly the same. Getting up in the morning, knowing that the only thing I have to look forward to is lying back down and counting one more day off the calendar, is a mini-war itself.

That being said, Bandee did get one more mission before he was told he wouldn't be traveling anymore, so soak this up while you can:

---

[44] **NCO,** or **noncommissioned officer**: an enlisted soldier who has proven himself or herself worthy of authority; unlike Commissioned Officers (COs) who have a commissioning ceremony and an elongated training period, NCOs are entrusted with authority by way of rank. In the U.S. Army, any enlisted soldier with the rank of Corporal (E-4) through Sergeant Major (E-9) is considered an NCO, while Privates (E-1) through Specialists (E-4) are considered junior enlisted.

The chaplain and I went off to revisit the soldiers in Jaji, a place I hadn't seen since April. Our arrival seemed to be perfect timing: just two days before we landed, a soldier from the small COP had been killed in an ambush on a convoy. And though that's quite a regrettable episode, when all things are considered, there were some blessings mixed in with the tragedy. You see, the ambush wasn't just your ordinary ambush where a few Taliban get together and attack a convoy; no, this ambush was massive! Dozens of RPGs were launched, at least 11 Taliban were involved, and the soldiers' Cougar was getting hammered; even its bullet-proof windows were shattered. To make things worse, the unit had run out of ammo during the firefight. The soldiers in the attack braced themselves in their vehicles, expecting death to befall each one of them. At one point, the Platoon Leader started laughing out loud, which was his natural reaction when he finally accepted that, despite all his years of training, he was about to die and there was nothing he could do about it.

Not too long after, though, air support came in and saved the troops from certain death or capture. Two Taliban were killed and nine were detained. The American forces lost one soldier, and a few others were injured.

As for the nine detainees, they were all released the following day because it was deemed that there wasn't enough evidence that they had been involved in the ambush... despite the soldier witnesses and the detainees' hands being covered in gun powder. And where were those detainees released? Right where they came from... just outside the wire of this COP in Jaji.

In the midst of my slumber one night in Jaji, I was abruptly woken up to the shouting of soldiers running outside the hut I was staying in. I hadn't heard an explosion or alarm, so I shrugged it off and rolled over to get more comfortable in my sleeping bag. But, I didn't get any shuteye: instead, an officer casually walked into the hut to announce that the

> COP had been hit by indirect fire (specifically a rocket), accompanied by some small arms fire.
>
> I jumped out of bed and threw my body armor on over my skivvies, grabbed my rifle, and went outside to see how I could help. The QRF were already in their fighting positions. So much of me doubted that we had actually been under attack because I hadn't heard or felt anything that remotely resembled a rocket attack, nor did I hear gunshots. Within minutes, it was announced that the situation had been dealt with and that we could all go to bed.
>
> The next morning, a mostly-intact rocket was found within our COP; it was obvious that it had been shot from the small village in Jaji where the detainees were dumped back into. But, the reason I didn't hear an explosion was because there was none: the rocket was a dud. The previous night, I had gone to sleep quite annoyed, grumbling to myself that if the Taliban were going to attack us, the least they could do is improve their aim and shoot their rockets over by my hut so I could confirm we were really under attack. Little did I know that, it wasn't their aim that failed, it was their weaponry.

Bandee seemed to have brought his sour luck back with him. On the same night he returned to Gardez, CH Fardpot and I were talking in the chapel when our late-night conversation was interrupted.

KPUUUH!

I opened the door to investigate the explosion, and instead saw a bright light making its way towards the ground that was just a few hundred meters away.

I instantly recognized it as an illumination round, which is simply a mortar round that lights up the sky as if it were daytime while it gradually drops back to the earth, fastened with a parachute that allows it more hang-time. While illumination rounds aren't destructive like high-explosive mortar rounds, their act is often followed by an appearance from their faster-moving, more-lethal, higher-octane mortar cousins after the illumination round has exposed the enemy.

CH Fardpot and I took a moment to glance at each other, sharing the same thought that maybe the mortars were coming from our own range at the hands of coalition soldiers doing night-firing practice.

KPUUUH! KPUUUH! Ku-KPUUUH!

No longer interested in reflecting on what kind of mortars were coming our way or from whom they were being shot by, the chaplain and I began sprinting to safety. I had just come from the shower a few minutes prior, and so I was wearing flip-flops, which made it difficult to run in the darkness. But it didn't take long for us to realize that we were the only ones reacting to the situation. No alarm; no soldiers running to bunkers. It turned out that our initial suspicions were correct: the ones firing the mortars were our own soldiers.

I breathed a sigh of relief that the explosions weren't directed towards us, yet was disappointed that my one moment of bodyguarding had been a fraudulent experience.

Not much later, I was zonked out in my humble little tent, but my midnight siesta didn't last long. An hour into my sleep, the FOB emergency alarms began to blare and intruded my deep coma. I woke up, annoyed with the series of training events that were interrupting my night. I wasn't worried about the seriousness of the situation because I had never been attacked while in Gardez. Not to mention, I hadn't even heard an explosion.

I threw on my body armor with the fervor of a drunk zombie, and I affirmed to the other tent occupants that we were just undergoing another training simulation.

"Nobody else heard an explosion, right?"

They looked at me, shocked at what I just asked, meanwhile rushing to get their armor on. They scoffed, "This isn't a drill! How did you not hear that explosion?"

My undead carcass resurged with vitality as my eyes widened and I quadrupled my pace, not wanting to be around the tent the next time a rocket claimed its dominion.

I double-timed to the bunker where I knew my chaplain would probably be. I couldn't see anything because my eyes hadn't adjusted to the black of night.

"CH Fardpot?" I called out. "Is CH Fardpot in here?"

Like a child hesitant to respond because he's afraid his mom is gonna lick her hand and wipe his hair in front of all his friends, CH Fardpot softly answered.

"Yes."

So, I joined my irked chaplain and everyone else in the bunker.

After a couple hours passed, an announcement was disseminated that we were clear to go back to bed and get whatever sleep we could. And so, just as if a bunch of kids had been called in from recess, we emerged from the bunkers half-awake, dragging our feet to wherever we each laid down our heads.

Later, we found out that while we had been sitting in relative safety, just a few miles down the road closer to inner-city Gardez, another base was being actively engaged with multiple rockets. FOB Lightning had been christened with one single rocket that exploded near my tent, yet I somehow slept through it.

◊

Joanna, I have a prayer request that may come off as selfish. Today, I'm not going to ask that you pray for our protection. I don't ask that you pray for the success of our mission. I don't even ask for your prayers for the future of Afghanistan. Because, in all honesty, I'm too exhausted to even pray those prayers myself at this point, and I'm not going to ask you to pray for something that I'm not committed to praying about with you. What I ask you to pray is the same prayer I've been shouting to God for the past weeks:

that we are given deliverance from this country. Right now, most of the 33rd Brigade soldiers no longer have a real mission: sure, there may be busywork that's being done, but for all intents and purposes, our mission is complete. Our tour is done. And instead of being able to celebrate that reality back at home, we're still here for reasons that are beyond my comprehension.

I'm not relenting on my promise to you that I'll be departed by September. After all, I only make such a bold promise because I have a bold God who promised it to me, first. And though I still believe I'm going home early, even despite the rumors (and for some soldiers, realities) of extensions, I would appreciate your help in getting me home early, too. I don't ask for your prayers because I'm afraid it won't happen, I ask for your prayers because I want you to be invested in me coming home early, too. Pray this prayer with me, and you'll not only be joining me in this prayer, but you'll be joining several brothers and sisters who are praying this prayer. We've done our time, our mission is complete, and now it's time to go home. The Georgia National Guard has things under control. We're just in their way at this point – and Georgia's made it clear that they agree.

So, that's my request to you: please pray that God softens and changes the leaders' hearts so that they may understand the unnecessary strain they're putting upon soldiers and their families. With our prayers to God, these hearts can be changed. Remember, "the king's heart is in the hand of the Lord; He directs it like a watercourse wherever He pleases."[45] That verse is more important than ever for us.

Together, you and I can be amazed by this small leap of faith. And while God will hear my prayers alone, how much more will He hear ours together.

I miss you,

Your Future Husband (whom apparently can sleep through a rocket blast)

---

[45] Proverbs 21:1

.:13:.

The Promotion

January 2010

It felt strange wearing my uniform again. After chopping off my locks and shaving my bushy beard, I found myself back in Marion, Illinois, reporting for weekend duty.

I stood outside the armory, staring at the American flag flapping on its pole. There was a lot to get done before sunset, but for a moment, 50 glimmering sun-stained stars paralyzed me.

"Hey, chap ass!"

Breaking my paralysis, I turned around to see the face of MAJ Metheny, an officer I had long-respected but hadn't seen since the deployment began. He was an awfully candid character, always on the move as if the unit's every task depended on his ability to get his work done. Yet, he was somehow also willing to shoot the breeze with any soldier who crossed paths with him as if his short stature was indicative of his place on the military totem pole.

"Carries a whole new meaning, don't it, SGT Geist?"

I saluted MAJ Metheny, and he shot a quick salute back at me and then shook my hand.

"Yes, sir. Yes, it does."

We kept our attention on the flag, rather than each other.

"Last time our infantry unit went to Iraq, we lost one soldier. *Just one*," MAJ Metheny emphasized. "But that one loss hurt like a bitch. Having lost six this time around…"

He didn't finish his sentence, just shaking his head.

"Say, SGT Geist, where were you stationed in the sandbox?"

"Sir, I spent most of the tour in Gardez, on the east side. I spent a month or so in Kabul, and then just short of a month in Herat."

"Ah, *Herat.*" MAJ Metheny laughed, now turning to me. "What an armpit of a place."

"You spent some time there, sir?"

"Me? No, not me. I spent my whole tour fobbited up in Kabul. Pretty glad I didn't have to waste any time in Herat. You said you were there near the end of the tour?"

"Yes, sir, that's correct."

"So, were you there the night that..."

"Yes, sir. I was there. You heard about that?"

"*Ha!* Everyone heard about that blitzkrieg. What a thing to have witnessed, huh, SGT Geist?"

"Yes, sir, it sure was something."

"That all happened *right* at the end of the tour, right? It was August or something, wasn't it?"

"August 18th, sir. It was a Tuesday morning. The first one hit a few minutes after midnight."

"Good thing you made it out safely. You know, I was just talking to CPT Zollar about that situation. You know Zoll, right?"

"Roger, sir. I'm quite familiar with CPT Zollar."

"Ol' Zoll, he's survived so many deployments, I think his balding head would be thick with hair if it weren't for the stress he's been through. On this deployment, Zollar was the commander of the... uh, what's that called? I can't believe I already forgot that damn acronym."

"...SECFOR, sir. The Security Forces."

"SECFOR, that's the one. He told me about that night."

"Oh, yeah?" A smile cracked on the corner of my lip. "What did he say about it?"

"He was telling me how, on that night, right after the first explosion, he and SSG Sidney were getting ready to go check out the Northern Expansion of Camp Stone. Just before they stepped into the north side, though, they heard a bloodcurdling scream; some soldier was calling for a medic because one of the foreign forces had gotten hit by shrapnel. So, Zollar and Sidney went over to take care of the foreigner, and *right after that happened,* a mortar rocked the Northern Expansion."

I nodded my head, listening to the story.

"If that soldier hadn't hollered for a medic," MAJ Metheny concluded, "then Zollar and Sidney would've been wiped out. We'd have eight fallen soldiers, not six. Zollar's sure of it. It's just one of those things, you know."

"God wasn't done with their lives yet," I appealed.

"Maybe. Maybe they just got lucky. Ah, but shit, sergeant. I can't think of the name."

"Name?"

"The soldier that flagged them over; the one who saved their lives. What was that fucker's name?" he thought aloud. "What's his name, SGT Geist?"

MAJ Metheny gazed at the flag as if its stripes would give him the answer he sought. If he had instead noticed the ear-to-ear grin that had grown on my face, he would've realized I knew exactly who the soldier was that he was referring to. Rather than just telling him the soldier's name, a piece of me wanted to keep him mulling over it.

"Oh well," he gave up. "More important things to take care of today."

"It was good running into you, sir."

"It was good running into you, too. Oh, SGT Geist, there's something I've been wondering."

"Sure, shoot."

"When you were in Afghanistan, why'd you do what you did?"

I was baffled.

"Why'd I do *what*, sir?"

"Send that letter to your congressman. Why did you go to such great lengths?"

I remembered I had told a select few people that I was planning on writing a letter to my congressman about the dog killings, but after COL Staar encouraged me to go through the chain-of-command instead, I never went that route.

"Sir, quite honestly, I'm not sure what you're referring to."

"*Ah*, it's no big deal, SGT Geist. It's not really my business anyway."

"Sir, please. What are you talking about?"

"I was just disappointed to hear that you wrote a letter to your congressman, begging to get yourself home early."

My jaw dropped; I was more dumbfounded than if an apple had fallen on my noggin in the middle of a desert.

"*What*?! Sir, that never happened; that's a complete bastardization of the truth. When I returned to Kabul in August, I went to the company commander and requested to be manifested for a flight home. On two separate occasions, I pleaded my case to her, and both times my requests were vehemently denied. After that, I stopped fighting the issue altogether. The verdict was in, as far as I was concerned; I didn't fight the issue after that. I wouldn't have ever written a letter to my congressman about such a selfish issue."

MAJ Metheny nodded, no longer willing to look me in the eyes anymore. I wasn't sure if he believed me, but I was more frustrated that someone would slander my name like that.

"MAJ Metheny, who said that happened? Who told you that I had done that?"

"I can't get in the middle of this, SGT Geist. I really would rather not get involved."

He shook my hand again.

"SGT Geist, I'll see you around the armory."

◊

I walked onto the drill floor and, trying to shrug off the indignation from the conversation with MAJ Metheny, took a deep breath in, appreciating the familiar smell of tobacco tar and grimy mop heads. It was bittersweet being at my home unit again. I loved seeing old faces from friends who had been sent off to different parts of Afghanistan than me, but there were a few faces that weren't there. For me, the most notable absence was that of Jared Southworth. The drill floor felt so much less-spirited without his energy lighting up the room.

"Miss you," I muttered under my breath as I looked over to where he would have been standing with his platoon.

"SGT Geist?"

I turned around to see "Doc," our unit's longest-tenured medic. He was a short man nearing his 50s, and everyone in the unit appreciated his heart of gold. When he had gone on the deployment, he often articulated how frightened his wife was of something happening to him; she was dependent on him and the strength he brought to his family, and consequently, I always dreaded that something bad would happen to him, knowing how damaging it would be for his family.

Doc had been one of the first Marion soldiers to get home. After all, it was only July when he had been hit by an IED, inflicting serious brain damage.

"Hey-*hey*, Doc! It's good to see you. I've been praying for you."

Doc lit up like a kid given a lollipop.

"Well hey, thanks SGT Geist! Hey, you haven't seen a storage box with my name on it, have you?

"Sorry Doc, I haven't."

"Aw, that's alright. How's the wife?"

"Oh, we're still not married. But she's doing good, thanks. How's the head, Doc?"

"It's getting better. When they released me from that Walter Reed Hospital, it was one of the best days of my life. But now I just have trouble."

"Trouble? With what, Doc?"

Doc's face drooped, now appearing less like an excited little boy and more like an ashamed old man.

"Well, I get these intense mood swings now. And I can't remember things sometimes. I don't notice the memory loss, but my wife does."

"Oh, Doc, I'm really sorry to hear that. We were all worried sick about you when we heard about the blast. I've been wondering about you often since I've been back."

"That's kind of you, SGT Geist. I do appreciate that, sincerely."

"So what are you doing here anyway? Is your Purple Heart ceremony today?"

"Oh, me? Naw, SGT Geist. The Purple Heart is still getting processed. I'm just here to pick up some gear. Which, by the way, you haven't seen a storage box with my name on it, have you?"

"Uh, *no*, no I haven't, Doc. I'm sorry."

"Aw, that's alright. Heads up, SGT Geist, looks like someone's flagging you down."

I turned to see a soldier jogging over to me and snapping to parade rest, folding his arms behind his back.

"Relax man. What can I do for you?"

The soldier dropped his hands.

"There's a phone call for you, sergeant."

"Thanks bud, I'll be right there."

As the soldier hurried away, I turned back to Doc and shook his hand.

"Doc, I really loved seeing you again. And I hope your head gets better; don't get too discouraged about it."

"Thanks, SGT Geist. It was really good running into you."

I started heading towards the office area when Doc called after me.

"Hey, SGT Geist, real quick. Sorry, but I just had a quick question. You haven't seen a storage box with my name on it, have you?"

Sadness consumed me.

"Doc, I'm really sorry. I haven't. With all my heart, I wish I had. I just… I hate not being able to help you, Doc. I wish I could've prevented… your box from getting lost. It breaks my heart."

"Aw, that's alright."

◊

Sitting down in the office chair by the phone, I grabbed my cup of tea and took a gulp. Call it an acquired taste or call it a cruel psychological trick my mind was playing on me, but I now found myself sometimes drinking tea of my own will.

After wetting my throat, I picked up the phone.

"This is SGT Geist, 2-130th Infantry Battalion Chaplain Assistant. How may I help you sir or ma'am?"

"SGT Geist, my name's Sergeant First Class (SFC) Donnelly. I'm up at the 108th Brigade out of Riverside, Illinois."

Oh, man. I couldn't believe it. The 108th Brigade was the unit I had dreamt being a part of. I had been looking for opportunities to be moved into their unit for years.

"SFC Donnelly, what can I do for you?"

"SGT Geist, I hereby offer you a transfer to be our brigade chaplain assistant. This comes with a promotion to the rank of E-6, Staff Sergeant. Congratulations."

I was at a loss for words. Not only was he offering me a transfer to the unit I most wanted to be a part of, but he was offering me a promotion to Staff Sergeant, the rank I had been working my tail off for since the very moment I was promoted to Sergeant back in 2006. Beyond the personal gains, I also knew that I was apt to take on the responsibilities of this job; I was perfectly conditioned for this position.

"SFC Donnelly, thank you, thank you very much. I'm excited to hear this offer," I paused for a moment. "But, I'm afraid I must decline. Thanks for your time."

I began putting the phone down, expecting to hear him say "No problem, have a good one," allowing me to promptly hang up.

"Wait SGT Geist," he blurted out instead. "Why are you declining? I don't understand what's going on."

Taken aback by his concern, I explained my perspective.

"SFC Donnelly, are you aware that I'll be discharged from the Army in April?"

"Yes, I'm aware, but with all the years you've already put in, I can't imagine why you wouldn't want to continue your career and beef up your retirement benefits."

I paused again to think about how to diplomatically express myself.

"SFC Donnelly, when I was 17 years old and was given the enlistment contract, I picked up a pen to sign it. I was a fool; the Army didn't want ink, the Army wanted my blood. And now I have no more blood to give you."

"You regret your enlistment, SGT Geist?"

"Absolutely not, sergeant. Enlisting was one of the best decisions I ever made in my life; I entered the Army as an immature boy and have since become a globally-conscious young man. I've been pushed past what I once believed were my limitations, and now I'm a responsible soldier. But I'm also exhausted; the military has drained all my energy. I'm sick of leaders wrapping a chain around my neck to prevent me from ever using my own discretion and, not to go soft on you, but I want to learn how to care for others again. I don't believe I can learn that here. Uncle Sam told me that if I was willing to go on a deployment for him, then he'd offer me a college education. He got his deployment; I got my education. And now I'm just ready to move on with my life. I'm done with the politics here."

"Politics? You realize that no matter where you go, you'll find politics? You're *always* going to have a boss choking you out. What you're not understanding is that if you decline this position, I'm going to have to give it to a less-qualified soldier. This opportunity is a once-in-a-lifetime thing; soldiers would kill to be in the position you're in. I don't know how else to say it: we don't want anyone else for this job right now. What do I have to do to get you to agree to this promotion?"

"Sergeant, I gave the military several chances to keep me. I asked them to send me to their bodyguard school so I could be better-qualified to train junior chaplain assistants; I was denied. I asked them if they would re-class me to an infantry position; they ignored me. There was a promotion opportunity over a year ago; the brigade offered it to a soldier they were buddy-buddy with that had four years less experience than me as a chaplain assistant. Did you know that I went eight months without getting paid at one point? The only time I don't get ignored by the military is when they want to pressure me into doing something I'm not already contractually bound to. Uncle Sam did everything he could to get me to sign up, but once I did, he tossed me to the ducks like a piece of stale bread. I can't play the game anymore. I'm throwing in the towel."

"Listen, SGT Geist. Will you listen and keep an open mind for me, just for a moment? I'm sorry you're frustrated, but I need you to logically consider this."

He was pulling out all the stops to convince me to accept the promotion. The least I could do is listen to his reasoning, giving him a chance to change my mind. I continued sipping my tea as he discoursed.

"Listen, SGT Geist, you were one of the youngest sergeants in military history when you got promoted. Now I'm offering you a chance to be one of the youngest Staff Sergeants in the Army today. Imagine what your career would look like if you kept on this path. You already have six years under your belt; you could retire by the age of 37! Think about it: you could really make a name for yourself, SGT Geist."

To be fair, he was right. It truly was a prime opportunity, something that I'd never have another chance at again if I declined now. By refusing this promotion, I'd be passing up an opportunity that many soldiers worked for and never achieved, and extinguishing my military career all-the-same. I realized at that moment that the only thing that should compel me to refuse the promotion would be if getting to spend extra time with my family was more of a priority than progressing through the ranks and making a name for myself.

"Thank you, SFC Donnelly," I said. "But I get out of the Army in April, and I'm not looking back."

.:14:.

Go West, Young Man!

1 August 2009

Hello, dolly!

We've arrived in August, and as I've said all along, I'll be home before this month fizzles out, despite the Army still telling me otherwise. Every day, I'm told that it's more and more of a reality that I won't be home early. Amidst such defeating assertions this week, I decided to fast for a short period; for nearly 50 hours, I didn't eat anything in an attempt to appeal to God and display my dependence on Him to the point of denying my body its worldly needs. By the end of the fast, I barely had the strength to stand up, but wanted to make a statement to God about how much I trust Him, even in a war zone.

Most days, I can grit my teeth and just take the discouragement from Big Army, but there have been times when I've been anxious about my prognostication. Because, when I think in logical terms, the reality smacks me in the face: the idea that I will be getting home early is impossible. It just is. How in the world could it happen? It can't. It's impossible.

One day, I was sitting in the chapel's office alone, dealing with these desolate thoughts, when I felt compelled to pick up a Bible, as if I knew there was a specific message from the Lord waiting for me today.

But which Bible? We have many translations here: New King James Version, New Living Translation, New International Version, The Message, to name a few. I pondered for a moment which translation I should grab for today, and an image popped in my head of one of the New Living Translation Bibles we have here, and so I hobbled to the chapel shelves and sought it out.

There I found two New Living Translation Bibles sitting on the shelf; identical versions of the same Bible. The one on the bottom was tucked away in the shelf, while the one on top was sticking out as if it was asking to be taken.

I went to go grab the one on top, but not before something inside of me whispered, "No... not that one... pick the one on the bottom..."

So instead of going for the Bible that was sticking out, I reached and took the one on the bottom.

I didn't know exactly where to be reading, so I kept flipping through pages of the different books in the Bible. I quickly fiddled through Genesis, 2 Samuel, Psalms, Song of Songs, and Isaiah, but still couldn't figure out what I was "supposed" to see today. Somewhat frustrated, I closed the Bible and just clutched it in my hand and said out loud, "God, where do *You* want me to read? What do I need to see today? Where should I be looking?"

That's when I felt prompted to open the cover of the Bible. On the inside cover was a hand-written note, penned by whoever donated the Bible from America to here in Gardez. It read:

> "Dear Soldier, thank you for your sacrifice in keeping our country safe! May God Bless! Matt 19:26, pg. 750"

I thumbed to page 750 and skimmed down to Matthew 19:26.

> "Jesus looked at them intently and said, 'Humanly speaking, it is impossible. But with God everything is possible.' "

Yup. It's true. My early return is absolutely impossible, humanly speaking. So it's a good thing my Commander doesn't play by those rules.

◊

Since I last wrote, Gardez has been quiet for the most part, probably because of the upcoming elections that are later this month; right now, the Taliban are planning their attacks, not executing them. Elections are a dangerous time in any Muslim country, and this country is no different, especially considering last year was Afghanistan's deadliest year on record since the turn of the millennium, and 2009 is on track to even surpass 2008 in that regard. Come August 21st, Afghanistan will make international headlines because of its elections.

There has been one day that was the exception to Gardez's quietness: July 21st. I imagine you may have seen Gardez in the headlines when you woke up that morning because the city was riddled with suicide bombings throughout the entire day. The American forces responded by launching bomber aircrafts in the air, attentively surveying the city below for any kind of terrorist action. By the end of the day, several terrorists had been killed (as well as some of our partners from the Afghan National Army), but there were still about seven suicide bombers at large in our city. You can imagine that it was not a good day to be in Gardez. In fact, by early evening, I was advised that our FOB was the target for a large-scale attack. The threat was so serious that the soldiers on the QRF were all staged and ready to react.

I didn't want to get caught in an attack while being incapacitated like I was a couple of weeks ago, so instead of going to bed, I stayed up in the chapel with my body armor and weapon within an arm's reach, trying to stay vigilant as late as I could. Fortunately, the weather was on our side and was just as attentive, forcing a ceasefire on all potential Taliban activity by threatening a thunderstorm throughout the night. There were constant flashes of lightning outside, and though it was pitch black, it was obvious that the sky was overcast. It began to pour rain around 1:30am as a menacing thunderstorm pulled through the city. I figured that was Mother Nature's way of pledging her vigilance over FOB Lightning, so I retired to my tent as the storm raged throughout Gardez.

Meanwhile, our brother Bandee finally got to go on one final mission he'd been itching for. We found out that while all the 33rd Brigade soldiers may be out of the east, there's still a presence of 333rd Military Police (MP) soldiers, a separate company from Illinois that's been operating out of Salerno. So, Bandee hopped on a bird, flew to the now-familiar Salerno, and immediately was put on a mission with the MPs:

> The mission was straightforward: the MPs were going to patrol around Salerno, stop at a small ANA outpost to drop someone off, swing over to an ANP compound to train the Afghans how to do a military vehicle search, and then head on back to the FOB. We wanted to complete this mission as quickly as possible because it was a Thursday afternoon (which is the equivalent to our Friday nights in America that kick-off the weekend). This meant there would be more Afghans present than usual, and "idle hands are the devil's

playground." Not to mention, Khowst Province is a historically volatile region for coalition forces.

Everything went smoothly for the first ten minutes of the mission.

We were about five minutes away from the ANA outpost when our small convoy found itself on a bridge in Salerno. It was a vulnerable spot in which attacks could come from a barrage of areas: from the rooftops, from the side of our vehicles, or even from under the bridge.

Below the bridge was a ravine that had a 20-to-30 foot dropoff. Initially that plunge may not seem overly treacherous, but when you consider you're in a Cougar that weighs 14 tons, a 20 to 30 foot dropoff would be quite deadly.

Avoiding the dropoff, we turned safely onto a road that was perpendicular to the bridge. Or, at least three of the four wheels were safely on the road. As for the rear passenger wheel... the one that I was seated directly above... it was hanging in mid-air as our Cougar had missed the turn-off.

In less than a moment, a handful of reactions transpired: the Cougar started rolling on its side, and we braced ourselves to roll off the bridge and into the nasty little ditch below. We were taught at Fort Bragg that after a vehicle teeters to a 25° angle, a rollover is possible, and at a 45° angle, a rollover is imminent. Though we couldn't be sure that we would surpass the 45° mark, we grabbed onto whatever we could to minimize the impact that this 14-ton vehicle might have on us. While we knew that we'd probably sustain injuries from such a devastating fall, it wasn't clear if any of us would be killed. As for the gunner, well... his fate was sealed.

We continued to tip sideways as the only sound we heard was that of the Cougar's engine struggling to push forward to negate the fall.

5° angle.

VROO!

10° angle.

VROO!

15°.

VROO!

20°.

VROOO!

25°.

VROOO! VROOoOOoO!

30°.

VROOOOOOOOOoOoOoOoOooOooOooOoooo!

35°.

Just before our freefall to the ravine below, with my teeth interlocked and eyes sewn shut, the Cougar stopped moving altogether. We weren't moving forward, but we weren't rolling down to our possible deaths, either. We remained there motionless, just on the brink of the point of no return; that is, just under the 45° angle mark.

The three of us in the back swiveled our heads around at each other, anxiously remaining steady so as not to cause the Cougar to finish tipping into the ravine.

First, we shared a moment of tense silence, immediately followed by uproarious laughter flooding the Cougar.

The medic cried out, "This *isn't* funny!"

I think we all agreed, yet the laughter continued.

The medic helped himself to a chuckle, and one of the passengers said, "This ain't funny, I thought we were rolling."

I concurred, "Yeah, I thought it was a rollover."

As our nervous laughter continued and our Cougar undetectably teetered, we recognized that we were as stable as we were going to get. We all started unbuckling our harnesses and we busted open the door, crawling out the back of the Cougar and swiftly into the streets of Salerno as if we were a pack of red fire ants whose sanctuary in the sand had been disrupted.

We knew we weren't in a good situation. Here we were in the middle of Khowst Province, starting to get surrounded by droves of Afghan onlookers, and a million-dollar vehicle was inches away from rolling down a steep ravine.

Our vehicle commander announced that he needed a volunteer to pull security on the far street, and within seconds, I was at the edge of said street with a readied weapon, visually sifting through the Afghan crowds for potential threats. There was a large abandoned metal box in close proximity to me: for what purpose it usually had, I don't know, but on this day, it was my sole cover in case we got ambushed.

An ANP officer pulled security with me at the edge of the street, and in an attempt to win over any nearby guerillas that might be in the area, I began a dialogue with the locals using the simple Dari and Pashtu words I've learned. I called out to the children, asking "What's up?" I conversed with the elders, "How are you?" and "I am also fine, thank you."

As I maintained my sector, reinforcements rolled up to our location and began working on pulling the Cougar's wheel back on solid ground. I continued scanning, seeking out hateful eyes amidst the children, adults, and oxen roving around us.

After about an hour of frying under the ill-mannered Khowst sun, I glanced over to our Cougar to see it getting pulled forward. Our Cougar's front bumper was chain-linked to another Cougar's rear bumper, and while flooring the front Cougar's gas pedal, our nearly-tumbled Cougar inched its way forward as well. Eventually, the wheel that had missed the road was now back on. We had successfully recovered our vehicle.

I shook hands with the ANP officer, profusely thanking him for his assistance, "Tashakur, sir. Tashakur, tashakur very much."

I hopped in the back of our vehicle, and within minutes, we were driving off to continue the rest of our mission, which went flawlessly thereafter.

SGT Bandee's MP mission will certainly be his last – at least here in eastern Afghanistan, where we won't be stationed much longer because of news that you may have recently read about back in Illinois.

A few days ago, another Marion-based soldier was killed in Herat. But SPC Gerrick Smith wasn't killed by an IED or a rollover or a rocket. He was killed by a gunshot wound; the bullet was expended from his best friend's weapon (while they were in his own hut, nonetheless). If you think it's unbearable when a soldier is killed by an enemy, imagine how it must feel when you find out it was friendly fire. The details of the situation are sketchy, but an investigation is currently being conducted to figure out how this accident happened.

However it actually went down, I can't help but feel that SPC Smith's death is a microcosmic example of the problem with keeping the 33rd Brigade in Afghanistan. Here's an American soldier who served out his combat tour, yet he still found a way to die. *Did the Taliban hunt him down?* No. *Did a terrorist drop a rocket on his head?* No. *Well, was it at least because of a rollover during a combat mission, a helicopter crash, or even some natural cause?* No, no, and no. Instead, SPC Smith was just the victim of hanging around an unsafe place too long.

The soldiers in Herat are having a difficult time coping with the tragedy, and so the ministry team has been requested to move out of the east and into the west to support the soldiers out there. And so, tomorrow, CH Fardpot, Bandee, and I are scheduled to get on a bird to get to Kabul so we can catch a connecting flight over to the west.

Personally, I'm excited about this transfer because I believe that I can't be any less useful in the west than I am here in the east now; I want to be with my soldiers. And so, for the rest of my tour, I will be in Herat, Afghanistan.

But exactly how long is the rest of my tour? Well, not even the leaders at Camp Phoenix are sure. But any way you look at it, we know that it's soon. Even if it turns out I'm a madman who claims to be able to hear God's voice but is actually insane, I'm coming home fairly soon. And if it turns out that what I believe is right and I get sent home earlier than anticipated, I'm coming home extremely soon. Hence, it's only natural for me to mull over my time spent here in Afghanistan.

As I get ready to leave FOB Lightning, I realize that I have so many meaningful memories in Gardez. There's one memory in particular that I won't soon forget: I was standing on our flightline one afternoon when I was able to see a direct result of the success of my dog crusade; a puppy was running around the helipad, getting petted and playing with soldiers who were laughing at his goofy rambunctiousness. A smirk came over the corner of my lip: this puppy trusted the soldiers, and now I could feel confident that that trust wouldn't be broken anytime soon.

But when I leave this war-torn country altogether, there are really three particular things that I'm going to miss. And it's not that I can't get these things at home, it's that I can't get these things to the same degree.

First of all, I'll miss the night skies here. Think about it: I'm 8,000 feet in the sky in a spot where bright lights are forbidden, so you can imagine what the heavens look like after the sun retires for the day. The moon is terribly beautiful, and when she's absent, then you have the countless stars in the sky. Watching a shooting star fly over your head is not abnormal, and the clarity of the constellations would blow your mind. In America, I look at the stars and force myself to wonder about their creation, but in Afghanistan, I look at the stars, and *they force me* to wonder about their creation.

The second thing that I'm going to miss is the mountains. Going from a flat state like Illinois and traveling to a mountainous region like Gardez was a real culture shock. Thinking about the snow-capped mountains of the winter to the misty mounds of the spring to the bare rocky giants of the summer, I doubt I'll ever see anything like these natural beasts ever again. I didn't expect I would better appreciate beauty by going to war, but that's what happened.

The last and greatest thing I'll miss from Afghanistan is the hospitality, and specifically the hospitable people. I can't stress how well I was treated here by the locals. These Afghans weren't interested in treating me as if I was their brother, they were interested in treating me well *because I am* their brother. There's a huge difference between the two philosophies. If America ever sees poverty like this country has endured for thousands of years, then maybe her people will truly understand what I mean by this.

Until then – our wagons are heading west, and only God knows what's in store for the rest of this journey and when it's going to end. In the meantime, I'll keep serving my time until I'm told my time is up.

As for you, please continue praying for us troops. Many have become exhausted and are more-than-ready to go home, but each day we stay here is one more chance of going home in a cargo box instead of on a plane seat. May God grant us deliverance, but only when the time is right according to His will.

Thank you, and God bless!

Love,

A Guy You'll Be Seeing Extremely Soon

Moments after the near-rollover in downtown Salerno, July 2009

.:14:.

Beyond Repair

March 2010

I thumbed down the list of symptoms printed on the pamphlet, adding up how many I had. The list wasn't all-encompassing, but at least touched on the most common problems.

- Trouble falling asleep and/or staying asleep
- Nightmares and/or night tremors
- Seeks adrenaline
- Numbness / Withdrawal / Lack of emotions
- Emptiness
- Expecting to die young
- Physical fatigue
- Suicidal or violent fantasies
- Loss of faith in others; detachment from family and friends
- Increase in use of alcohol
- Increased irritability
- Outbursts of anger
- Hypervigilance; always being armed with a knife or gun
- Easily startled by loud noises
- Reduced concentration
- Avoidance of things that remind you of the traumatic event

It said that if you had most of these symptoms, you should seek treatment for post-traumatic stress disorder. I counted that I had 15 of the 16 symptoms; the one I lacked was the last symptom listed, and I lacked that one because there was no trauma to avoid. I didn't *have* a specific event that was haunting me. I wondered, is it possible to have PTSD without the "TS" part?

There was a phone number listed at the bottom of the page that said I should call if I found myself suffering from PTSD-like symptoms, a number specifically for military veterans. I knew that I probably should call it; I'd felt so disconnected from the rest of the world since my return. As I contemplated making the call, I glanced at the clock and saw that the electronics store would be closing soon, and I still needed to pick up my camera that they had seized a week ago to fix. My attention turned from my emptiness to my errands.

I hopped in my car and laid my foot down on the pedal so I would fly over hills. I guess this is what the list meant by "seeks adrenaline," though this symptom was the least of my concerns on that pamphlet. Once I arrived, I wasted no time getting to the technical customer service desk.

"Name?" asked the team representative.

"Geist. I was the one with the camera that had the cracked lens."

"Oh right, Geist." He knew me by name because this was the second time I had requested it to be fixed; the first time they sent it in, it was sent back without being repaired because they had somehow missed its defect.

After he handed over my camera, I turned it on and took a picture; the image was skewed so I looked into the lens to find it had a crack.

"Uh, excuse me," I told the representative. "The lens is still cracked."

"Oh, it is?" he asked as he looked at the camera. "Yeah, you're right. Hmm. Well, I guess we'll have to send it back in again."

"What?" My patience melted like butter on a hot Herat day. "This'll be the *third* time I've sent this camera in. I don't want to send it in; I want it to be fixed."

"Well, there's not a whole lot we can do."

My calm demeanor dropped to my ankles, baring an ogre underneath.

"I'll tell you what you can *do*, kid. You can give me a camera that's not defective. I'm sick of not having a functional camera."

"I understand, but this is policy. I can't just give you a camera."

"You agree that it's busted, right? I mean, we're not disagreeing that it has a problem, right?"

"Right, there's a problem with the camera. We're not arguing that."

"But you *are* arguing with me. Can I take home a good camera today or not?"

"I'm sorry, but there's nothing I can do."

"Go get your manager."

The representative left, his manager taking his place a few minutes later.

"Hey there, I'm the manager here," he said. "What can I do for you?"

"You can get me a new camera. I've sent this one in twice now."

"I'm sorry, but technically, we aren't allowed to give you a brand new one until they fail to fix this camera a total of seven times."

"S... *seven* times? So you're telling me I'll have to deal with this BS up to *four* more times?"

"No, because I'm sure they'll get it right this time."

"No they won't," I raised my voice. "I want to leave with a new camera today. I'm talking about *right now*."

"Sir," he calmly replied, "we can't just give you a new product. If we do that, we're essentially buying you a new camera. We eat that cost."

"So why don't you eat that cost, then refurbish this camera and sell it? It's basically brand new. If you're so confident they'll fix it, that should pan out just fine."

"That's not how it works."

"That's how it's going to work *today*," I lightly smacked the counter with my fist. "I'm sick of coming here and dealing with this crap!"

"Sir, I'm trying to help you here, okay? There's no reason to get aggressive over this."

My knuckles were turning white on the counter and my whole body tensed up.

"*Aggressive*? Maybe you're not understanding what I'm saying." My volume was increasing with each word. "I'm telling you that I'm not sending this camera back to some tech guru flapjack who can't even identify a cracked lens."

"Sir, you have to understand…"

I cut him off, "Go get me a new camera, dammit!"

I figured other employees and customers were turning their heads in my direction to see the commotion, but I refused to avert my eyes from my prey, lost in a fantasy of jumping over the counter and choking this man in hopes that it would get my point across. The manager recognized the pure rage in my eyes, perhaps understanding that my anger had little to do with the camera.

"Okay," he whispered, "okay, let's calm down. We're going to go get you a new camera, okay? But you need to know that you're being hostile here. I'm trying to help you; there's no need to be abusive towards me. We'll get you a new camera."

"Thank you," I told him as he left to go to the back room. A minute later, a teenage worker came to the desk holding a brand new camera.

"S… sir… here's your camera." His voice wavered as he fidgeted in place. "But, uh, sir, we'll need your credit card, sir. Not to ch… charge you, of course, sir. It's just to have it on, you know… to have it on record, sir."

"No problem," I said as I handed him the credit card, leaving right after they gave me my new camera.

◊

On the way home, I felt a pathetic mess. What was I becoming? I wasn't like this before my tour. Here I was during what *should* have been the most exciting time of my life, about to separate from the Army, graduate from college, and marry the woman of my dreams. So why was I so broken?

As soon as I got home, I threw the camera in my closet and picked up my list of PTSD symptoms to examine them again. Not allowing myself to think my way out of it, I called the number on the bottom of the page.

RING! RING! RI...

Just as fast as I mindlessly called the number, I hung up.

You don't have to do this. You're stronger than this. What could they do to help anyway? You don't *have PTSD, do you? Before you even left to go to Afghanistan, people that didn't even know you were telling you that you'd come back and be suffering from PTSD. Aren't you just falling victim to a self-fulfilling prophecy?*

It didn't matter either way. I desperately needed help. In a moment of hope that I could be normal again, I hit redial.

RING! RING! RING! RI...

"Suicide hotline. This is Larissa."

"Larissa, hi. Uh, I think I made a mistake. I didn't mean to get a suicide hotline."

"How can I help you?"

"Well, I got this number from a pamphlet that the government sent me. It said that I should call this number if I found myself suffering from PTSD-like symptoms. Is there anything you can do to help?"

"Well, sir, I'm not sure there's anything I can do for you. This is just a suicide hotline. You say that you have PTSD."

"No, I *don't* have PTSD. But I'm experiencing some of its symptoms. That's all."

"Are you in danger of hurting yourself or someone else?"

"No, Larissa. I'm not going to hurt anyone."

"Are you in danger?"

"No."

"Then perhaps I can direct you to get an appointment at the VA Hospital?"

"You can't help me, Larissa?"

"Well, I *want* to help you. We can get you help by setting you up with the VA Hospital."

I had already tried that avenue for my back problems. I went to the VA and told the doctors about all the pain I was having, how I couldn't sleep well because my back and tailbone were in such pain. They took a couple of x-rays and decided that I didn't have a problem, and that if I did, there was no reason to believe it was service-connected.

I reasoned that, if the VA had denied me assistance for an overtly physical problem, how much less likely they were to help me with an intangible issue like having symptoms of PTSD, especially when I couldn't even identify the "TS" part of my problems. It had fatigued me enough just to make this phone call, so there was no way I had enough patience to cut through the VA's red tape.

"Uh. No, Larissa. I know how to set up appointments at the VA already. I've done it before."

She sensed the sadness in my voice.

"Sir, I want to help you."

"It's, uh, fine. It's okay. I'm fine. My mistake, Larissa. I called the wrong number. I'm sorry."

"Sir, are you okay?"

"Yes," I said through my choked voice. "Thank you."

I hung up. Though reinforcing my loss of faith in others, Larissa did help me do one thing that I hadn't been able to do since my return from Afghanistan: I bawled my eyes out, crying real, warm tears.

I was just like my old camera: busted in the way I viewed the world, defective no matter how many people tried repairing me.

.:15:.

The Last Hurrah

21 August 2009

Welcome to the wild, wild west! I'm at Camp Stone in the desert plains of Herat, Afghanistan, where it hasn't rained since April and the heat is the fiercest combat that most soldiers face. If you want to feel how hot it is here, one soldier suggested trying this: start your oven and set it to 400°. While it's warming up, go stick your head in your freezer. When your oven hits 400°, quickly pull out of the freezer and open the oven, then stick your head right outside of it. In Herat, a "cool" day is a 95° day.

But, Herat is by no means the hottest place in Afghanistan. Bandee can testify to this after he went on a mission to Farah, which is south of Herat:

> Farah makes Herat feel like a winter wonderland. While I waited for my flight back to Camp Stone, I sat in the shade for 30 minutes and still found myself getting dizzy; it was *at least* 100° in the shade. I thought it wouldn't get much worse than that. That is, until I had to actually board my ride back.
>
> After our flight came in, all of us boarding lined up in front of the engine's exhaust, the bunch of geniuses we are. We weren't only wearing all our protective gear and backpacking our rucksacks (which adds at least 10°), but we were also in the wide open, getting beat down by the sun's volcanic rays. It was a cruel tag team, the sun and exhaust working together to make us drop. It's hard to say exactly how hot it was, but I can assure you that it was well-above what humans are meant to handle at extended lengths. If you want my best guess, it had to be over 200°; it was like being fully-clothed in a sauna that scorches out flames.
>
> When we finally moved from the dragon's breath and into its belly, I was so dazed I felt like I was a ghost gliding onto

the aircraft, not a human taking steps. I say with confidence, never in my lifetime will I be hotter than I was in Farah.

And come winter, I won't be complaining about the cold.

But, Bandee was grateful to go on a mission down in Farah, especially because he got to experience a combat landing on his flight back to Herat:

The purpose of a combat landing is to land in a manner that would befuddle any attempts to shoot the plane out of the sky.

Our descent began not with a gentle light flashing, advising us to strap our seatbelts, as is done on commercial airlines. Instead, our descent began with our entire aircraft nosediving towards earth as if our wings had been snipped. It felt less like we were in the process of landing and more like we were in the process of crashing.

After a few minutes of careening down, the plane began circling around in the air. If you had the gumption to look outside the window, you'd see that the aircraft was nearly on its side. We continued circling towards the ground in a fashion much similar to that of a bug that was caught in the swirling flush of a toilet. The G-force kept us still in our spots, meanwhile the aircraft was creating a Fibonacci sequence[46] in the sky.

---

[46] **Fibonacci**: a mathematical algorithm often used to enhance architecture and other art. Found in basic nature, yet its complexity and aesthetic beauty so marvelous, the Fibonacci sequence has even been used to argue for intelligent design. In terms of creating the sequence in the sky, an aircraft would appear to plunge in a skewed spiral motion.

I looked across at some of the others on the craft. One pale passenger had been punched in the gut with nausea as he puked into his hand; others just closed their eyes, unwilling to appreciate this moment that made every roller coaster I've ever been on seem dull.

When the wheels finally hit ground, everyone was rattled around because of the potent impact. As we unloaded, most of the passengers looked like they were ready to kiss the ground, à la Pope John Paul II after a flight.

While the west is much hotter than Gardez, it does have one upside for soldiers: it's remarkably safer. When I arrived, I was told that Camp Stone hadn't been attacked in years, and the combat deaths are minimal compared to the other parts of the country. Unlike in the east, many of the roads are paved here, which lessens the likelihood of an IED attack tenfold because there are fewer spots to hide the bombs.

The reason that Herat is so safe is because the Afghans here are more worried about tribal wars than the Global War on Terrorism. We're somewhat near the Iranian border, and so any violence that goes on is usually between an Iranian tribe and an Afghan tribe. In fact, the anti-tank mine that killed medic SPC Talbert last month was an anomaly; it's believed that the mine wasn't even placed by the Taliban, but instead was a hidden remnant from the Russian invasion of the 1980s.

So, while violence does exist here, it has less to do with the war on terror, which is neither condoned nor condemned by most of the natives; rather, it's just a fact of life, and they choose to stay out of it.

That being said, that doesn't mean that the Taliban are absent. They still roam around, but they are considerably undermanned compared to some of the hotspots around the country. If the Taliban attacks in the west, it's usually very calculated because they know they don't have many men to lose.

As safe as Herat is, though, the Afghanistan national elections have upped the ante. Elections in any terrorist-infested country are always an ugly process, usually concluding with a leader being elected at the price of many innocent locals and several coalition troops' lives.

I could tell you about how the elections went around here, but instead, I'll leave it up to the man himself who had a front-row seat to the election's combat operations. After requesting to go out on missions to support the elections, Bandee was charged with the duty of securing an ANP base so operations could go smoothly. For about three days before the actual voting, he was constantly going out on missions to reconnaissance the area he would be securing, as well as patrolling an area where enemy activity had been reported. Without further ado, I once again turn your attention over to Nicholas Bandee:

> As our team left Camp Stone yesterday morning for the recon, we weren't off the base for more than a minute when we found a dead Afghan lying in the middle of the road. Because I was the gunner, I got a good look at him as we passed. He was belly-up, and his arms and legs were spread apart. The peculiar thing was that the death was like a "Disney death," where no indication of blood or gore is present. His face and body were completely intact, yet he was clearly dead. As we inched by, a group of ANP scooped him up off the side of the road and dumped him into their truck. All of us on the security team hoped that this wasn't an omen about the coming days, but we all feared that this was a message from the Taliban about the violence that was going to erupt over the next week.
>
> We drove by a woodline where there have been reports of mysterious bright lights at night, and we scanned the area as best we could without inserting ourselves into unnecessary risk. We kept a distance as we monitored the area, scanning for anything suspicious. We knew that there was enemy activity in the exact area we were looking at,

and one of our primary duties on election day would be to suppress any attacks that might come from here.

As we continued monitoring the woodline under the blistering Herat heat, a bomber aircraft swooped down past the woodlines and dropped a flare into the thicket. After we decided that we couldn't dismount and head into the woodlines without inadvertently walking into a minefield or some other impassable crisis, we continued patrolling our area. We didn't come across anything else worthy of noting, but judging by our short soiree, it was obvious that the elections in a few days were going to be a tense experience. But at the same time, we knew that we had to pull security in this undesirable area, otherwise Taliban could easily take control of the situation in our area of operation. We weren't about to let that happen.

After we returned back to Camp Stone from our day-long patrol, the team offered to let me just lock up my armor, helmet, and ammo in the vehicle so, when we had to go on our next mission, I wouldn't have to lug all that equipment from my tent to the vehicle again. Because we could get called out on an emergency mission during these high-intensity times, I thought it best to keep my gear locked up in the vehicle. After all, Camp Stone hasn't been attacked in years, what were the chances that that streak would be broken tonight? Besides, even if there *was* an attack, I was confident that it wouldn't persist for more than a few minutes at most. After everywhere I've been and all I'd been through, the thought of an actual crisis on Camp Stone was laughable.

After I locked up my gear in the vehicle and returned to my tent, I tried relaxing my mind and body a bit, knowing that the next few days were going to be serious business. By the end of the night, I was more than ready to rack out until my body would wake me up the next morning.

I laid my head down on my pillow and closed my eyes just after the stroke of midnight. I began my nightly ritual of chatting with God about concerns that arose throughout my day when I was interrupted with a familiar (yet unwelcome) sound.

Whiiizzzzzz... ***kpuuuh!***

I gave God a raincheck and ran outside to check for damage. There was smoke and dust in the air covering the stars, and it was obvious that whatever just launched at us had hit within the confines of Camp Stone. I picked up a light jog as I headed towards the chaplain's hut, not stressing about the attack because it had landed nowhere near me.

Had I only known what the next two-and-a-half hours had in store for me.

I ran into a bunker near the chapel, trying to find CH Fardpot. He wasn't there. I sprinted across to another bunker. Again, no luck. I certainly didn't like this hide-and-seek game because my armor, my helmet, and all of my extra ammo were still locked in the truck from earlier that day; wearing just a pair of nylon daisy-duke shorts and a sleeveless t-shirt, I was exceptionally vulnerable.

It was the third bunker that had the surprise of a lifetime waiting for me. I ran inside, and instead of finding CH Fardpot, I found a naked Italian soldier whose head was gushing with blood. He had a crimson trail from the top of his head that dripped down his cheeks, into his goatee, and across his shoulders. In a quivering voice, he softly cried out to me, "Help me. I'm hurt."

I ran from the bunker and as far into the open as I could to ensure someone would hear me yelling at the top of my lungs.

"*MEEEDIIICCCCC!*"

CPT Zollar (the commander of the base's SECFOR team) and SSG Sidney (the supply sergeant) heard my cry and hurried over to the casualty with me. They had been seconds away from investigating the Northern Expansion of Camp Stone for personnel, but instead deemed that the wounded soldier was the higher priority, following me to the bunker.

CPT Zollar began assessing the Italian soldier's wounds; it seemed the injury wasn't critical. The soldier had been in the shower when the rocket exploded, and some shrapnel had broken through the wall and cut his head open.

While CPT Zollar and SSG Sidney tended to the soldier, I continued my search for the chaplain. After searching two more bunkers, I found CH Fardpot and told him there was a wounded soldier who needed care. It had been several minutes now since the initial *whiz* and *boom*, so we agreed that we could probably make it safely to the casualty.

As I escorted CH Fardpot over to the bunker, a distinct launch was heard...

Fa-THOOP!

...followed by a shrill whistle.

WooooooooooooOooOooOoOoOOOOO...

A mortar was heading towards Camp Stone and would explode in a matter of seconds as the chaplain and I were caught in the wide open.

We sprinted towards safety as CPT Zollar screamed for us to get into his bunker. The mortar was flying right above our heads...

...fwap...fwap...fwap...fwap...fwap...

...its wind vibrations slapping my face as I bolted to the bunker. I was less-than-confident that I'd actually make it in time, so in one last attempt to outdash an untimely demise, I sprung into the bunker...

...... ***KPUUUH!***

...the mortar exploding within 100 feet of us, piercing our ears with the sound of death. The chaplain and I made it in, not a millisecond too soon.

We all remained in the bunker, realizing that this attack was far from over. CPT Zollar was told over his radio that the mortar had exploded in the Northern Expansion, which created a sobering moment for him, as that's the destination to which he and SSG Sidney were heading toward when I had called them over.

"Sergeant," CPT Zollar somberly spoke, "thank you. You just saved my life. Had you not called us over to this casualty, we would be in the Northern Expansion right now."

SSG Sidney agreed, "He's right. Really, sergeant. Thank you. You saved us."

Fa-THOOP!

Our sentimental moment was cut short as everyone in the bunker ducked down and prepared for another pestilent round heading towards Camp Stone.

WooooooOooOooOoOoOOO...... ***KPUUUH!***

Feeling the ground shake, we knew that it hit close, but we were all still in one piece.

Then another launch...

Fa-THOOP!

...another trill...

WooooooOooOooOoOoOOO......

...another deep breath...

... ***KPUUUH!***

...another miss and another exhalation of relief.

The next time we heard a launch...

Fa-THOOP!

...it became obvious to us that we were in for a long night. The whistle sounded like it was going to be nearly right on top of us...

Woooooo...

...and I huddled with those nearby me in the bunker. There I was, my left hand holding onto an Afghan interpreter and my right hand holding onto the hairy back of a naked, blood-soaked Italian...

...*OooOooOo*...

...meanwhile a mortar ruled with authority over the nighttime sky, trying to find someone to wallop. Right before pounding the earth, there's usually a quick moment where a mortar will stop whistling and leave you with nothing but your thoughts.

...*OoOOO*...

In that one-to-two second period where all sound seems to cease, I prayed the most beautiful prayer I've ever prayed in my entire life. It consisted of two words, but I only had time to roll it into one.

"Godplease!"

...... ***KPUUUH!***

We flinched at the explosion and looked around, instantly appreciating that we were still intact. But would we be so lucky next time?

We remained in that bunker for what seemed like forever, but eventually we were given the "all clear," indicating that the attack was over.

I emerged from the bunker and surveyed the chapel for damages to our sanctuary.

The chapel wall had a hole in it with debris all over the pews. It had been hit by some pretty fierce shrapnel, but the chapel walls wouldn't be irreparable.

After assessing the chapel, I ran over to the team I had gone out with earlier that day and asked them for the keys to the truck so I could grab my armor, but during the attack, they had lost the keys to the specific truck that had my gear in it. There was nothing they could do about it, and if we were to be attacked again, I'd be on my own without my armor, helmet, or ammo. I just crossed my fingers and hoped that that's all that was in store for us tonight.

I heard people murmuring that one of the Camp Stone storehouses had been blown up from the first explosion, so I sought it out to see for myself how badly it had been destroyed. It wasn't hard to find... about 30 people were crowded around it, taking pictures and videos of it. As soldiers shone their flashlights on the obliterated building, I was stunned that nobody had been killed nor maimed, save for our friendly neighborhood naked Italian-man.

Fa-THOOP!

Dread overcame me as someone yelled "Here it goes again!" Like a street gang's drug deal discovered by the police, everyone scattered to the four winds.

Woo...

I hustled to find a bunker, knowing that if a mortar dropped anywhere near me while I didn't have my armor, then I'd quickly find myself with an undesirable posthumous award. But as I ran…

…ooo…

…I couldn't find any bunkers because it was so dark. I continued barreling forward like a frantic gorilla…

…oOo…

…and when I realized I just passed a bunker, I turned around as fast as I could…

…oOo…

…but slipped to the ground because I lost my footing on the rocks…

…oOo…

…and I got up as quickly as I could, but I knew it was too late. I wouldn't make it into the bunker…

…OoO…

…so I flung my body against a concrete wall…

…OoOOO…

…and curled into the fetal position to brace myself for impact.

…… ***KPUUUH!***

My t-shirt flapped against my skin as the noise of chaos dissipated into silence. I dared to open my eyes, finding that the terrorists had missed me again by a few hundred feet. I sighed a breath of relief and uncurled, then strolled into the bunker while trying to ignore the irritating ringing in my ears. But not even a second after I made it into the bunker…

Fa-THOOP! Woo...

...I found myself needing to take cover. I interlocked my hands over my head (as if that would offer more protection than the bunker was already providing) and tried analyzing how close the mortar was going to land (a most unpleasant chore).

...ooooOooOooOoOoOOO...... ***KPUUUH!***

After I realized that I had again been spared, I raised my head and squinted at the dark faces accompanying me in the bunker. Everyone else were either American contractors or foreign military. A couple of them nodded at me, as if to say, "Welcome to the party."

Fa-THOOP!

Emphatic groans and one person yelling "*incoming!*" concealed the mortar's hiss.

KPUUUH!

I tried encouraging the others by revealing a little-known fact about mortars.

"Well guys, if we can hear the whistle, at least that means we're not on its *exact* impact trajectory."

Fa-THOOP! Woooo...

Despite what I just said, hearing the mortar's whistle wasn't exactly a comfort to any of us. I whispered under my breath, "*incoming*," tired of this hackneyed routine.

...OoOOO...... ***KPUUUH!***

Another two mortars immediately launched in succession.

Fa-THOOFa-THOOP!

*WooooWoOOoOOoOOOOOOO****OOKPUKPUUUHH!***

They were coming without relent and, each time, sounded even closer than the last, like they were going to drop right on us. Yet, each whistle sounded closer than the last, as if the Taliban somehow knew where our bunker was and were closing in on us. It was so frustratingly antagonistic. We couldn't fight back... it was like playing a land-version of the game *Battleship* with that cheating cousin who never gives you a turn to fire back, though nothing about the explosions felt like a "game." Only making it worse, these Talibs had better accuracy than any terrorist I'd encountered before. They were dropping their rounds almost right on us, precision that was unheard of by untrained militants.

To our relief, bomber aircrafts started buzzing about in the air, teaming with helicopters hovering over the desert below. I thought we would be done now that the cavalry had arrived; to my dismay, the reinforcements hung around for only a few minutes, and after deeming the area now a safe zone, whizzed off.

The skies that were clamoring a moment ago were now shrinking in noise; it waned quieter, and quieter, and quieter, and quieter, until I could even hear my slow breathing.

I held my breath, listening for anything other than peace.

But there was nothing but *silence*.

Only total *silence*.

Just *silence*.

Si...len...ce.

Si...len...ce.

Si...

...len...

...ce.

Si...

...len...

...Fa-THOOP!

Like a lightning bolt striking a beach during a sunny and cloudless day, a mortar whistled its way down to Camp Stone.

...oOooOooOoOoOOO...... ***KPUUUH!***

Then another.

Fa-THOOP! Wooo...

Nobody even cared to call out "incoming" anymore; it was pretty obvious to everyone at this point that we had incoming fire, and calling it out certainly wasn't going to affect where that mortar was going to land or our fate that would follow.

...oOoOoOO...... ***KPUUUH!***

We were emotionally fatigued. Where did our air support go? Why was the quick reaction force not lighting them up? How did these terrorists catch us with our pants down?

While waiting for the next launch, I had a revelation: almost every explosion had rocked our immediate area... not one projectile sounded or felt like it landed over 400 feet away from where we hid.

I devised a quick plan.

"Hey," I got everyone's attention in the bunker, "the next time they call the 'all clear,' get to the other side of Camp Stone. They haven't been hit all night."

I felt a little more at-ease after my advice was acknowledged, but I knew the soldiers in all the other nearby bunkers probably hadn't been close enough to know where the mortars were landing. Someone had to tell them. Someone had to warn them. But who would be willing to run along the impact zone to get the word out?

I knew it had to be me. After all, I had spent the entire attack in the same 500-foot radius, and nearly every rocket and mortar landed right on top of me. I knew better than anyone. This was my responsibility.

I crept outside my bunker and scanned the sky for flying objects, carefully listening for a whizz or a whistle. When I saw nothing and heard neither, I zipped to the next bunker with my head down.

"Sergeant?" one soldier exclaimed as I appeared behind him like a ghost. "Where did you come from?"

"Hey guys, listen up real quick," my mouth spoke almost quicker than my brain registered what I needed to say. "I've been on this side of the camp all night, and *every* rocket or mortar has landed in this area. Next time we get the 'all clear,' get over to the other side of Camp Stone."

I heard a few unsettled "okay's" and confused "alright's."

"Hey, are you guys all okay?" I asked as I tried regaining a steady breathing pace.

"Yeah, we're all fine. Thanks sergeant. Are you doing okay? Hey, are you just wearing... *where's your armor*, sergeant? You might as well be naked! If you get hit, you'll..."

I scurried across to the next bunker, feeling the wind go up my shorts as I dashed. After repeating myself there, I made a ducking sprint across the impact zone. I continued zigging and zagging until I had told all five bunkers that had been getting the brunt of the attack. When I found the fifth and final bunker in the area, I leaned against the concrete wall and slid my spine down until I found myself sitting on my butt, and I remained there until the attack was over.

Just after 2:30 in the morning, we were given the "all clear."

I was the first to follow my own advice. I hastened away from where we were getting peppered and into a safer area on the base, which just so happened to be near my tent. I gazed at the sky and marveled at its beauty. It was, in fact, the most beautiful and clear sky I had ever seen in my entire life. Yet, it was also the most frightening sky I'd ever seen. There were shooting stars galore, which on any other occasion, I would've stayed out all night and gawked at. But tonight, that wasn't the case. Each shooting star prompted me to hit the deck as I expected it to be a mortar that was blotting out the sky. Similarly, each passing vehicle outside the base sounded like a whizzing rocket, inciting my heart to skip a beat.

I knew I couldn't spend my entire night being paranoid of all the "what-if's" and "could-be's." I was as safe as I was gonna be, understanding that if a rocket or mortar hit anywhere near my tent, everything inside of it would be annihilated. But, I didn't have much of a choice. I couldn't very well stay awake until the sun rose and then still somehow conduct combat operations efficiently in the morning.

I laid my head down on my pillow and finished my prayer to God that I had started hours earlier. There was a lot to thank Him for. Throughout the entire attack, not a single person was killed, and the only injury was that of a naked Italian whose head was grazed with a piece of shrapnel. In a two-hour period, the entire camp had been sprayed by some of the most accurate Talibs with whom I'd ever crossed paths, and I began to recognize how astronomical the chances were that none of the mortars that got dropped in our backyard pierced my body. The morbid thought gave me a renewed desperation for God and His goodness to me, because without His provision, I could've just been a grease stain on the back corner of Camp Stone tonight.

The following morning, the damage was surveyed in full. It turned out Bandee's approximations were right: there were several new dimples in the vicinity of where he had taken cover, along with a few more just outside the base in that same general area.

That day, all of us at Camp Stone found ourselves on our toes, the lack of sleep paradoxically rejuvenating us with energy. Soldiers clung to their rifles and knew exactly how far away their armor was at any given point. Contingency plans were crafted prior to getting into the showers. Tower guards were extra attentive. Bunkers were mentally noted. And, most beneficial to Bandee, his team found the vehicle key to unlock his gear.

But the election wasn't over; Bandee still had a job to do:

> The day after the attack, our team went out on another recon at the same location we'd gone to before. The route was eerie, as the town that had been so populated just the day before was now a ghost town… never a good sign. Also, along the way, we came across a group of Afghans huddled around a jingle truck[47] at a gas station. When the Afghans saw us, they all panicked and frantically loaded up the truck and fled from the scene, some running, some jumping onto the fleeing truck, and one speeding away on his motorcycle. They were gone before we could even turn their direction in our Cougar.

---

[47] **jingle truck**: a truck customized with colorful decorations. Commonplace in central and southwest Asia, these trucks often have chains and pendants dangling from the bumper that cause a "jingle" sound.

That same night, we all anticipated another attack on Camp Stone. But, no attack was launched on us. The Taliban probably knew that Camp Stone would be on high-alert and well-prepared to counterstrike any offensive they might instigate, and they were right; that night, there was an unspoken truce between us.

The following day, I was a gunner using the 240B machine gun as we traveled to the small ANP-run base we'd be overseeing. We settled in for the long haul once we got there; we weren't going to be leaving until after the elections tomorrow, which meant this was where we'd be spending the night.

As the sun went down on the election's eve, we heard several guns firing in the distance, and one soldier witnessed a firefight between Afghans ensuing right before his eyes. But, our mission was to protect the soldiers on our base, not to chase down any unrelated skirmishes. So, we let the firefight be. It wasn't our fight to fight.

During the night, each of the soldiers had to pull shifts manning turrets. My shift was going to be from 0200 to 0500, so I tried going to bed around sundown the night before. I was luckier than I had been when I traveled to the Middle of Nowhere in the east back in April, because this time, I didn't have to sleep on the ground. I was given a cot, and because this place is crawling with camel spiders and scorpions, I was grateful for it.

I didn't get much sleep, though. We knew going into this thing that we were probably going to get attacked, and the situation wouldn't be good: we only had our vehicles to provide cover, no bunkers. And because we were sleeping out in the open, if an attack happened on us like it had earlier this week, then there would be a large chance for American casualties. The shrapnel of such an attack on uncovered soldiers like ourselves could easily turn deadly in a matter of seconds.

Needless to say, unease prevented me from deeply sleeping; every noise jolted me wide-awake.

VROOOOooooooooooooooooooooooooooooooOOOOOOOO...

Rocket attack?

...OOOOOOOOOOOOOMMMMMMMMMMMMmmmm!

No, just a Cougar being fired up.

Fthup. Fthup. Fthup. Fthup. Fthup. Fthup. Fthup...

Talib sneaking up on me?

...Fthup. Fthup. Fthup. Fhtup. Fthup. Fthup. Fthup.

No, just an ANA soldier making his rounds.

"CHA-TOOR-IST-EE KANDOW SARDEH!"

What the mother... a surprise attack?!

"Bolle! Bolle!"

No, just one Afghan shouting up to the guard tower... right next to my cot.

Keeping my eyes half-open while trying to sleep, I witnessed well over ten shooting stars whooshing over us, each one alarming me to a full alertness on my cot.

At one point during the night, I woke up to what looked like a falling star hovering several hundred feet above me. If it was a mortar... which I suspected it was... I knew that it probably had a hangtime of about seven seconds (at least judging by the mortars from the attack a few days ago), and it obviously had to have already been in the air for several seconds considering how high it was. My mental clock started counting down.

T-minus 4 seconds.

My heart beat four times faster when I saw that it was coming straight down on top of me… and that I wasn't hearing a whistle.

T-minus 3 seconds.

There was no bunker nearby me, and even if there had been, I certainly didn't have time to outrun the vivid round.

T-minus 2 seconds.

At best, all I would've been able to do was roll off my cot and hide under it, just hoping the mortar overshot me.

T-minus 1 second.

I knew I hadn't reacted quickly enough: my fate was sealed. If it wasn't going to pass over me, I hoped the flaming ball of death would at least knock me out quick and painlessly.

Here it is; the silence before the end.

Except, moments later, I was still alive. I peeked up and saw the mortar still in the sky; it had barely moved anywhere.

Yeah, this "flaming ball of death" was a *mortar* alright… an *illumination mortar*… gently gliding its way to the earth, being guided down by a cute little parachute. Apparently, it had been shot by one of our own guys who thought they saw enemy activity in the woodlines. The would-be blast's flare sizzled out before it got anywhere near me. I rolled over and fruitlessly tried getting back to sleep.

When my shift to pull security came up, it was actually welcomed because at least I no longer had to pretend I might get sleep if I tried. The first hour of my shift was quiet, but it wasn't long after that I was alerted to what I thought could be enemy activity. Through my night vision goggles, I saw lights moving around in the woodlines. I called it in on the radio and continued to monitor it, knowing I was more-than-equipped for an attack: I had a .50 caliber gun, an

M249 light machine gun, a frag grenade, and two M4 rifles at my disposal. Any Talib that wanted to mess with us would be given the opportunity to see their Allah.

Squinting to study the activity up ahead, I realized that the lights weren't flashlights as I had originally thought, but were several headlights from a convoy. However, I doubted that they were American trucks because it seemed too early for missions to be starting.

I counted that there were between six to nine vehicles in the group, and they were somewhere between 800 meters and 1000 meters away, heading towards us. Eventually, they drove to the woodlines we had scanned a few days prior, and then they parked and turned off their lights. For about a half-hour, I couldn't spot them anymore until three more vehicles came down the same road and did the same thing: they pulled up to the woodlines, parked, and turned off their lights. So, I estimated there were about 9 to 12 vehicles in the woods with their lights off. I couldn't tell what they were doing, but I figured that, if they were enemies, they were either offloading equipment for an attack or just rendezvousing at the spot, underestimating the functionality of my night vision goggles. I called it in again so everyone on our team would keep their attention on it.

For the next several hours, I scrupulously scoped the trucks. The team leader of our mission called for a dawn stand-to.[48] At this point, it was near the end of my shift and the trucks in the distance all turned their lights on again and left the area. I still don't know exactly what went on in those woodlines,

[48] **stand-to**: a military practice in which soldiers are prepared to respond to an attack at the crack of dawn and/or dusk; historically, enemies are inclined to attack the moment the first ray of light hits at dawn and/or just before the last ray of light leaves at dusk.

though there's a good chance it may have just been friendly forces out extra early for election day.

At 5:00am, a new gunner came and took the role over, but I couldn't focus on anything but the trucks, so I jumped on top of the Cougar with my binoculars and kept scanning for threats. The sun was coming up, and if we were going to get an early-morning Taliban wakeup this election day, then it was going to happen within a few minutes.

But to my surprise, no attack occurred.

The rest of election day, we had no drastic activity take place, either. We remained vigilant all day, and as the sun began setting after the polls had closed, we headed back to Camp Stone because our mission was complete.

The ride back was nostalgic for me: it would be my last time I'd ever be a gunner for a combat mission, and, in fact, it would be my last combat mission at all. As strange as it sounds, I was a bit disappointed that this was the last time that the Taliban would have a chance to try to kill me in their home country. To sit up on top of the turret, scanning the streets for enemies, knowing that a bullet could pierce me any moment... I felt so alive. Tangoing with death rejuvenates the soul, and this was my last dance. This was my last moment of feeling like a true soldier. This was my last gasp of air. This was my last hurrah.

If Bandee's account of election day seems anticlimactic compared to the assault on Camp Stone, that's because it is. We had all anticipated lots of carnage as the Afghans voted all day, but no blood was poured in our area.

That being said, this is one story where I can appreciate the anticlimactic ending.

I ask you to prayerfully consider the future of Afghanistan. This country was torn apart by the Russian invasion of the 1980s, and all that was left behind was a perpetual state of laziness, corruption, and poverty. These things have become a zeitgeist in Afghanistan, an inconvenient but insurmountable blockade to the nation's success. But even though that's all that was left of this country, the Afghan people restored their desire to rebuild their country, and they've welcomed America's help to achieve that dream. The Afghans have been commendable in their efforts to transform their country into a place they can be proud of, and yesterday's elections are proof: the Afghan people knew the countless risks of voting, and then saddled up anyway over to the polling stations so their voices could be heard, revealing a true longing for a country where they can live without fear.

So there you have it. The polls are closed and the results are in. If you're curious as to who won, they've already announced their winner: it's the people of Afghanistan for believing in and fighting for a free country of their own.

Like Bandee, supporting this election mission was the last important thing I had to do before I come home. At this juncture, I only have one mission left to tend to. It's called Operation: Return to Joanna.

Speaking of which, I'm sure you're wondering about my status of getting home. Well, I'll put it this way: I've been told that I'll return to Camp Phoenix in the next week and begin outprocessing. On September 6th, I'm scheduled to be on a flight to Manas, Kyrgyzstan, and I could be there anywhere between one-to-five days while waiting for a 20-hour flight to Fort McCoy, Wisconsin, where I'll continue the demobilization process for up to three more days. The morning after I finish the paperwork in McCoy, I'll get on a bus and get dropped off at an armory in Illinois where family can pick me up that evening. So according to Big Army, I can anticipate being in my home between September 10th (at the very earliest and only in the implausible situation that nothing goes wrong) and September 16th (at the very latest and only if most things don't go wrong).

But I shrug these dates off. I don't care if the Army tells me that it'll take at least four weeks for me to get home. If it only took my God six days to create this entire world, then I also believe that He has the power to get me home much sooner than what the Army has told me.

Do you?

Love,

Homeward Bound

The Camp Stone storehouse that had gotten destroyed by the initial explosions in the wee hours of August 18, 2009; another mortar was launched within seconds of this picture being snapped

.:15:.

Midnight Slaves

May 2010

Lloyd had followed through on his promise: he had fetched a cardboard box from the library dumpster and leaned it against the wall. He now slept beside it, cradling his daughter into his chest to protect her.

I set the cardboard on the concrete slab, positioning it so it would offer the most padding while carefully trying not to wake Lloyd or his daughter. I draped my ratty blanket over my body as I laid my head down on my travel pillow. The pillow had supported my head throughout my time in Afghanistan, and now its purpose was restored as I tried going to sleep on the steps of the St. Louis Public Library.

For tonight, I was homeless.

At the beginning of the semester, Joanna and I felt called to found a ministry: one night every week, we would gather a small group of college students and head to the streets of St. Louis to seek out its homeless citizens to offer them sandwiches, granola bars, juice, and water. During the wintry months, we'd additionally hand out hot chocolate, heavy clothes, blankets, and foot and hand warmers. By doing this, we built relationships with the disenfranchised, so much so that they began to look forward to seeing us every week. It's true that some just looked forward to the food and drinks we were bringing them, but others couldn't wait to see us again so we could pray for their needs and hand out Bibles. Our mission was to show the forsaken that God hadn't turned a blind eye to them; that He cared enough to send people to offer them sustenance amidst their plights.

We called ourselves the Midnight Slaves.[49]

Every week after we ran out of supplies, as our group of Midnight Slaves would drive back to campus to retreat to our warm beds and pantries full of food, I would look out the car window and see homeless men and women trying to fall asleep on metal vents, a source of heat during a cold night. It was a distinct separation between the Midnight Slaves and the St. Louis homeless; we came to help them, but we certainly weren't one of them.

For one night, I wanted that to be different. I wanted to be one of them, to show them that I wasn't superior to them. I wanted to prove that I was their friend.

I drove into the city on what would be the last night of the Midnight Slaves. Except, this evening would be a little different: regressing to my freshman roots of when I roamed the city just across the river by myself, I was alone this night.

Slinging a backpack full of sandwiches, water, and Bibles over my shoulder, I hiked up the steps of the library, one of the homeless hotspots during the spring and summer months. I knew most of the people there by name, though new faces popped up every week.

"Hey, Lloyd!" I called out.

Lloyd turned around while setting up his cardboard box-of-a-bed and grinned at me as he crouched on his hammies.

"My man, Danger! How you doing brother?"

"Not bad, not bad. How's the little lady doing?" I looked over at his pre-teenage daughter who rarely spoke, despite my best attempts to start a conversation with her. She trusted Lloyd and Lloyd alone.

---

[49] **Midnight Slaves**: name derived from Romans 6:22.

"She's not doing so well, my friend. She's been getting these headaches, *these…*" he threw his hands in the air, "…*these* migraines, I guess. Caused her to have a seizure once. We have a towel, but nothing to dampen it so we can put it on her forehead. That's why we really appreciate your water, man."

"Speaking of which," I pulled out several bottles from my backpack. "Here you go, brother."

Lloyd took the bottles, nodded his head, and smiled again.

"So, you're graduating this week, right? This is the last time we'll see any of you?"

"Unfortunately," I nodded, "that's the case. This is the last time."

"That's cool, man. You're off to bigger, better things. Congratulations on your graduation," Lloyd wanted to be happy for me. "So this is it, then? You're going to finish handing out sandwiches and head back?"

"Actually, Lloyd… I was hoping that I could maybe stay out here?"

His eyes furrowed in confusion, so I clarified.

"I was hoping that I could spend the night with you guys."

"Absolutely!" Lloyd emitted a delighted laugh, slapping his hands together. "You see this spot right here? You'll sleep right next to us. We got your back tonight, brother. You just stay close to us and we'll make sure you're safe."

I couldn't help but smile at his excitement. Lloyd offering for me to sleep near him was the equivalent of someone opening up their home for me to spend the night as a guest.

"Hey Danger, I'm going to go grab you a bed, alright? You're handing out sandwiches now, right?"

"Yep, that's the plan."

"Go ahead and do that, and when you get back here, you'll have a spot laid out for you."

"Thanks a lot, Lloyd. That's generous of you." I was more appreciative than I was probably showing. If he hadn't offered to get me a cardboard box, I wouldn't have known where to get one.

I continued handing out sandwiches to the regulars. I strolled to the entrance of the library, where an elderly black man named Mr. Humble pinned himself against the door. It was an appropriate name, considering his circumstances. Mr. Humble was always appreciative of the Midnight Slaves.

I continued down to the Scottrade Center, where the St. Louis Blues play their hockey games. Despite being a fan, I had come to resent Blues home games as the building's security would force the homeless people to vacate its premises during scheduled events. With several heated vents and an overhang to repel rain, the Scottrade Center was a favorable sanctuary for those living on the streets.

The Blues had missed the playoffs already, so on this particular night, I was able to find my friend, David, lying down on one of the massive Scottrade vents. The Midnight Slaves affectionately called him Eli in reference to the titular character that Denzel Washington played in The Book of Eli. Like Eli, David was able to rattle off Bible verses as easily as I could rattle off the ABCs. But, David was also a tormented man who had intense mood swings, so you were never sure if you would get Bruce-Banner-David or David-the-Hulk on any given night.

When I approached David, he was sound asleep. He often had trouble resting, so I set down a water bottle and a couple sandwiches and went on my way without disturbing him. He'd wake up in the morning and know the Midnight Slaves had been there.

I trotted eastward towards the Gateway Arch and found a man discretely hiding in the shadows of a construction site.

"Hey," I called out to him. "Are you hungry?"

The man emerged; he was a familiar face, but I couldn't recall his name. He was wearing a camouflaged parka, an authentic Army jacket that had been phased out of the military a few years ago. I used to own one myself, but had given mine away to some shivering homeless man several months ago during a particularly bleak, wintry night.

"Why are you asking if I'm hungry?" the homeless man interrogated.

"Because I got food for you if you want some."

"You think I'm needy?"

"These sandwiches are for anyone who wants them."

The man looked at me suspiciously, then continued to reprimand me.

"You guys come out here every week, and have I ever asked anything of you?"

"No, sir. No you haven't."

"Exactly. You *ask* me if I want a sandwich, and I've said yes before. I didn't ask *you*. You asked me."

"You're right," I tried shrugging off his ungrateful attitude.

"So, I don't *need* anything from you, you understand?"

It was hard to tell if he had just had a bad day and was now using me as a soft target for his spite, or if he genuinely had a beef with me for supposing I could help him.

"No worries, man. I'm not trying to offend you."

"So you can be on your way now."

"No problem, friend. But can I ask you the same thing I've asked you before?"

"What do you want to ask me?"

"Would you like a sandwich?"

The man hesitated a moment. I could tell he wanted one, but he was letting pride get in his way.

"I don't need your sandwich," he carped. "I don't need anything from you."

I nodded my head as he stared me down. Before I departed from this bitter man, I looked at his jacket one last time. It had a nametape sewn over its right chest: "GEIST."

"That's a nice jacket," I complimented him and then continued on my way, feeling the heat from his gaze on the back of my neck.

◊

I circled around the city, coming upon a new face and held out a bottle of water.

"Hey, sir, would you like some water?"

The dark-skinned man stared at me with uncertainty.

"Sure," he said. "Sure, I'll take one."

"You hungry, friend?"

The man became less hesitant towards me as I showed him that I had a turkey and mayonnaise sandwich for him.

"Yes, man. Yeah, I can definitely use a sandwich."

"Do you want a Bible?"

"Ah," he understood my purpose now. "You come in the Name of the Lord. Yes, please, I'll take a Bible. What's your name?"

"I am Danger," I said as I extended a Bible to him.

"Danger!" he exclaimed. "Your name is Danger? Yo, that's nuts. Are you messing with me? Now I know a man named Danger! If your first name is Danger, *I don't even wanna ask* what your middle name is! Hey, shouldn't you be at the *bay?* You know, 'keep danger at bay.' Or, how about this, 'anger is only one letter away from danger.' "

I politely laughed; it wasn't uncommon for someone to react to my name by cracking a few jokes.

"Ha, I like you man. My name's Joe. It's nice to meet you."

"Hey Joe, it's good to run into you. Are you living out here on the streets?"

"Yeah," he said. "I'm trying to do better than this, but yeah, this is where I'm at right now. I got laid off."

"I'm sorry to hear that, Joe. Times are tough; I know it isn't easy."

"You got that straight, Stranger Danger."

"Can I offer you a prayer?"

Joe's eyes lit up.

"Yes, please, Danger."

"Dear Lord," I said as Joe closed his eyes and I laid my hands on him. "Please keep Joe safe on the streets tonight. It's not a safe place…"

"No, it's not," Joe muttered under his breath, shaking his head.

"…and I ask that You reach Your Hand down and protect him as he lives out here."

"Protect me, Lord. Protect me."

"Please keep his belly full and let him have plenty of water to drink. Increase Joe's opportunities and change his circumstances…"

"Oh, Lord, change them!"

"...and may Joe cling to You and know You better. Help Joe get a job..."

"Yes Lord, please help."

"...but may he continue to cling to You as his circumstances get better. We ask that Your will be done, not ours, and we ask this in your Son's Name..."

"In the name of Jesus."

"Amen."

"Amen."

I lifted my hands off Joe who simply smiled at me.

"Danger, Danger, Danger. You know what?"

"What's that, Joe?"

"Look at yourself. You're here, giving me food and water and praying for me."

"Right..."

"Hey, you could be at the baseball game, like the rest of the kids your age. Hey, you could be at a bar. Hey, you could be living it up. But no, you're out here, caring for me. God bless you, brother."

"Well, Joe. You know what the difference is between you and me?"

"What's that?" he leaned in, eager to learn my secret.

"One paycheck."

Joe smiled.

"I've been to the ball game before, Joe. It's a lot of fun, but the game eventually ends. If I was watching the ball game right now, I'd be missing out on an amazing opportunity. An important opportunity; a *meaningful* opportunity. We spend so much of our lives chasing after the wind, and I've learned that the hard way."

It was true. In my life, I had felt there were only a handful of truly meaningful things I'd done. Pursuing Joanna after God told me I'd marry her was one, deploying to Afghanistan was another, and now, reaching out to the people living on the streets of St. Louis was the third case.

"I hear you brother, I think most of us learn that the hard way. Hey," Joe went on, "thanks for coming out tonight, Danger."

I smiled and shook his hand, then continued down the streets.

Just past the St. Louis Soldier's Memorial Military Museum, I found two men cackling back and forth with one another. One was a black, built man sitting with his legs crossed in the grass, and the other was a white man with a long, gray beard leaning against an oddly-placed tree. I sat down next to the two of them. I was uninvited, but they didn't seem to mind my presence. I began to wonder if they even noticed that someone had sat down next to them at all.

I didn't say a word, just listening to what they had to say. For the most part, they were just shooting the breeze and telling jokes, though the white man's demeanor struck me as if he had some kind of military background. The relaxed-but-alert way he was sitting and the terminology he was using were dead giveaways that he had once been in the service.

"Mike, I'm going to find some cigarettes," the black man said. "Do you want any?"

The white man shook his head, and the black man wandered off. It was not uncommon for me to see a homeless person search the streets for half-smoked cigarettes. They would pick it up off the ground and smoke the rest of its life, then return the butts to the ground.

"So, your name is Mike?" I asked the white man.

"Yes sir, that's me, I'm the Mike," he slurred. I could smell the alcohol on his breath. He wasn't quite drunk, but he had obviously had more than one drink.

"Would you like food, water, or a Bible, Mike?"

"Sure, I'll just take a water and a sandwich," he accepted, yet seeming disinterested in me. I handed him both, and he set them down in the grass. He was sitting in damp dirt, which soiled the back of his pants; not that he would've been otherwise presentable.

"This is a good sandwich," Mike said after taking a bite. "Can I have another for later?"

I handed him one, and he said "Thanks," but I still wasn't connecting with him. I was just a soup kitchen to him, a vending machine that produces food and drink.

"Mike, can I ask you a question?"

"Shoot, man," he said with his mouth full.

"Were you in the military?"

Mike looked into my eyes for the first time and abruptly stopped biting his sandwich. He pulled the food away from his face, studying me.

"Have I talked to you before?"

"No, Mike. This is the first time we've met, friend."

"How did you know?"

"It's your demeanor. I had a feeling you were in the service."

Mike coughed into his dirt-stained arm.

"Army. Vietnam War."

An unkempt Vietnam veteran who was living on the streets and had turned to the bottle to get him through his days. I was talking to a walking, breathing American cliché.

"Me too," I responded. His eyes widened in confusion, so I clarified. "Well, not Vietnam. Afghanistan for me. I just got back."

"If you're in the Army, then how do you have a beard?" he interrogated.

"I'm out now. Actually, I just got out. A few weeks ago, in fact. I haven't shaved since then."

"What was your discharge?"

"Honorable."

"Good," Mike nodded in approval. "Mine too."

Mike continued munching his food, but now had a different attitude towards me. He accepted me now.

"So, kid. You learn anything over there?"

"Heh," I let out a single tone of amusement. "I learned how to pray with my eyes open."

"Useful trick out here, too," he quipped as he took another bite of his sandwich. "You wanna know something?" he asked, but didn't let me answer. "I went to Vietnam when I was 19 years old. *Nineteen!* I was just a baby."

"Did you like it?"

"Hell no. You crazy, man? I was 19! I liked my soldiers, but I hated the officers. Were you an officer?"

"A noncommissioned one."

"What rank were you?"

"Sergeant."

"You're fine then. I'm talking about the real officers, the commissioned ones. I hated them."

"Yeah," I related to him. "I can understand that frustration. There're plenty of officers that shouldn't be in authority positions."

"You're talking my language, man! You know what you're talking about. I was in Vietnam, and this freaking General, man. Damn Four-Star General came to our base. This old fuck tells us all these rules we have to follow. Man, he didn't know what we'd been through! I'm telling you man," Mike began clutching his sandwich so firmly that the mayonnaise-laden turkey was sliding out. "This General comes down from his crystal palace and tells us how to run things? What does *he* know?"

I simply nodded my head, afraid to interrupt Mike's tangent. His voice was amplifying with each word.

"And then I go back home, and I've got nowhere to turn to. My country sends me off to *Viet*-fucking-*nam,* tells me to kill these Vietnamese who are just as young as me, and then sends me back home and says I'm a danger? *I'm* a danger?! I'm *unstable*? You *made* me a fucking danger!"

Mike's eyes filled with fury, and I could tell he was having trouble channeling his anger. I would've been afraid, but I knew he wasn't lashing out at me; he had wounds still trying to heal beneath the skin.

"I didn't want to go," he shouted at me. "But they sent me anyway! And then they wouldn't help me."

kpuuuh! kpuuuh! kpuuuh!

A series of loud explosions startled me as I lunged to find cover behind the tree. It only took me a moment to realize that they were just fireworks coming from Busch Stadium. The St. Louis Cardinals had just won their baseball game.

Mike continued ranting, his mind back in Vietnam and yet somehow unfazed by the explosions.

"Nineteen! You damn know-it-all General, telling me how to fight. Fucker."

Mike was fuming, breathing heavily and trying to regain composure. I shared in his pain; his frustrations were not foreign to me. For a moment, Mike's anger roused my own animosities.

Mike had a condescending Four-Star General who criticized his competence and questioned his capabilities; I had CH Fardpot who praised me to my face and wrote glowing acclamations on my evaluations, yet belittled me in front of soldiers and, as I found out after I returned to my unit in Marion, also slandered my character behind my back. Mike had labored to be the best soldier he could be, only to find himself scorned by a leader who had no idea what he had been through. I poured my heart into being the best soldier I could be, only to find my unit thought of me as a liability because CH Fardpot painted me as a bungling nitwit, perhaps so he wouldn't have to share the acclaim for our widely-successful ministry. Mike returned to a nation of ungrateful Americans who villainized his war efforts; I had returned to a university full of smug students who felt they were entitled to their education, and in my first week of classes, even had a professor tell me that America deserved the September 11th attacks because of our involvements in the Middle East. Mike had struggled to survive a vexing conflict where every day was a divine gift, then returned to his own country to find that his life suddenly lacked significance; I, too, had known that agony all-too-well.

More than anything, I had gone to Afghanistan aspiring to be a hero. Instead, I returned feeling weaker than when I had left.

A moment ago, a homeless man named Mike and a Midnight Slave named Danger were innocently conversing with each other. Now, we were two frenzied war veterans involuntarily sharing our greatest rancors, ready to explode like a pair of IEDs triggered together.

Instead of being a minister to a victim of mental torture, I activated a couple of timebombs in downtown St. Louis.

You've gotta diffuse this, I told myself. *You can deal with your own demons later, in the same way you subdue them every night. But for right now, focus on Mike. You cast him back to Vietnam; let's bring him back home now.*

I peered into Mike's seething face and, muzzled with a loss for words, didn't know how to stop him from ranting.

"I'd *kill* that fucking General. Mudder-fucker. I would take his…"

"Well," I blurted out to interrupt Mike, searching for the words to lull his fiery tangent, "if it makes you feel better…"

Mike was about to erupt, his magma eyes fixating on mine in hopes that I had something helpful to say, words that would alleviate his contempt for that General, something that he could take with him and whip out of his back pocket whenever he needed comfort, a punchline that had enough rain to diffuse an agitated volcano.

"…he's probably dead now."

Mike silently stared at me, freezing to process what I just said. When he grasped my words, he chortled with belligerent approval, slapping his knee, gasping for air in between his snorting.

"Ha ha, *haaaaaa*! Ha *haaa!* I like this guy!" he hollered behind himself, as if there was someone nearby to share our conversation with. Mike couldn't contain himself; instead of unleashing the molten lava, I had managed to flare up all the hot gas.

I chuckled along with Mike until his laughing fit calmed down.

"Mike, can I pray for you?"

His eyes widened and I could read his thoughts: *You would do that for me?* I clutched Mike's shoulder and began praying. I asked for forgiveness for Mike, I asked for his bitterness to be wiped away, and I asked for peace in his life. I knew exactly what Mike wanted from

God, as it was a prayer I had often prayed for another jaded war veteran.

"Amen," I finished, looking at Mike.

"Thank you," he wheezed, tears falling down his cheeks.

◊

Sifting through my bag, I realized I was running low on supplies and it was getting late. I headed back towards the old library to spend my night as a homeless man. As I strolled up the steps of the library courtyard, I heard a familiar voice call out to me.

"Well, I'll be! It's the Danger-man!"

I smiled and walked over to my friend, giving him a handshake and a half-hug.

"Warren, how's life treating you?"

Warren was an intelligent man who was a victim of the crashing economy. He had gotten laid off at work, and was evicted from his apartment shortly thereafter, pitting him as a resident of the St. Louis Public Library.

"Danger, things are great. Where's everyone else?"

"It's just me tonight, friend. Do you want a sandwich?"

"You know it, man. I don't mean to beg or anything…"

"You want an extra sandwich, Warren?"

"You know it, man! Last sandwich you gave me was so delicious, I almost bit my fingers off."

I smiled at his accolade. Somehow, a turkey with cheese slapped on mayonnaise-slabbed bread was culinary art.

"Hey, Danger-man, let me ask you a question. Do you remember the last time you were with me, you prayed for God to bless me with a job so I could get an apartment again?"

"Sure, Warren. Tell me about that."

"Do you know how long I've been praying that same prayer, that I'd find a job?"

"How long?"

"Too long. I haven't had a job in two years, my friend. Two *long* years. But you know what? Last week, you prayed that prayer for me, and the very next day, I got a job."

"Warren, that's awesome! Congratulations my friend!"

"No, thank you, man. And you know what? Not only did I get a job, but when I went into work the first day, they were so impressed with my skills that they guaranteed I would have swift upward mobility if I kept up my performance. They said I would be promoted early and often."

I didn't know what to say. While I didn't expect God to abandon Warren, I also didn't necessarily trust that a job would fall into his lap in less than a week, let alone a day. Once again, God made a statement about my modest expectations of Him.

"Awesome!" I marveled. "I'm so happy for you."

"Are you heading home now?"

"Actually, I'm staying here tonight. I'm going to be with you guys."

"Really? Wow," he said, his face bloating with surprise. "You know what, this is a dangerous place, man. Where you sleeping?"

I pointed over at Lloyd, "Just yonder."

"I got you, man. I'll watch out for you tonight. Nobody's gonna mess with you on my watch, you feel me? If anyone messes with you, I'll be there. But Lloyd's a good guy, too; you'll be fine with him."

I wasn't too worried about getting hassled, but I appreciated his enthusiastic support.

"Thanks Warren. I appreciate that."

"I'll be here until I go to work in the morning. Hey, you have a good night, my man. I'll be here all night, just let me know if you need anything."

I lumbered over to the cardboard box Lloyd dredged up for me, a symbol that I had truly earned his trust. I quietly set up my bed and lied down to go to sleep for my one-night episode as a homeless man.

Before I went to sleep, I admired the freckles burning in the sky. Though the stars not as luminous, I was reminded of Afghanistan, and particularly the night I left the Terps' hut for the last time. After I had said my final goodbyes to everyone, I had dragged my feet towards my tent, gazing up at the stunning fireballs hanging over Gardez as I heard a voice cry out to me.

"Danger!"

I turned around to see Rambo Three jogging my way.

"Danger," he said as he put his hand on my shoulder, "Danger, remember: 'When I die, see the sky. No cry; just *bye-bye*.' "

I smiled at my friend and, after giving him a rough pat on the back, walked out of his life.

Now staring at the same sky that hovered over Afghanistan, I missed so much about that country. I missed my Muslim friends. I missed its countryside. I missed feeling alive. And I missed feeling like I was a strong person. I hadn't felt strong in months; I was a mess. Though my nightmares were less frightening and their frequency slowed to a trickle, I still wasn't happy with my state of mind. I was angry with the world, and I didn't know why. Would I end up like Mike, still bitter 40 years later? Where was his family? Did he push them away so far that they stopped trying to communicate with him?

After allowing my mind to whirl in circles for an hour, I tried focusing on calming my breathing. The night began unusually warm; the day had been hot and the evening was temperate. But after I went to sleep, the warmth dissipated into an uncomfortable chill that prevented me from falling deep asleep. If it wasn't the cold, then it was the *fthup-fthup-fthups* of footsteps that would propel me into high alert, a vigilance I hadn't felt since Afghanistan. When I heard these footsteps, I'd wake up and look around, seeking the sources of shadows until I could confirm there was no threat.

At the crack of dawn, I felt someone kicking at my feet. My back throbbed from the hard ground.

"Hey, man." It was Lloyd. "We gotta get going. Security's gonna kick us out of here any minute."

Lloyd and the rest of the homeless group moved all their stuff about three times a day: they'd migrate towards a church that offered them breakfast in the morning, spend the afternoon in what's been dubbed "Homeless Park," and then head back to the library's courtyard after the building closed in the evening.

Unlike my homeless friends, I didn't have to do this. Instead of having to move everything I own several times throughout the day, I got to drive home in a heated car, prance into my apartment stocked with food, take a nap in a comfortable bed where I knew I was safe, and study for a final examination that would earn me a Bachelor's Degree, further distancing myself from ever needing to involuntarily sleep on the streets.

Though it had been delayed by several hours, the distinct separation between the Midnight Slaves and the St. Louis homeless continued.

.:16:.

The Forsaken One

31 August 2009

I woke up to the sunlight seeping through the holes in the tent, marring my eyes. It was a bright and beautiful Kabul morning on August 29th, but I had no will to wake up. God had forsaken me, and I was angry with Him. I was already told that I wouldn't be flying out of Afghanistan until September 2nd, and flying "home" home wouldn't happen for who knows how long. There was no use in hoping for an early release at this point: simply put, my departure from Afghanistan happening before September was an impossibility.

Talk about an abysmal pain, Joanna. Being told that I'm not coming home early is a bummer in so many ways. I mean, it's obviously a bummer for both of us in that we want to see each other as soon as possible. But it cuts deeper than that. Yes, I desperately want to hold you, but more significantly, I don't want to be a false prophet. I told you (as well as our friends and family and anyone that would listen) that I would be coming home early. I went out on a limb of faith and stated the improbable – *nay*, the *impossible*. And being wrong about it pours embarrassment on me, completely discrediting me: I become a punchline; just a joke. And not just to you and our family and friends, but to God. I begged you and so many others to have faith in what I was saying; to disappoint those who trusted me makes them all fools, too. My parents put all the deposits down to make sure I was enrolled in school and had an apartment to live in for this semester. You trusted what I said, believing in this prophecy and praying for it to happen, going out on a limb of faith yourself. So many family and friends who don't have faith birthed a "wait-and-see" attitude, having no confidence in what I prophesied, yet deep down, hoped that *just maybe* it would come to pass. *Just maybe* they could see an act of faith produce fruit.

So you see, none of this was ever just about me. Convincing others that God had spoken to me and then being wrong about it, potentially damaging others' already-fleeting faith? I disclosed this prophecy to you and everyone else because I believed God told me to. I wanted you to be amazed by Him when this came to pass; but I knew that if I was wrong, I would've generated hurt and confusion instead of help and encouragement.

Not to mention, what does this mean for *me?* To say that I heard the still voice of God and *be wrong about it?* Woe to me, Joanna. Woe to me![50]

I'm getting ahead of myself: let me back up, because I never even explained my arrival to Kabul in the first place. I had departed Herat and arrived at Camp Phoenix just eight days ago from today. When I arrived, I was met by the head chaplain of the 33rd Brigade, CH Stanford. He's the officer who decides when my mission is complete, and when you prayed for changed hearts within the 33rd Brigade leaders, he's the first person that God needed to touch. However, it was unlikely for CH Stanford to become tender towards my situation, considering the flack he caught for my dog crusade. I had burned my bridge with him just two months ago when I defied his request to not pursue my animal rights campaign. Yet, now I needed him to be empathetic towards my situation, despite what I put him through. And if his heart wasn't changed and willing to send me home early, then the game was over. The buck stopped there.

But the buck didn't stop there. When I walked into CH Stanford's office, the first thing he relayed to me was that he was going to do what he could to let me go home early. He knew that I was enrolled for the Fall 2009 semester in school, and he explained that he felt I had already sacrificed enough by missing what would've been my graduation year to instead cooperate with this deployment's demands. He told me to focus on getting home as quickly as I could, which was an order that I was eager to fulfill.

After CH Stanford agreed to let me go home, he had to talk over the issue with two leaders that had much more authority, that being the Chief of Staff of Task Force Phoenix (to whom I'd also been a pain because of my animal rights fight), as well as the colonel who was taking care of all flight manifests. Both leaders had tender hearts: they empathized with my

---

[50] Matthew 7:15-20 decrees death and destruction to false prophets.

situation and agreed to get me home on an earlier flight than I was originally scheduled.

But not everyone had a tender heart. The last person who had to approve the early release was my company commander who, though outranked by everyone I had already talked to, technically had more direct authority over me. When I approached her and told her that the higher-ups authorized me to leave early, she shot the idea down, making it clear she had no intentions of letting me go home before September. She told me that I was scheduled for a September 2nd flight out of Afghanistan, and although that was still earlier than I was originally scheduled, it wasn't before September as I had thought I heard God tell me. I was downcast, but trusted that God would still find a way to get me on a flight earlier than September 2nd.

After I was denied my August release, I went through the motions of handing in my gear to the Camp Phoenix supply sergeant in hopes that, if a flight suddenly became available, I wouldn't be unprepared to leave. And so, after turning in the same exact unspent bullets that I was issued back in December, I was ready to go at a moment's notice in case the company commander's heart was changed. After I finished the last of the paperwork I had to do, I anticipated hearing of some kind of deliverance that I would be granted, but it never came. I even received an email from a college professor informing me that my absence from his class was unacceptable and that he was going to drop me from it, a course that I calculated I had needed to obtain my degree.

In hopes that this plight would be the catalyst to tenderize her heart, I told my company commander that my course enrollment was at stake. But it was just as hardened as ever: she told me that my school issues were my problem, not hers.

No flight home. No early release. No miraculous happy ending.

And that's why I woke up two days ago with such a spiritual hangover; for the first time this deployment, I accepted that I had been wrong about the prophecy. Unless the company commander suddenly allowed me to leave, and I somehow got manifested for a mystery flight that no one had known about until today, then I wouldn't be going home early.

So, on that day the sun was seeping through the holes in the tent and marring my eyes, I finally dragged myself out of bed around lunchtime and headed over to the computer lab to kill several hours. But shortly after I arrived, CH Fardpot frantically tapped me on the shoulder to tell me that some changes had been made and that I needed to finish turning in my weapons and my ammo. I told him that I was finished with all of that, and I left the computer lab to straighten out whoever was ordering me to accomplish tasks I had already completed.

While trying to get to the bottom of the confusion, I ran into CH Stanford.

"Sir, do you know what's going on? CH Fardpot told me that I have to return some equipment and finish my paperwork. I've already done all that, though."

"Well, Geist, the unit is just trying to make sure you're ready to leave," he explained, then further clarified, "they just want to make sure you're able to get on your departing flight tomorrow."

I began trembling and felt nauseous. Had I really just heard what I thought I did?

"Sir, I'm not sure I'm understanding..."

"You're manifested for a flight home tomorrow, Geist."

Yes, it was true: the company commander had suddenly allowed me to leave, and I somehow got manifested for a mystery flight that no one had known about until today.

My eyes began welling up with tears and I ran to the nearest bunker and braced myself to accept what just happened: I would be heading home *tomorrow*, and even though I had become faithless, God still proved true to His promise. I began crying into my hands, thankful for God's goodness and disgusted at my faithless attitude. In believing that God had forsaken me, I had instead forsaken God.

I traveled to Kabul International Airport in the early morning of August 30th, and by the end of the day, I was on a flight to Manas, Kyrgyzstan, which is the last stop that our 33rd Brigade soldiers need to make before arriving at Fort McCoy, Wisconsin to finish outprocessing and go home.

When I arrived in Manas last night, I was told that I would be home and ready to return to school by this weekend. Had I not been allowed on this flight, I wouldn't have arrived to Manas until the night of September 2nd, just missing the last flight to Fort McCoy for another six days, which would've meant I wouldn't have been home until long after Labor Day, which would've meant I would've had to battle for the privilege to stay enrolled in all my classes. But God's version of "early" allowed me to get home just in time: because I've already been delivered from Afghanistan, I'll instead be going home much earlier than I was ever told I should anticipate coming home. If this seems stunning, then good; it stuns me, too. For every one soldier who's been sent home early for non-emergency reasons, I can point out thousands more who have been extended during the Global War on Terrorism.

I now feel at peace with the timetable set before me; I finally feel that this is what God must've been referring to when He said I'd be home "early" back in December. Just a few days ago, I lacked this peace; everything seemed out of place, and I didn't feel that I was getting home as "early" as I was meant to be. But now, I finally feel I'm exactly where I should be, where God had intended me to be all along.

In January of this year, just a few weeks after I felt God whisper to me that I would be home early, I knew that I needed to just have faith and enroll for school this coming semester. And it was by faith that I did that very thing. And it was by faith that my parents put a deposit down for my apartment, understanding that if I was wrong about this, they'd be out hundreds – maybe thousands – of dollars. It was by faith that I told you about this situation and asked you to have faith of your own. And it was by faith that you prayed along with me, begging God to change the hearts of the 33rd Brigade leaders, including key leaders who were strong opponents to me just a couple of months prior.

Let's assess the situation as it stands today. Because I enrolled for my senior year in college, I was granted the opportunity to go home early. Because my parents faithfully trusted my word, I have an apartment to shelter me for the schoolyear. Because I told you about my situation, accepting the fact that I might seem like a nutcase, you were aware of my prophecy months ago and inevitably became involved as the story developed. And because of your faith in accompanying me in my prayers, the hearts of the 33rd Brigade leaders were changed.

Had faith been absent, then I wouldn't have enrolled in school, and therefore would've had no reason for an early release. Had faith been absent, I'd not have an apartment to shelter me. And had faith been absent, the 33rd Brigade leaders would not have been concerned with my situation because their hearts would still be hardened.

Here's the bottom line: without faith, I would have no miracle to speak to you about today. There's a verse that speaks to this phenomenon: "We do not want you to become lazy, but to imitate those who through faith and patience inherit what has been promised."[51]

Meanwhile, it was through my faithlessness that God proved His dominion this month. I had underestimated Him, forgetting that my God is a God who holds true to each and every one of His promises. And in that way, God taught me the greatest lesson of all: He is ever-present in a world that constantly tries to push Him out.

That's the way I look at it. Perhaps that's not the way others are going to see it. I mean, there *is* a chance that my early release was coincidence. I know some people might look at it that way. Some might say "it's just *three-and-a-half weeks*, that's not very early anyway." Well, tell that to a soldier who's been on a deployment for a year. Believe me, one week early is nearly one eternity early.

But I can't prove to anyone that this wasn't all coincidence, and I can't prove that my definition of "early" is the correct definition. And so, what remains then?

---

[51] Hebrews 6:12

Only faith remains. Nobody can “prove” that God was the reason I’ll be home early. All we can do is take the evidence provided and decide whether we’re willing to make that leap to faith or not.

Look.

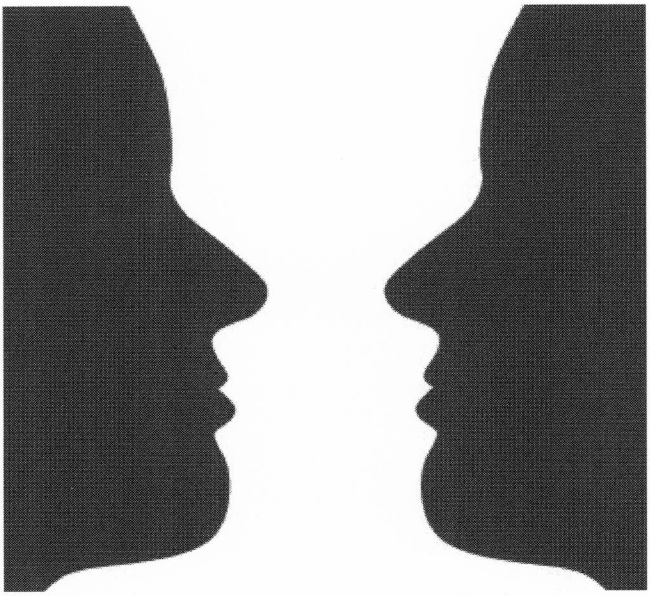

I know it’s an age-old optical illusion that you’ve undoubtedly examined before. But tell me, what do you see? Are those faces in there, or is that a vase? Depending on the way you look at the situation, you may see different things. Often in this world, much like in this picture, one way to look at a situation is much more prominent than the other. Sure, you’ll probably see the face quicker than the vase. But if you ignore the face and look hard enough, you’ll see the vase. But which were you meant to see? The face, or the vase?

We have so many moments where we have a face and a vase right in front of us. And the face is obvious, yet we still try our hardest to only see the vase. In fact, some of us allow ourselves to become completely blind to the face, so that even if we tried focusing on it, we’d still only see that vase in front of our eyes.

So let me ask you something – when you look at this situation and the events leading up to my early deliverance, do you see a face or a vase?

My greatest hope for you is that you don't walk away thinking that you only saw an empty vase.

I will be praying a special prayer for you tonight. Tonight, as I lay my head down on my pillow, I'm going to request that God puts you through persecution. I pray that you will soon feel the torment of what it can take to stand up for what you believe. I pray that someone will try to harm you because of the One you claim allegiance to. Believe me, I know how cruel that sounds; I've thought about it. But when I think about the underground Christians who have to daily fend for their lives because they believe in a Savior amidst a country where the reigning religion emphasizes a deity of an impersonal nature, I realize those underground Christians are so much stronger than most American Christians could ever wish to be. When you know you could die for your beliefs, your faith becomes something more than a family tradition or a societal identity. Remember the interpreters who risked their lives by merely having a Bible in their possession? I wish that every Christian would know that intensity so that perhaps they could feel true faith, the kind of unrelenting faith that bears great fruit despite its great bruises.

During my flight to Manas, I had a lot of time to think about Gardez, a place that my heart will always hold sacred. I thought about the interpreters, and I prayed a prayer for them. There's little chance I'll have contact with them again; Afghanistan doesn't have a postal system and the Terps have limited Internet access at best. I thought about the night before I was to fly to Kabul, when I sat to eat dinner with them one last time. As they all joyfully shouted amongst each other across the table, I solemnly grazed my eyes on each one of them, thankful for their existence and their place in my life. I held up a large slab of bread in front of them, and I broke it and handed a piece to each of them. My prayer was that they'd remember the things I had told them of Jesus; my belief is that they will. My desire is that some of them would allow the joy of Christ to permeate their lives; the truth is that I won't ever know. My hope was that I would see them again on earth; the reality is that I probably won't. And so, together, we ate the bread and drank our drinks, celebrating our last supper with one another.

Now that I'm in Manas, I've had much time to reflect on this deployment as a whole. And because this base is one of the main hubs that ports soldiers in and out of Afghanistan, you either get seasoned veterans who have served a long tour but are now on their way back home, or you get inexperienced soldiers who've never been to Afghanistan but are on their way into the country for a long tour. As I've traveled around the base, I've noticed the more novice soldiers: the ones without combat experience who are still fumbling around trying to figure out how to get their bulletproof plates to fit in their vests. As I gander at these soldiers without any combat patches, it amazes me to think that just nine months ago, I was on this same base, but wearing their unsoiled boots. I feel pity for them – many of them have no idea what they're getting into, and it's certain that my eyes are resting upon some who won't survive the year ahead. But at the same time, I know that they're doing something that has to be done, something that ensures the future safety of this allied nation. They are doing something that was asked of them by their own country, as well as by Afghanistan. They are sacrificing a piece of their lives to rebuild a country that's been torn apart by tyranny and oppression. They are the watchmen of this generation, running towards the flames in an effort to douse one country's pain, offering their blood to accomplish that mission.

As I look out at the soldiers, I don't know whether they know all that or not. But, it doesn't really matter.

They're about to find out.

Love,

Someone Who Saw a Face

.:16:.

Stop the Bleeding

July 2010

I glanced at my hand on the steering wheel, studying my wedding ring and not being able to help but smile. I had always hated wearing rings, but this one was different: it looked so sharp and yet was so lightweight I barely noticed it.

But after today, I wouldn't be wearing it again for awhile. Joanna and I weren't married yet. I was just wearing the ring to get a feel for it; to make sure I liked everything about it. At the end of the day, it would go back in its box until a ringbearer presented it to me at an altar.

Joanna kept staring at me, smiling. I smirked right back at her, knowing there was a lot to be giddy about: we had just graduated together, and in a couple of months, we'd be married. None of this would've been able to happen if I hadn't gotten home early.

Glancing at Joanna, I reminisced getting off the plane in the Midwest. On that September morning last year, I brushed through the terminals, scanning for Joanna and my parents. I didn't have to look long: I found my parents a few feet away from me, but lost sight of them as a crazed Cougar surprise-attacked me, leaping into my arms and wrapping her legs around me as I spun her. I was on U.S. soil again, holding the woman of my dreams as a gate behind me closed for the last time, stranding me in a place that was far, far away from war.

But the deployment wasn't done yet. The four of us zipped across the state to the outprocessing stations at Fort McCoy that same Friday. It was already 11:00am, and outprocessing had to be done by 5:00pm that afternoon. If it wasn't, then I would have to hang around Fort McCoy until Tuesday, as the base was shut down for Labor Day weekend. I was told I needed to be in attendance at college by that Tuesday, or I'd be dropped from class, needing to enroll the following semester instead. Instead of a May 2010 graduation, I could've been looking at a December 2010 graduation. Instead of a September 2010 wedding, I'd be married sometime in the uncertain future. Being home "early" hinged on outprocessing being completed by 5:00pm that Friday.

When I arrived to Fort McCoy, I was instructed not to expect to finish outprocessing in one day.

"It's never been done," I was told.

"It's a three-to-five day process," many explained.

"Impossible!" they cried.

Well, yes. Humanly impossible.

Five hours later, I had finished outprocessing. In my hands, I held the official orders declaring my mission completed. The deployment was supposed to continue for at least another 24 days, but that didn't happen for me. I was done.

I looked at the clock: it was 4:27pm. Had my deployment lasted just 34 minutes longer, my entire life would've been stalled for another several months. God said that I would arrive home "early." That's all He told me, "early." Well, it turns out "early" was a 34-minute difference from being "late." And God's version of "early" turned out to be right on time for me.

That very evening, I walked into my warm home, a testament that God's promises are true and trustworthy.

◊

puuuh!

Hitting a pothole, my mind returned to the present and, out of the corner of my eye, I saw Joanna still grinning at me with excitement. I couldn't blame her; there was just so much in our future to be excited for.

Our excitement fizzled as we had to slow down past what looked like a traffic problem. All the vehicles in the single lanes inched along beside a car that wasn't entirely on the shoulder; a wheel-and-a-half were hovering over a drop-off that led to a nasty little ditch below.

I noticed there were people standing around the sidelined car, gawking inside the driver-side window. A trail of gas was leaking from a dump truck that was also off-road just ahead. The fresh gas was creeping down the hill towards us. I jumped out of our car when I realized this accident had to have happened just a moment ago.

I ran to the car that was delicately placed on the shoulder; there was an elderly man trapped inside. Not trapped in the sense that he was physically weighed down by an immense piece of debris, but trapped in the sense that he was physically unable to move because he was immensely weak. His arm was ripped open and his head was sharply angled towards the ditch below. Though I didn't know what transpired, it looked bad: there was blood on the left side of the car interior, debris of the car all over the road, and rugged skid marks from the dump truck that weaved from outgoing traffic to incoming traffic back to outgoing.

A few witnesses of the accident were huddled around the driver's side, probably because the passenger side was an unsafe place to be; if the car tipped over, anyone standing on the passenger side would be crushed.

I opened the passenger door and moved a briefcase to slip in and sit beside the old man. From this position, I couldn't see his arm, but I was told it was bleeding pretty bad. From the driver's side door, Joanna told me that there were slabs of skin embedded in the door.

One of the witnesses announced that the victim was gushing too much blood, so I started taking off my shirt to improvise a tourniquet until I was informed that the dispatcher on the other end of the 9-1-1 call said not to apply a tourniquet. My military training told me that this was a situation in which a tourniquet was necessary, but not wanting to be held liable for disobeying police orders, I didn't dare do it.

I looked at the man and felt helpless; if I wasn't allowed to treat him, what was I even doing inside his car?

I kneeled on the passenger seat towards the victim and tried making small talk.

"Sir, I'm here to help you. What's your name?"

"Richard," the man slurred.

"Alright Richard, help is on the way. You're going to be alright."

There was an awkward silence between us, but I wanted to keep him talking. If this man were to fall asleep, the chances of his survival would decline exponentially. And though from my viewpoint it didn't seem like a potentially fatal accident, I didn't want to chance it.

Richard broke the silence between us.

"I fell asleep," he sobbed. "I fell asleep."

"You fell asleep?" I asked, confused.

"I fell asleep while driving. My family told me this would happen. I was afraid of this."

Richard's head was at an unnatural angle because of the way his weight had shifted during the accident, and I knew blood must've been rushing to his brain. Besides the discomfort, Richard was expending his scant energy to hold his neck straight and, worst of all, was prone to incapacitation or even a stroke if he had already been suffering from a hemorrhage. Yet, I also knew that I should never touch a car accident victim, especially if it looks like they may have had neck trauma.

"Richard, how does your neck feel? Is your neck injured?"

"My neck is fine; it's my arm."

Taking a split moment to decide what recourses I had, I palmed his head and lifted it so his body would at least be at a more vertical (and therefore safer and more comfortable) angle. His head was like a large water balloon that had condensation on its outside: his temple was drenched and the sweat of this frightened old man dripped off my brand-new wedding ring. As I lifted his head, Richard didn't cry out in pain and seemed no less coherent, so I resolved that my decision to shift his neck had been a good one.

I noticed he was wearing VFW[52] pins.

"Are you in the VFW?"

"Yes, that's where I was coming from."

"Are you a veteran then?"

"Yes."

"Me too. What war did you serve in?"

"Two."

"My grandpa served in World War II. Where were you stationed?"

"I don't want to talk about it!" Richard gurgled.

"Okay, okay, that's no problem." My mind raced to find topics to talk about to keep him awake, but I couldn't help but recognize how weak he was. Here was a war veteran who survived a combat zone and must've been so strong in his life, yet now he needed some scrappy kid to support his head.

---

[52] **VFW,** or **Veterans of Foreign Wars**: a nonprofit organization created to aid U.S. veterans.

I continued on, trying to find more conversation material.

"Do you have family in the area?"

"Two sons."

"Do you want me to call them?"

Richard's eyes lit up in excitement, and for that split moment, he seemed lucid.

"Yes, please!"

I called Joanna over and had her sift through Richard's briefcase to find his address book. As Joanna stepped away to search, a paramedic hopped into the seat behind Richard.

"Sir, do you know where you are?" the paramedic asked.

In a tone that reflected great shame, Richard responded, "Yeah, I'm in my car…"

"Do you know why you're here?"

"I got in an accident."

"He said he fell asleep," I informed the paramedic.

"Thanks for being here," the paramedic nodded. "I think we can take it from here."

His fresh hand replaced my now-flaccid hand, and I slipped out of the car the same way I came in.

Joanna waved an address book, pointing to the phone number of one of Richard's sons.

As the phone rang, I wondered to myself what I would tell his son, but my thoughts were cut short when a cheerful voice spilled through the other end of the phone.

"This is Kevin!"

"Hi Kevin. My name is Danger. I'm calling you because your father has been in a car accident. He's fine right now and seemed stable last I saw him. He was conscious and talking and was aware of what happened. But his arm has been cut badly and he's shaken up."

"Okay, where are you?"

"We're east of Fairfield on Route 60. The paramedics are trying to get him out of the car to transport him to the hospital right now."

"Where are they transporting him?"

"Um… I really don't know."

"That's okay. Thank you so much for calling, I'm on my way."

"Okay Kevin, drive safe."

The phone call ended, but the conversation did bring up an important question: where was Richard being transported to? No one in the immediate area knew the answer, and I didn't want Kevin to come to the crash site and nobody be there to tell him what was going on.

"Joanna, we need to figure out where Richard's going in case they're gone when Kevin gets here."

"Okay, but should I put this back in his car?"

She held up a miniature-sized flag that had been lying in the road with the rest of the debris. It was an American flag, but it wasn't red, white, and blue, but rather brown, gray, and black because of how worn it was.

"There's too much going on in there," I told her. "We can give it to him later."

"There's an officer just standing around over there," Joanna pointed out. "I'll go ask him which hospital Richard's going to."

I clutched her shoulder and halted her, saying, "No, let me. I don't want him to be rude to you."

The officer was in his early 30s, a stocky but stumpy man. As I approached him, I realized he looked strikingly similar to my late buddy, Jared Southworth. I got the impression that this cop wasn't a rookie, but he was no seasoned veteran either.

"Officer, do you know where this man is being transported to?"

"What?" asked the cop.

"Do you know what hospital this man is being transported to? His son wants to know where he needs to go."

"How does his son know?" he quipped in annoyance.

"He was called after the accident happened."

"Who called him?"

"I did."

He turned his body towards me and crossed his arms.

"Why would you do that?"

"Because it's his son, officer. He has a right to know."

"Not right now he doesn't."

"Officer, it's his *son*."

"I understand that, but now his son is gonna come to the crash site and see his dad in this bad shape. Why would you do that to him?"

"Officer, that man is sitting in his car, *bleeding to death*, and asked me to call his son. I wasn't about to deny his request."

"Why didn't you just let us take care of all that?"

"You weren't here."

"Yeah, well now his son is going to be out of his mind, speeding to get here, and might cause an accident. If that were to happen, you could be held liable for that accident. You've caused havoc for this situation. Next time, just let the police handle it."

I felt myself getting fired up; Joanna says she can tell by my face when I'm being engulfed by rage. I become a bull: my jaw droops and then locks, and my eyes furrow as hot air seeps through my nostrils.

But the officer didn't seem to care, goading me with condescending taunts of "*toro*" and flirting with the idea of wildly waving a red cape.

I reminded myself that I wasn't an animal. I'm a human. And humans are subject to arrest.

"Officer," I exhaled, "do you know where this man is being transported?"

"No, they won't know that until…"

"That's all I needed to know," I said as I walked away.

The gas from the dump truck had now leaked down the hill and under our own car's engine, so I had Joanna move the car to a nearby pub. The pub's parking lot was empty as Route 60 had been closed down for over a half-mile.

As firefighters, paramedics, and police swarmed Richard's car, another officer approached me. Whereas the younger, stumpy officer oozed inexperience, every indication was that this older officer had been a cop for decades.

"Are you a witness to the accident?" the seasoned officer asked.

"No, sir, we just stumbled upon it right after it happened."

"Are you family?"

"No sir."

"Then I'm going to have to ask you to clear the area."

"No problem sir. By the way officer, do you know where he's being transported?"

"The victim is being sent to Condell Medical."

"Thank you, sir. Just so you know, the victim's son is on his way right now."

"He is? Thank you so much, we'll look for him." He began to walk away, but promptly turned around a second later. "Oh, and by the way, was the victim conscious when you talked to him earlier?"

What does he mean, "earlier?"

"Yes officer, he was coherent."

"Alright, thank you very much for your help."

"No problem. Thank you, officer."

As I wandered towards the pub, I called Kevin again to see where he was. I could hear the wind flapping on the other end of the phone.

"Hello," an anxious Kevin said.

"Hi Kevin, it's me again. I just wanted to tell you that they're transporting your dad to Condell now."

"Condell? Okay, I'll make sure to head over there if I don't see them."

"Great, great, glad to hear that. I'll let you go then."

"Thank you so much."

"No problem, Kevin. Take care."

Joanna and I drove east as the ambulance disappeared from our view.

A few minutes later, Richard was dead. Kevin was the one who told me the bad news; I had called him later in the day to see what his dad's status was.

"Kevin, I was just calling to see how your dad's doing."

"He passed away," Kevin had said, much more somber than when we first spoke.

"*Oh*, Kevin, I am so sorry. I'm *so* sorry Kevin, that's not what I expected to hear."

"I know," Kevin choked out. "You talk to someone one minute, and the next they're gone."

I apologized to Kevin for his loss, telling him that his family would be in our prayers. He was profoundly appreciative that Joanna and I cared enough to stop and take care of his dad while he died.

"I'm just so grateful you were there," Kevin gushed. "You were a Godsend. And you were probably a great comfort to him, to have someone to talk to. In fact, you were probably the last person he ever talked to."

That hit me hard. It felt like a huge responsibility was just thrown onto my shoulders, yet one I could no longer fail or succeed at. It was just a responsibility, one that would remain dormant.

Kevin also took the time to explain what had ultimately killed his dad. Richard had fallen asleep while driving and swiped the truck, then swerved towards the ditch we had been hanging over while the liquid gas flooded the street. Apparently Richard's arm was a lot worse than I was able to see from where I had been talking to him. Richard had somehow gotten pinned by the steering wheel, and when the paramedics rescued him out of the car, the pressure on his arm was no longer there, and so he bled to death quickly thereafter. He died almost as soon as he was put into the ambulance. The newspaper would cite "internal injuries" as the official cause of death.

◊

Six days later, Joanna and I showed up at Richard's wake. With my heart pounding so hard it felt like it was trying to make a prison break, I introduced myself to Richard's son.

"Kevin? I'm the one who called you."

Kevin seemed emotionless, and I wondered if he was offended that Joanna and I came to the memorial service.

This was not the case.

"Danger! Thank you so much. Let me introduce you to my wife."

Kevin called his wife over, and all he said to her was, "This is him."

Kevin's wife instantly knew who I was. Her eyes filled with tears as she hugged Joanna and me.

"Thank you for being there. We tried finding who you were, but couldn't."

"I'm so deeply sorry for the sudden loss you're experiencing," I told them. "I know Richard lived a long and fruitful life, but I doubt this is how anyone would've wanted his passing to happen."

Kevin nodded his head.

"Yet," I continued, "I find solace in the fact that Richard seemed to be at peace during his last moments. He was fully aware of what had happened, and even expressed that he wished he had listened to you, his family, in your urgings for him to give up his license. But at the same time, he wasn't overwhelmed with regret, but rather had a calmness I would've never expected from a man who was suddenly thrust into his final moments without warning."

"You know," Kevin said, "I just hope he knew that I was on my way. I hope he knew in his heart that I was going to be with him."

"Well, it's funny, because it was *you* guys that were his final concern. I realize now that he knew he was going to die that day, but he wasn't panicking about that. Instead, he just wanted peace with you; he lit up when I asked if I should contact you. A man who knows he was dying shouldn't spark with excitement the way he did, but that's what happened. To me, that says so much about the bond you had with him, that you would be so heavy on his mind in his last moments. As he lay dying, his last request was to get you by his side. *You* were his last thought."

Kevin's eyes grew wet.

"I didn't know Richard," I exhaled, "but I can't help but believe he would've wanted you to have known that."

I gave Kevin and his wife the tattered flag that Joanna had picked up, the one that had been launched from Richard's car during the crash.

"I wanted to hand this to you personally."

Kevin looked at me through his tears.

"Thank you."

◊

I lied down in bed that night and considered everything that had happened over the past few days. I couldn't help but wonder if Richard would still be alive if I had applied that tourniquet against the dispatcher's wishes. I wish I had refused to leave his car, so I could've kept talking to him; someone to keep him conscious.

My thoughts turned from sadness to anger as I considered the young cop who had the audacity to chastise me for doing what I could to help. He accused me of causing havoc. *Havoc!* If I was in that situation a hundred times, I would've made the same decision every time. I had no regrets with my decision to create "havoc" for Kevin, only regrets with my decision to be polite when addressing the unsympathetic officer.

I found myself unable to get to sleep, too enraged to quiet my mind. I didn't have a handle on my anger: not just in this situation, but every situation. More often than not, whether there was reason to be or not, I was an angry person. Joanna noticed it the most, and though it hadn't damaged our relationship, it was at least straining it.

I realized how little control I had over my life. Before I went to Afghanistan, everything felt right: I had a sense of some control over my life and was a happy, warm person. But now, I had no control over my anger or life in general. Was I doomed to deal with death forever? Was I still prisoner to Afghanistan, a country that was thousands of miles from me?

Like Richard, I had survived a war that invigorated my life, but was a mere shadow of that strength now. I had held up Richard's head, but who would hold mine up?

That night, Richard and I had something in common: we were both cold.

◊

Exhaustion eventually overcame my body and flung me into a dream in which I was in an interrogation room. The older, polite police officer from a few days ago was sitting before me and wanted to get a witness account of what transpired during Richard's final moments.

"First," he said as he scribbled on his notepad, "why did you stop? You didn't even know this man. Why did you care about whether this stranger lived or died?"

It seemed a callous question.

"When a stranger dies," I articulated, "it's hard for anyone to care. Every newspaper all over the country has obituaries that speak to a handful of peoples' deaths daily. Furthermore, most of these obituaries are about old people who died. How can anyone notice the obituary of just another 86 year-old man?

"Yet when a stranger dies," I rubbed my chin, "one in whose survival you were invested, it hits a bit harder. Not as hard as a family member's death would hit you, but a lot harder than your everyday stranger who you read about in the newspaper. When Richard died, I didn't cry, and I didn't cancel any of my errands. But I can feel a microcosm of the pain and bitterness that his family must be feeling."

I stopped for a moment to let the officer catch up on his notepad, then added, "This, and I'm reminded how breakable the human body is."

The officer grinned, asserting, "A good reminder for a boy named Danger."

I looked at the concrete floor and nodded, repeating, "A good reminder for a boy named Danger."

When I lifted my head, I found I was no longer looking at the mild-mannered police officer. Instead, it was his partner, the insensitive and rude one that resembled Jared.

"Well," the officer said as he crossed his arms, "it's too bad you stopped to help. Because of you, Richard is dead."

"You know that's not true, officer."

"Sure it is. You should leave that kind of rescue stuff to professionals; professionals like me."

I slammed my fist on the desk.

"*You* weren't *there*, officer. It was up to me, not you."

"Don't talk back to me, son."

"Don't call me son, officer. You're just as old as me. You're my peer."

"I'm not your peer," the green officer quipped. "You know that. You know me, I'm Jared."

I jumped out of my seat and grabbed the officer by the collar.

"How dare you! You are *not* Jared Southworth. Take that back, you phony."

"I *am* Jared."

"You might seem like Jared in appearance, but you're not *half* the man that he was."

"At least I'm a man," the officer sneered, "unlike you."

"You don't know anything about me."

"Sure I do, kid. I know this much: you're *weak*."

I lifted the officer up and slammed him down on the ground.

"I am?" I asked as I pounced down on him, grabbing his head and pounding his skull against the concrete until his ears leaked blood.

"Where were *you*?" I shouted as I pummeled his face until my knuckles looked like they had been walloping tomatoes. "Where the fuck were you when Richard was dying?"

I looked down at him, realizing he was unconscious and possibly dead at this point. But it wasn't good enough. He deserved more than that, so I pulled a knife from his uniform and began stabbing him in the chest.

"If you're such a professional, stop me now, you piece of shit!" I cried out.

SLISH!

I slashed his throat, the capstone to my rage.

I stood up and, breathing heavily, looked down at the busted corpse that was left below, spitting on his mutilated face.

"*Now* I've caused havoc."

I collapsed into the interrogation chair again and began to breathe, feeling my veins throbbing in my head. Out of nowhere, a piercing pain shot through my back as if the knife I had just used to murder the officer had found its way into my own spine. I scrunched my eyes shut, trying to ignore the sharp twinge. But it kept surging: my back was firing tiny little bullets through my entire body, except for my left leg, which was spared with utter numbness.

I opened my eyes and found I was lying in my bed in Zion again.

Now awake, I tried adjusting my position, but the pain only intensified.

"Gah!" I cried aloud. My back was on fire, but emotionally, I was calmed down. I didn't feel angry anymore; it was as if I got my vengeance on the officer in reality, not just in my dream.

I looked over at the clock. The crick hit at 4:00am, as usual.

Every now and then, I'd wake up in pain during the middle of the night. Most nights, it'd either be my back or my tailbone that felt like it was being roasted over hot coals, so I'd get out of bed and begin a ritual of stretching. I'd often envision myself as a human edamame, and if I stretched in *just* the right way, I could pop the stubborn stinging right out of my body like a soybean pops out of a pod. Usually, this eased the inflammation enough to allow me to get back to sleep.

As I sat on my butt in my pitch-black room and reached my fingers towards my outstretched toes, I contemplated the journey I'd been on since I'd been back from Afghanistan. I'd been in America nine months now – the Georgia National Guard, whom had replaced the 33rd Brigade, was even home by now. Had it really been that long?

I winced when I sat on my tailbone after I gave up on my stretches, unable to pop the bean of tension out of my back this night. I lied down on my side so I wouldn't put any strain on my coccyx, which was the other source of aching. Stretching usually helped temporarily limit the pain in my back, but other than alleviating pressure altogether, there was no remedy for my tailbone.

Resting my head on the carpet, my eyes adjusted to the blackness. I squinted under my bed, seeing what looked like a six-inch ruler misplaced there. I grabbed it, and feeling the Velcro on my hands, realized it wasn't a ruler at all. It was a nametape.

I read it aloud.

"Bandee."

I missed seeing that nametape on a uniform. But I wouldn't see it again.

Bandee. He no longer lives. He's gone.

That's not true, Bandee silently whispered, as if he was a ghost inside of me who awoke from his dormant state when I grabbed his nametape. *I'm still here.*

No, Nick. I left you in Afghanistan by yourself.

You didn't leave me, Danger. I'm still with you.

Not anymore. I used to see your face when I looked in the mirror. Now I don't even know that man.

Why? What's happened to you? Why are you so angry?

I wish I had an answer for that. I can't help it; I'm just angry.

This isn't the first time you've turned to violence in your dreams. It's insatiable, Danger. It's not good.

But I always feel better when I wake up. When someone does me wrong, I don't lash out at them until I go to sleep, where I can do whatever I want to them and not cause anyone harm in reality.

You've channeled your anger to be unleashed in your dreams.

Precisely. And I wake up and feel great afterwards.

That doesn't change the fact that you still get angry. Remember what they say, "anger is only one letter away from Danger."

Are you using a cliché to try to help me?

What makes a cliché a cliché? I'm just pointing out that you've lost so much sleep being angry.

Well, maybe that's just my curse for surviving Afghanistan. But at least nobody's getting hurt.

For now, they're not. But what if your anger leaks out into reality?

It won't, Nick.

You're being naïve. What you've done is discovered a bandage for your anger. But bandages lose their adhesiveness and fall off.

And at that point, there won't be a wound there anymore. By then, I'll have healed. It'll just be a scar.

But what if it's not?

Dammit, Nick! Just go away!

You weren't angry like this before your deployment. You've changed.

Of course I've changed, Nick. I went to war. *Nobody comes back from that the same.*

But now during the day, you're one person; at night, you're someone much darker. You're living a double-life.

Ha! You know what that's like better than anyone, Nick.

Danger, you need to figure out how you can beat this. You don't need to be dependent on these violent dreams.

But if I'm not dependent on these dreams, then I got nothing to combat my rage. I'm impotent. Nick, I'm just empty. I have no inner strength.

You don't need to try to be strong in yourself; be strong in the Lord.

Nick, all I ever wanted was to be strong like you. Not like you for a day, or for a week. But like you for the rest of my life. You're everything I wanted to become when I enlisted. I wanted to be strong. I wanted to be worthy. I wanted to be unafraid. I wanted to prove that I wasn't the same pathetic kid that I'd been all my life.

You wanted to be a hero.

Yes, for anyone. Anyone that would let me be their hero.

You're Joanna's hero.

I stopped to think about that statement. Was it true?

I am… I'm Joanna's hero.

Remember the day you left to go to Fort Bragg? With tears welling in your eyes, you passed under that oversized flag?

I knew what he was talking about.

Yes, I remember, Nick.

What did you think to yourself then?

I said that I wouldn't go back home without becoming a hero first.

But at what point does someone become a hero? You've already said yourself, you never thought of me as a "hero," per se. You thought of me as just a guy you share the same blood with. Someone you share exactly the same thoughts with. We're exactly the same. Yet you envy me.

I envy you because of your qualities, Nicholas Bandee. Not because I think of you as a hero.

But am I not a hero?

I don't know, are you?

What makes a hero, Danger? Does doing the right thing in one fleeting moment make you a hero?

Being a hero isn't about reacting in one specific moment. Being a hero…

…is about how you act over the entirety of your life. A hero becomes a hero because they have substance in their character.

Not because they made a good choice during one critical moment. A hero…

…defends the defenseless. A hero lives for a purpose greater than themselves. A hero makes sacrifices. A hero…

…strives to love people in the way that God loves people. Yes, a hero will probably make that one good choice during that one critical moment that may save or end a life. But a hero…

…is so much more than one moment. A hero is a lifetime hero…

…not a momentary hero.

Danger, you are Joanna's hero.

And you live, Nicholas Bandee.

I live within you.

Bandee lives.

Be strong, Danger.

I am Danger.

I am Bandee.

Bandee lives within me.

I am Bandee.

Bandee lives.

I am…

…Bandee.

"I am Bandee."

.:17:.

In Memory of Bandee

4 September 2009

"Joanna, why don't you head into my room? I'll be there in a minute."

I watched her skip up the stairs and into my room. I glanced over at my dad and spoke softly enough so that my voice wouldn't carry up to my fiancée.

"Dad, this is going to take a minute. I need to tell her."

My dad nodded in acknowledgement, having been the only one who uncovered the truth.

"Tell her what?" my mom inquired as my dad's hand guided her to the kitchen to give me a moment with Joanna.

◊

I entered my room and there she was, sitting on my bed. It was a dream come true: Joanna was just a few feet away from me, not thousands of miles away. I sat down next to her, still wearing the same uniform that I had put on days ago when my trip home began.

"Babe," I began as I rubbed her soft cheek with my coarse palm, "there's something you need to know."

She nodded, "Okay..."

"Joanna, do you remember Bandee?"

"Yes, of course I remember Bandee."

"You traveled vicariously as Bandee told his story. Did you like reading Bandee's stories?"

"Of course I did," she exhaled in frustration, annoyed that I was asking questions that I obviously knew the answers to. "Please. What are you getting at?"

"Of course you liked reading Bandee's stories. He had a story worth telling, right? That's why I relayed his reports to you. Not many soldiers get to do what Bandee has done."

She nodded again.

"I want you to meet someone."

Her eyes widened.

"Bandee is here tonight. Are you ready to meet him?"

"Wait, what?" her voice deepened. "Bandee's here?"

"Do you want to meet him?"

It was almost as silly of a question as when I asked her on the playground if she would be willing to marry me.

"Well, yeah!"

I reached my hand into my pocket and slowly pulled out a nametape. I ripped off the "GEIST" nametape on my uniform and replaced it with "BANDEE." Taking Joanna's trembling hand, I spoke softly, "Pleased to meet you."

She shook her head, whispering "No."

"Yes."

"Stop it. You're confusing me."

"You're not confused."

"Stop this."

"Joanna, Bandee has no past. And Bandee will never have a future. Bandee was just a blip in the present. Bandee..." I swallowed the lump that was collecting in my throat. "Bandee is not a real person."

"No, no, no..."

"Nicholas Bandee is a fictional character I made up. But the stories you read from him aren't fictional in the least. Everything you read were true accounts from real experiences."

"No, please. Don't do it. Don't say it."

"Joanna..."

"No..."

"I am Bandee."

"*No*, you're *Nathan*. You're Danger!"

"Yes, I am. But I'm also Bandee. I am Danger; I am Bandee."

Her lips trembled with contempt and her eyes poured tears as her mind wrapped around the truth. An alternate dimension replaced her reality; the image of her fiancée lying on a cozy bed was replaced with a rugged soldier using a rock as a pillow; my cups of coffee transformed into a canteen of grubby water; my twiddling thumbs became my trigger finger; my nebulous reports on enemy attacks became my fight to survive them.

Joanna thrust her head into my chest – into Bandee's chest. She wept on the nametape, clutching my shirt as she cried. I stroked my fingers through her hair, rubbing the back of her head.

She looked up at me, "It was *you*? You were the one who traveled all over eastern Afghanistan? You were on the black roads? IED alley? The KG Pass? All those... *those combat patrols*! Along Pakistan, in Pirkothi! The Bermel attack... the Salerno rollover... the... the assault on Camp Stone? That was *you*? All you?"

"I know you might be angry. I'm..." I looked into her face; it seeped excruciating anguish. "I'm sorry."

"Why did you lie to me?" she grabbed her cheeks.

"It... I couldn't just... please," I petitioned, "you have to understand that I believe it was necessary. For a long time, I struggled as to whether or not I should tell you the truth. I eventually realized that the truth was too heavy for you. I was trying to spare you."

"You're going to have PTSD!" she wailed.

"No, no baby girl, I won't. What trauma did I go through? I can't have PTSD without the 'TS' part, right? Anything I went through that you could chalk up to producing Traumatic Stress didn't *upset* me, it *enlivened* me. All those instances you just mentioned were some of the most invigorating moments of my life. Joanna, if I really believed that God promised He would protect me, how could I possibly allow fear to seep in? Remember the story about Bandee going over the KG Pass? During that mission, I felt a comfort like none other. It felt like a bubble literally engulfed me, protecting me from all harm. Utter peace replaced fear of death. Trust me, you don't find peace in a situation like that unless God is present."

Joanna clawed at her face to wipe away her tears, leaving blotches of makeup smeared across her cheeks.

"Joanna, the night before I had to go over the KG Pass, I told the interpreters about my mission in the morning, and they all became so upset, telling me that they'd be praying for my survival. All except for Rambo Three, that is. He didn't seem concerned, so I asked him, 'Don't you believe I'll be in *khatar* tomorrow?'

"He shook his head, telling me, 'Danger will not die tomorrow.'

"I asked him, 'Don't you know how dangerous the KG is? How can you know I won't die?'

"Rambo Three shrugged his shoulders. 'Because,' he told me, 'you are gift from God.'

"He called me *a gift from God*, Joanna. I told him our love story that's so obviously been authored by God, and he believed the Lord wouldn't allow me to die until I married you. If he had enough faith, how could I not?"

"Did you know all along?" she grilled. "When did you know you'd be on missions?"

"Joanna, I always knew. From the moment they told me I was being deployed, I knew I wouldn't avoid those scenarios. I mean, I told you that I was deemed non-expendable. But *every* soldier is expendable."

"I can't believe I didn't figure this out. I feel so stupid."

"You're not stupid. I'm not surprised you didn't connect me to Bandee in my letters. Before I left for Afghanistan, I already had convinced you that I would be out of harm's way. And you wanted to believe I was telling the truth, so you only looked for reassurance that I was safe, not evidence that I was in jeopardy. It's like the picture I sent you: did you see a face or a vase?"

Joanna kept sniffling, taking everything in.

"In this case, you saw whatever I told you to look for. I tried to get you to look for fictitious comfort in each story. But if you tried hard enough, you would've been able to see the disturbing reality pop out instead. Both truth and deception were in there, but you didn't want to see the truth. And I didn't want you to, either. I pointed out the vase in hopes that it would draw your attention away from the face."

Joanna just looked at the ground, simply listening, not even blinking now. I couldn't tell if she was shocked or angry or any combination of the two.

"I hope you aren't mad, baby. But it was with Bandee that I was able to tell you my story, which I knew was a story that had to be told. It was only by lying that I was able to tell you the truth. Otherwise, I wouldn't have told any stories at all, as I know you would've worried more than it was worth to worry. I'm just a boy who tries to do what I think is right. It may not necessarily be right, but it felt like the closest thing to 'right.' "

She slowly nodded. I didn't know if that was a good sign or what.

"I wish you'd say something, babe."

She sat silent for a minute, then opened her mouth.

"Why did you do it? Why did you volunteer for all those missions? You knew how it would've crushed me if you had... if something happened to you."

"But we both knew I wasn't going to die."

"But you could still be paralyzed," she quipped. She wasn't making this easy, though rightfully so.

"Joanna, if I really believed what God had told me, how could I let anyone else take my place on a mission? How could I not jump at the opportunity to help a team who was going down a questionable path?"

"How could you not accept your role as Danger?" she mumbled, still concentrating on the floor instead of my face that she hadn't seen in so long.

"Exactly."

"But... I don't get... why *Bandee*?" she continued. "Why not Jones? Why not Johnson? Why'd you choose that name, Bandee?"

"Joanna, my deception has bound me to chains. I've been a prisoner to my lie from the beginning. And that's just it, Joanna. That's the meaning of 'Bandee.' You see, Bandee means 'prisoner' in the Dari language, and that name perfectly describes my year in Afghanistan. I've been held captive, a prisoner in body, mind, and soul. I've been prisoner to my lie. I've been prisoner to Afghanistan. I've been a prisoner to the Army's amoral protocol, a prisoner to my convictions, and a prisoner to my mission. I'm a prisoner for God, and prisoner to His awesome will. And I was a prisoner to my selfish lifestyle until I deployed and finally made a sacrifice that transcends my own life, and now I'm free! I'm finally a free man."

She kept shaking her head.

"I prayed. I prayed for Bandee so much."

"And God heard! Every prayer you prayed for Bandee was a prayer that God heard on my behalf. They weren't in vain. I know you've been praying for Bandee and me, as I've continually felt God's precious Hand in every situation I've faced.

"But now I'm home, and I'm alive. I can't say the same for 1LT Southworth, SSG Burkholder, SGT Stream, SSG Melton, SPC Talbert, SPC Smith, or any of my other fallen comrades, but God isn't done with me yet, which is why I can stand before you today."

She exhaled again, rubbing her temples as if she had a massive migraine.

"Joanna, God has prepared me to be a better son, brother, friend, husband, and father. And if God has put me through this much in just a mere 23 years, I can't wait to see what the rest looks like."

She fell silent for a moment, then spoke softly, "You need to stay. You can't deploy again. I don't want you to ever leave me again."

"*Deal*. It's done. My eyes have seen what they needed to see and my soul's been refined by it. Now, all that's left is my aching body that's ready to move on. I'm finished." I paused for a second, then added, "Can you forgive me?"

"Don't you mean, 'can you forgive Bandee?' "

"Bandee didn't do anything wrong to you. Bandee's only sin is that of not existing."

"That's a pretty serious offense."

She examined me as I let out a sigh.

"But," she continued, "I understand why you did it."

Joanna stared at my uniform, the nametape blaring back into her mascara-smudged eyes.

"Bandee," she shook her head. "It says 'Bandee.' "

I looked down past my chin as she tore off my nametape and tossed it under my bed.

"Can you put the right one back on?"

I grabbed my "GEIST" nametape again and slapped it back on my chest.

"There. Does that work for you?"

She smiled.

"Yeah, that's the one. 'Geist.' That's my hero."

My grin hid my Santa-caliber rosy cheeks.

"So, that's it then?" she asked. "Is that the only secret you've been keeping from me?"

My smirk faded as I realized there was still another matter to tend to. Joanna caught on to my sudden seriousness.

"What is it? There's something else, isn't there?"

"There is *one* thing," I confirmed.

Her face was grave, dying to know what was on my mind.

"Well," I explained, "before he departed, SGT Bandee had one last request."

I smiled, breaking her suspense.

"And what might this request be?" she smiled back at me.

"Bandee wanted me to give you a kiss for him."

"*Oh*, did he now?" she softly giggled, playing along.

"Yeah, he sure did, Joanna. *This guy* had the *biggest* crush on you. So, whadda say? Will you do it? Will you kiss me, in memory of Bandee?"

She had no qualms about fulfilling Bandee's final request, closing her eyes and slowly moving her face closer to mine. She smelled like vanilla, just as she had nearly a year ago on the night before I deployed. I cradled the back of her head into my palm and brought her in for a sweet and overdue kiss.

"I love you, Joanna."

"I love you, SGT Geist. My Kilmer kid."

"Hey," I reminded her as we stared into each others' smiling eyes, "I told you the pain would be temporary."

The true face of Bandee, as he performs combat operations in the streets of Bermel, March 2009

.: *epilogue* :.

Faith, Hope, Love
September 2010

"As I tied my shoes this morning, I spoke aloud to myself, 'This is the most dangerous day of my life.' "

"Well," my pal responded to me, "it makes sense. Today, you can die."

"There's just so much that can go awry today. I don't want to live with regret for the rest of my life because I failed to react to something."

"Hey, don't worry about it. You just focus on your job, and everyone else will do theirs. We're a team."

"I'm just afraid something's gonna blow up in my face."

"Nothing's gonna blow up in your face."

I exhaled a deep breath, wringing my wrists.

"You ready for this, buddy? We have to get this thing rolling. It won't kill you, okay?"

I nodded my head. He was right. I was well-prepared for this.

My friend held the door for me, and after we shared a collective nod, I burst through. I marched up the steps with urgency as I scanned the crowd before me. There were well over a hundred people there, many of them wearing a uniform not unlike mine. Everyone stared at me, waiting for me to make the first move.

I squinted, picking out familiar faces. There were many to be found: Joanna's family, my family, Joanna's best friend Corrine who flew in from Arizona, my best friend Matt, and even Mr. Ryan the gym teacher. In fact, not one stranger was present. For a fleeting moment, everyone who loved me was gathered in a single room to celebrate an event so astronomical that it could've only been orchestrated by the Creator of the universe, the culmination of an intricately woven plan that was set in motion long before I was even born.

There was only one person that was missing: *the bride*.

I nodded at my friend who had accompanied me to the front of the church, and we shot each other a pair of skittish smiles. Today, he wasn't just James Amos, my friend who takes too long to eat his hamburgers; rather, he was Pastor James Amos, a recently ordained minister making his debut in uniting two people in marriage.

And today, I wasn't just Nathan, the name I was born with; rather, I was Nathaniel Adam Joseph Danger Geist, having legally added Danger to my name a few days ago.

It was one year to the day since I returned home from Afghanistan, fulfilling the prophecy that I'd be home early. And now, the prophecy that I would marry Joanna, a prophecy foretold over four-and-a-half years ago, would be fulfilled. For today was my wedding day, and in a few moments, I would take the girl of my past and make her the girl of my future.

It was true, today was the most dangerous day of my life, even more dangerous than the day I treaded over the KG Pass with expectations of getting blown up. No matter what happened that day over the KG Pass, I knew I'd survive. But as of today, I felt mortal again. I could die at any moment.

Would this realization make me passive? Would I give into my weaknesses now, fearing death once again? Will I stop living my life dangerously? Will I stop living my faith dangerously?

No. I won't stop. I'm fully prepared to face any dangers, and I'm fully prepared to live and die for Jesus. A year ago, I had told Joanna that utter peace replaced fear of death. I thought it just held true for the duration of God's promise to me, but that axiom would always be true for me. God will protect me if He wants to protect me, whether or not I have an epiphany that makes me believe so.

When I was being attacked on Camp Stone, I made an important discovery of where the safest spot was on the base; I believed that those who stayed where they stood were doomed if another flurry of attacks got launched that night. It's possible I was wrong. It's possible I misgauged where the bombs were exploding. It's even possible a mortar could've landed right where I urged my fellow soldiers to seek shelter. But in my soul, I was convinced I had discovered a truth that could save lives. I knew something that others didn't. Someone had to tell them. Someone had to warn them. But who would be willing to get the word out?

I knew it had to be me. This was my responsibility. It will always *be my responsibility. I will continue to face peril if it protects others, and more importantly, if it brings someone to understand the Gospel of Jesus Christ. This is my call; this is the call of every Christ-follower in existence.*

The doors of the sanctuary flung open as everyone jumped to their feet. Looking as stunning as a star but as peaceful as a dove, my bride glided down the aisle, triumphant music welcoming her in.

I mustn't fear death. I won't fear danger. I must resist succumbing to my selfish desires. I was never meant to be enslaved to these things. My weaknesses cannot keep me from being free!

The sun's heat shot through the church's clerestory and beat down on my sable tuxedo, my body struggling to stand upright on account of my frail back. Obversely, the daylight illuminated the sanctuary and, vaporizing my shackles, released my soul from captivity.

By the grace of God, I must rise above my demons!

The closer my bride came, the harder it was to see as tears uncontrollably flooded down my face. Within moments, my bride stood before me at the altar; it was as if Beauty herself had donned an elegant white dress and clasped my hand with hers. After a special moment in which her shining face smiled into mine, we turned to the pastor to be united in marriage.

I am not prisoner to this land. I am not prisoner!

I am Danger.

Danger and Joanna Geist, September 4, 2010

How You Can Help

At the time of this book's publication, there still have not been any permanent changes to the policy that allows the killing of animals on FOBs as a means to remove them. While there was some high-profile dialogue in late 2009 to make killing animals on FOBs punishable under the Uniform Code of Military Justice (UCMJ), the conversations were short-lived and ultimately no action was taken.

But you can help. If you are outraged by the accounts told in this story, please contact the following people and organizations to express your concern.

The Humane Society of the United States:
http://www.hsus.org/contact_us/contact_cruelty_fighting.html

American Society for the Prevention of Cruelty to Animals (ASPCA)
424 E. 92nd St
New York, NY 10128-6804

Performing Animal Welfare Society
P.O. Box 849
Galt, CA 95632

Born Free USA united with API
1122 S Street
Sacramento, CA 95811

American Humane
63 Inverness Drive East
Englewood, CO 80112

Defenders of Wildlife
1130 17th Street, NW
Washington, DC 20036

The President of the United States of America
c/o The White House
1600 Pennsylvania Avenue NW
Washington, DC 20500

The Commander of Central Command
c/o The Department of Defense
1400 Defense Pentagon
Washington DC 20301-1400

Also, please don't forget about your local and state legislators. If you're not sure who your state legislator is, you can find that information on the following website: http://www.congress.org/congressorg/dbq/officials/?lvl=L .

To find your local representative, visit: https://writerep.house.gov/writerep/welcome.shtml .

Please note that I ask that you don't invoke the help of PETA. We wish to create legitimate change here, but not at the expense of soldiers or commanders receiving death threats.

A Note about Creative Nonfiction

This book falls under the genre of "creative nonfiction." Here's what that means: the occurrences in this story all really happened, though literary devices have been thrown in to make the story more compelling. For example, I talk about Joanna's tears flooding my room in the "Drowning in the Truth" chapter; I speak of a large fist crushing my soul in "Doubt, Despair, Pain"; I present my meeting with BG Jonah as a boxing match in "Please return to your seats, the intermission has concluded." As you can tell without me even needing to say it, Joanna doesn't have the supernatural ability to cry out a flood, no literal hand smashed my spirit to the pavement the night I left my family, and, *boy oh boy*, you can rest assured that I didn't actually prance into a Brigadier General's office with the intention of clocking him in the jaw. Yet, it was with these techniques that I was better able to get my point across. You knew what your protagonist was *feeling* without him having to explicitly state the emotions he was experiencing, keeping you better engaged.

I would contend that most products of nonfiction – including investigative journalism, school essays, and even news articles – use such literary devices to make their story better understood and more interesting, though not as often or as obviously as creative nonfiction stories do. A big difference between creative nonfiction and other nonfiction is *objectivity*. School essays, news articles, and journalistic stories are (theoretically) intended to be as objective and straightforward as possible. Creative nonfiction, on the other hand, is intended to get a point across *without molesting the truth*.

The term "creative nonfiction" has caught a lot of flack in the past because some authors have written fictional tales and powdered them with snippets of truth, and then they presented their material as "creative nonfiction." Writing a story that is *mostly* nonfictional is still fiction, in my opinion. For a story to boast "nonfiction" status, the story had to play out as presented without any gratuitous embellishing, only throwing *literary tools* – not *dishonesty* – into the story as needed.

So, to quash any notion that I've needlessly deceived my reader, I've chosen to outline the creative liberties I took to make this story flow better. No change was made without warrant, and it's my opinion that you would agree after reading why I made the few changes that I did:

◊ Rambo Three wasn't the name of my Terp, but a popular name that I'd seen at least a couple of Terps go by. I knew that it was imperative for my reader to connect with Rambo Three, and I felt it would make him more accessible if I gave him a name. Yet, for the safety of my Terp, I couldn't use either his real name or his actual nickname, which is why I went with a more common moniker.

◊ Furthermore, some of Rambo Three's comments didn't actually come from the Terp assigned to me. For instance, it wasn't Rambo Three who called me a "gift from God," but another Terp I was just as close to. While Rambo Three was the Terp I interacted with the most, I felt a closeness with all the other Terps, as well.

◊ My conversation with COL Staar took place over several meetings, not all in one sitting. However, it made no sense to interrupt the flow of the story to make this note.

◊ My meeting with BG Jonah was actually a meeting with two people: the Commander of Task Force Phoenix, as well as the Task Force Phoenix Chief-of-Staff. BG Jonah is the combination of these two people. The real Brigadier General was receptive to my concerns and well-prepared for the meeting, as any good General would be. The Chief-of-Staff was completely disinterested in the meeting, annoyed that I was taking time away from focusing on the soldiers on the ground, a perspective that I also can respect due to the intense responsibilities of his job. The reason I combined the two personalities into one was to simplify the number of characters my reader had to remember. Also, in reality, the meeting's importance was that I was confronting the Task Force Phoenix Commander, whereas having the Task Force Phoenix Chief-of-Staff sit-in on the meeting was of much less significance, despite his influence.

◊ The conversation with SFC Donnelly took place in the form of a series of emails over the course of a few days, not by a single phone call as depicted in the story. However, it was impossible to represent this form of communication in a way that still engaged the reader.

◊ Richard Kutz's accident did not occur in July 2010, but rather on September 14, 2010, just ten days after my wedding. However, to end on such a sad note would've deterred from the value of the wedding as the culminating point of the entire book.

◊ As angry as I was with the police officer on the day of Richard Kutz's death, he was never the subject of one of my murderous rampage dreams. However, because this chapter is the climax to the entire book, it seemed most fitting to present my dark dream at that juncture, especially considering it allowed the recipient of my violent fantasy to be an established character. In reality, it wouldn't have been unusual had the officer been a victim in one of my dreams, considering I'd "killed" other people in my dreams for much lesser offenses.

◊ Finally, conversational subject matters sometimes happened at different times than reported in the book, and even sometimes with different people. For instance, my dad didn't make the "you *are* a religious nut" comment, my little brother did. Percy wasn't the one who asked me why I never cuss, it was another soldier who did. The conversation with Warren on the last night of Midnight Slaves actually had happened a few weeks prior, with all the members of the Midnight Slaves being present. But, as you're hopefully gathering, expressing these details would've cluttered the flow of the story.

I realize that you just read an entire book in which I highlight my tendency to be a liar, so you may not trust me here, but for what my word is worth to you, this is the truth to this story. No other major details were altered than what I've listed here. I realize that some mind-bending events happened in this story, so much so that some might cry "foul" to this book's legitimacy. Whenever someone accuses me of exaggerating these events, I find it to be both a punch-to-the-gut and a compliment at the same time: it makes me a little sad that the content in this story is thought of as non-credible by a reader, but I also swell up with joy that God chose a bumbling fool like me to live out a story that was so unbelievable that some people actually doubt its authenticity. You see, I didn't "write" this story, my friend; God wrote it. I just listened to Him in February 2006 when He told me to start writing the details of what He was doing with my life. I had no idea what would come from this journal, but I did my best to obey the command of filling its pages with specific descriptions.

So, I reiterate that I didn't write this story any more than a sportswriter "writes" the results of a sports game. I wrote the book, not the story: my job was to report the events as they happened, just as any worthwhile investigative journalist would do. And that, my friend, is why I call this story a piece of *creative nonfiction*.

Emphasis on the *nonfiction*.

ACKNOWLEDGMENTS

No book is simply conceived and then missiled out in mass quantities like eggs on a chicken farm. I am Danger; I am Prisoner is no exception to this rule. My efforts are only the half of what has been poured into this piece.

First and foremost, I thank God for the abundant blessings He's given. I have no hesitation in telling you that this book would've never happened without the love of Jesus Christ transforming my life. God wrote this story; I just documented it as it happened. My only hope is that the time, money, and energy I've spent on this book is pleasing to Him.

I also want to thank my family and friends for all they've done to help me. Even though we've sometimes strayed from one another on matters such as faith, I've never felt for a split-moment that I didn't have your support. Thanks to all of you who received and read my emails while I was in Afghanistan, and thank you for standing by me when it might have been easy to forget about me.

Not the least of these is Joanna, the woman God set apart for me before we were even conceived. Joanna was not only one of the editors, but her support has been one of the most vital components to the manifestation of this story. While I was unable to financially support the both of us as I focused on this book, she became the breadwinner for our family. Joanna, my little Kilmer girl, my bride, I appreciate you more than you know. I love you dearly, baby. "Once a Cougar, always a Cougar!"

This section would become longer than the longest chapter in this book if I rattled off everyone who supported me in some way during the process of this publication, but because it's said that what you spend your time and money on is what you care about most, I am compelled to thank the following people for rallying around this book, investing in this story, and believing in me. The following people came through financially when I needed it the most: Matt and Lara Archibald; Corinne Boynton; Joan Brems; Ashley Cerone; Kurt and Melissa Clothier; Terri Eckard; Rakel Fairfull; Heather Ficek; Ted Gault; Ram Gopal; Lynn Gutter, Stuart Freudberg, and Carole Gutter; Julie Hamil; Sarah Jacobsen; Hannah Kline; Jan Love; Melissa Love; Christine Dugan Mika; Zaxxson Ernest Leonard Nation; Chuck and Janet Pearson; Sara Rekasis; Dustin Robb; Michelle Roberts; Dale and Vicki Schaul; Carl Schleyer; Julie Smith; Shane Spears; Chris and Laura Stephens; Matt Tomkowiak; Judy, Heather, Noah, and Melissa Turley; Elise Valdés; Gabby Williams; Kyle and Bri Wood; Kim Zinman; and of course Mike, Bridget, Jessi, and the late Ryan Carper for their exceptionally kind donation that defied my expectations. I am blessed to count myself a friend of the Carper family, as well as everyone I just listed.

Thank you to Kurt Clothier, who transposed the first draft into a coherent manuscript; your efforts saved me a lot of work, which allowed me to more quickly arrive at the final draft of this book. Thank you to the members of the Midnight Slaves who took the time out of their busy schedules to minister to the needs of the people of St. Louis. Thank you to Greg Walz for providing the Bibles for the ministry, and thank you to James Amos for being the pioneer that helped me realize the needs of the homeless people of St. Louis and East St. Louis. Thank you to Christen Ringhausen, who was the first person to consistently call me by the name "Danger"; without your serious commitment to extending the life of the namesake joke, I might never have become the Danger I am today. Thank you to Reid Stuck for catching a typo in the first edition of this publication. Thank you to the family of Richard Kutz, especially Kevin Kutz who provided me with candid feedback on the "Stop the Bleeding" chapter; though I only talked with your beloved Richard for a few minutes, I treasure that time and feel blessed to have been a part of his life, no matter how brief. Thank you to Tracey Kane for going above-and-beyond to assist me in securing an apartment on campus while I was still deployed – and making sure I got the best room in the building. Thank you to Tony "The Chuck" Grigonis for his help in the early fundraising and promotion of this book; you possess a unique set of skills, and despite the value of these abilities, you selflessly shared your knowledge without expecting anything in return. Thank you to Kim Zinman, Matt Tomkowiak, Corrine Size, and especially Ben Geist for helping put together the proposal-of-a-lifetime; I am indebted to you four.

Many editors with varying degrees of backgrounds came together and helped edit this book. Thank you to Holly Childers, Lauren Ennesser, Bernie Geist, Russ Miller, Aaron Newcom, Bruce Ollinger, Janet Pearson, Julie Smith, and Chris Stephens for their invaluable criticisms and suggestions.

Yet, there were four editors in particular who went above and beyond, critically impacting this book into what it is today. James Amos, Jeff Burd, Cory Fosco, and Emily Morrison, I thank you from the depths of my heart for willingly sharing your literary expertise and helping me understand the full potential of this story. Not only did you burn up much of your time, but you did so free of charge and without complaint. If it weren't for you, this book may have never taken off the ground. I believe God put you in my path for a reason. Thank you, friends.

But more than anyone, thank you to Bernie and Leanne Geist for their unhesitant and constant financial support of this book. Without your outrageously generous donations that served as life support during the most financially taxing times while I wrote, this book would've never been as polished as it is today. And the thing is, your belief in this book didn't even affect your support; you would've selflessly poured everything you have into this book based on the mere fact that I asked you to. Thank you for your unconditional love throughout my entire life.

Lastly, I thank you, the reader. Socrates is quoted as saying "the unexamined life is not worth living." If that's true, then you've made my life more meaningful by spending a portion of your time on this book. I wish to shake your hand some day and personally tell you that I appreciate your attention.

To everyone who made this book possible: *thank you.*

Good fight and good night,

DANGER!

Danger Geist

GLOSSARY

1LT: First Lieutenant (Rank O-2)
1SG: First Sergeant (Rank E-8)
ANA: Afghan National Army
ANP: Afghan National Police
BBIED: bicycle-borne IED
BG: Brigadier General / 1-Star General (Rank O-7)
CH: Chaplain
COL: Colonel (Rank O-6)
COP: command outpost
CPT: Captain (Rank O-3)
CSM: Command Sergeant Major (Rank E-9)
CSTC-A: Combined Security Transition Command – Afghanistan
DFAC: dining facility
ECP: entry control point
EOD: explosive ordnance disposal
FOB: forward operating base
GEN: General / 4-Star General (Rank O-10)
IED: improvised explosive device
KG Pass: Khowst-Gardez Pass
KIA: killed-in-action
MAJ: Major (Rank O-4)
MG: Major General / 2-Star General (Rank O-8)
MP: military police
MRE: meal ready-to-eat
NCO: noncommissioned officer
OCD: obsessive-compulsive disorder
POW: prisoner-of-war
PSD: personnel security detail
PTSD: post-traumatic stress disorder
QRF: quick reaction force
RPG: rocket-propelled grenade
SECFOR: security forces
SFC: Sergeant First Class (Rank E-7)
SGT: Sergeant (Rank E-5)
SIGACTs: significant activities
SOP: standing operating procedure
SPC: Specialist (Rank E-4)
SSG: Staff Sergeant (Rank E-6)
TIC: troops-in-contact
VA: Veteran's Affairs
VBIED: vehicle-borne IED

15066132R00213

Made in the USA
Charleston, SC
15 October 2012